TOP COW PRODUCTIONS COMPANY, PRESENTS...

THINK TANK

CREATED BY
MATT HAWKINS

&

RAHSAN EKEDAL

published by
Top Cow Productions, Inc.
Los Angeles

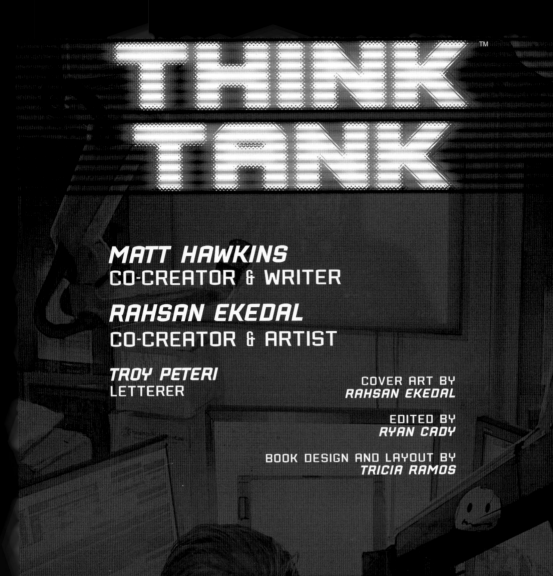

THINK TANK ™

MATT HAWKINS
CO-CREATOR & WRITER

RAHSAN EKEDAL
CO-CREATOR & ARTIST

TROY PETERI
LETTERER

COVER ART BY
RAHSAN EKEDAL

EDITED BY
RYAN CADY

BOOK DESIGN AND LAYOUT BY
TRICIA RAMOS

TOP COW PRODUCTIONS, INC.

Marc Silvestri - *CEO*
Matt Hawkins - *President and COO*
Bryan Hill - *Story Editor*
Ryan Cady - *Editor*
Ashley Victoria Robinson - *Assistant Editor*
Elena Salcedo - *Director of Operations*
Henry Barajas - *Operations Coordinator*
Vincent Valentine - *Production Artist*
Dylan Gray - *Director of Marketing*

To find the comic shop
nearest you, call:
1-888-COMICBOOK

Want more info? Check out:
www.topcow.com
for news & exclusive Top Cow merchandise!

IMAGE COMICS, INC.
Robert Kirkman – Chief Operating Officer
Erik Larsen – Chief Financial Officer
Todd McFarlane – President
Marc Silvestri – Chief Executive Officer
Jim Valentino – Vice-President
Eric Stephenson – Publisher
Corey Murphy – Director of Sales
Jeff Boison – Director of Publishing Planning & Book Trade Sales
Jeremy Sullivan – Director of Digital Sales
Kat Salazar – Director of PR & Marketing
Branwyn Bigglestone – Controller
Sarah Mello – Accounts Manager
Drew Gill – Art Director
Jonathan Chan – Production Manager
Meredith Wallace – Print Manager
Briah Skelly – Publicist
Sasha Head – Sales & Marketing Production Designer
Randy Okamura – Digital Production Designer
David Brothers – Branding Manager
Olivia Ngai – Content Manager
Addison Duke – Production Artist
Vincent Kukua – Production Artist
Tricia Ramos – Production Artist
Jeff Stang – Direct Market Sales Representative
Emilio Bautista – Digital Sales Associate
Leanna Caunter – Accounting Assistant
Chloe Ramos-Peterson – Library Market Sales Representative
IMAGECOMICS.COM

THINK TANK Volume 4
September 2016. FIRST PRINTING.

Published by Image Comics, Inc. Office of Publication: 2001 Center St., 6th Floor, Berkeley, CA 94704. $14.99
USD. THINK TANK™ 2016 Self Loathing Narcissist, Inc. All rights reserved. Originally published in single
issue format as THINK TANK: CREATIVE DESTRUCTION #1-4. "Think Tank," its logos, and the likenesses of all
characters (human and otherwise) featured herein are trademarks of Self Loathing Narcissist, Inc. "Image"
and the Image Comics logos are registered trademarks of Image Comics, Inc. No part of this publication may
be reproduced or transmitted, in any form or by any means (except for short excerpts for journalistic or review
purposes), without the express written permission of Top Cow Productions, Inc. All names, characters, events
and locales in this publication are entirely fictional. Any resemblance to actual persons, (living or dead),
events or places, without satiric intent, is coincidental. Printed in South Korea. ISBN: 978-1-63215-541-7

image

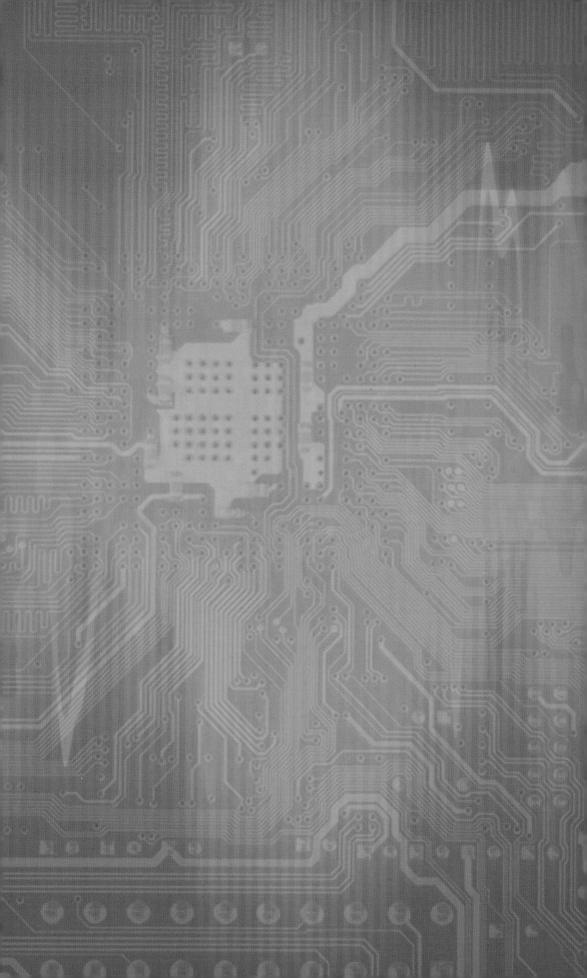

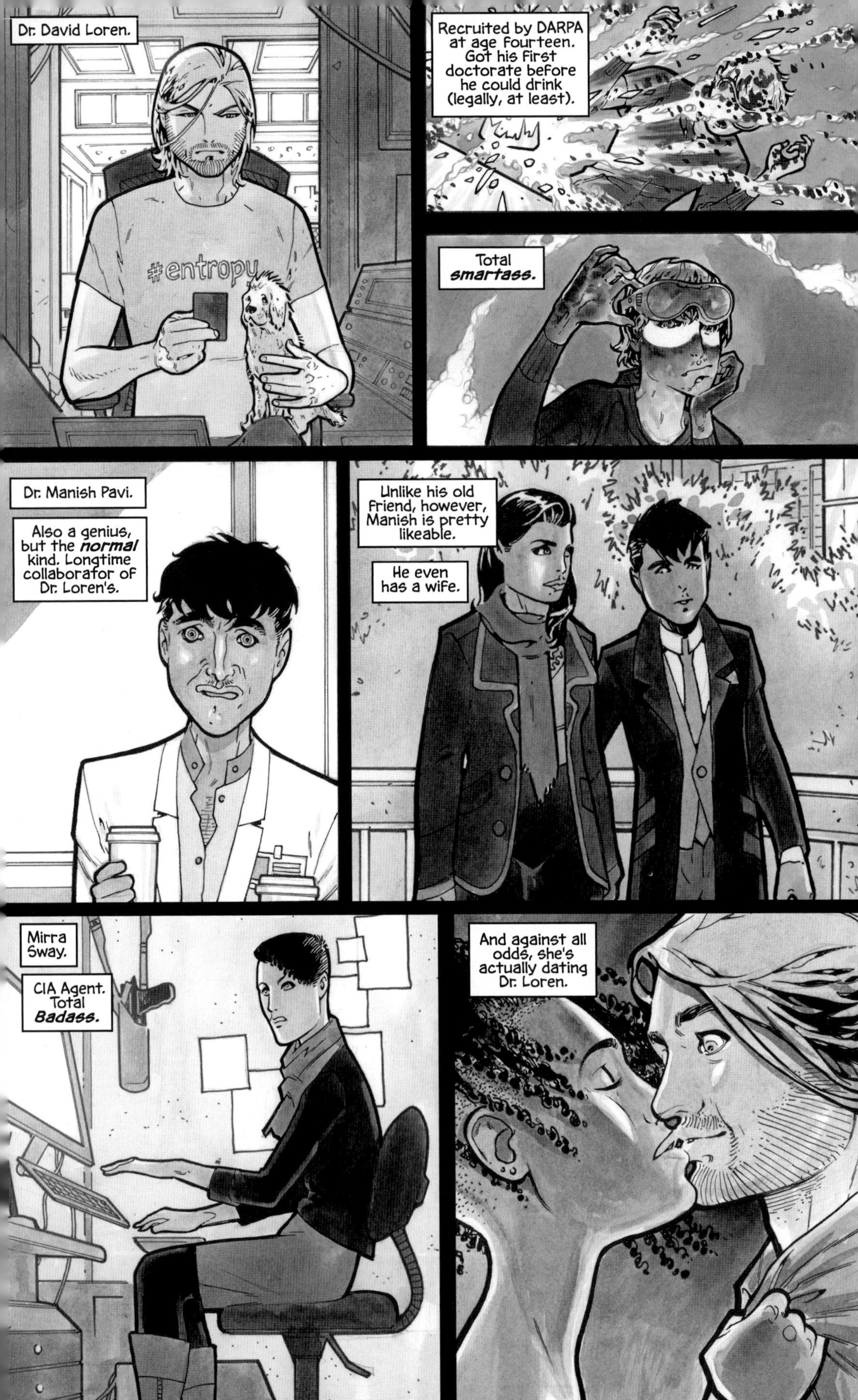

Dr. David Loren.
#entropy
Recruited by DARPA at age fourteen. Got his first doctorate before he could drink (legally, at least).
Total *smartass.*
Dr. Manish Pavi.
Also a genius, but the *normal* kind. Longtime collaborator of Dr. Loren's.
Unlike his old friend, however, Manish is pretty likeable.
He even has a wife.
Mirra Sway.
CIA Agent. Total *Badass.*
And against all odds, she's actually dating Dr. Loren.

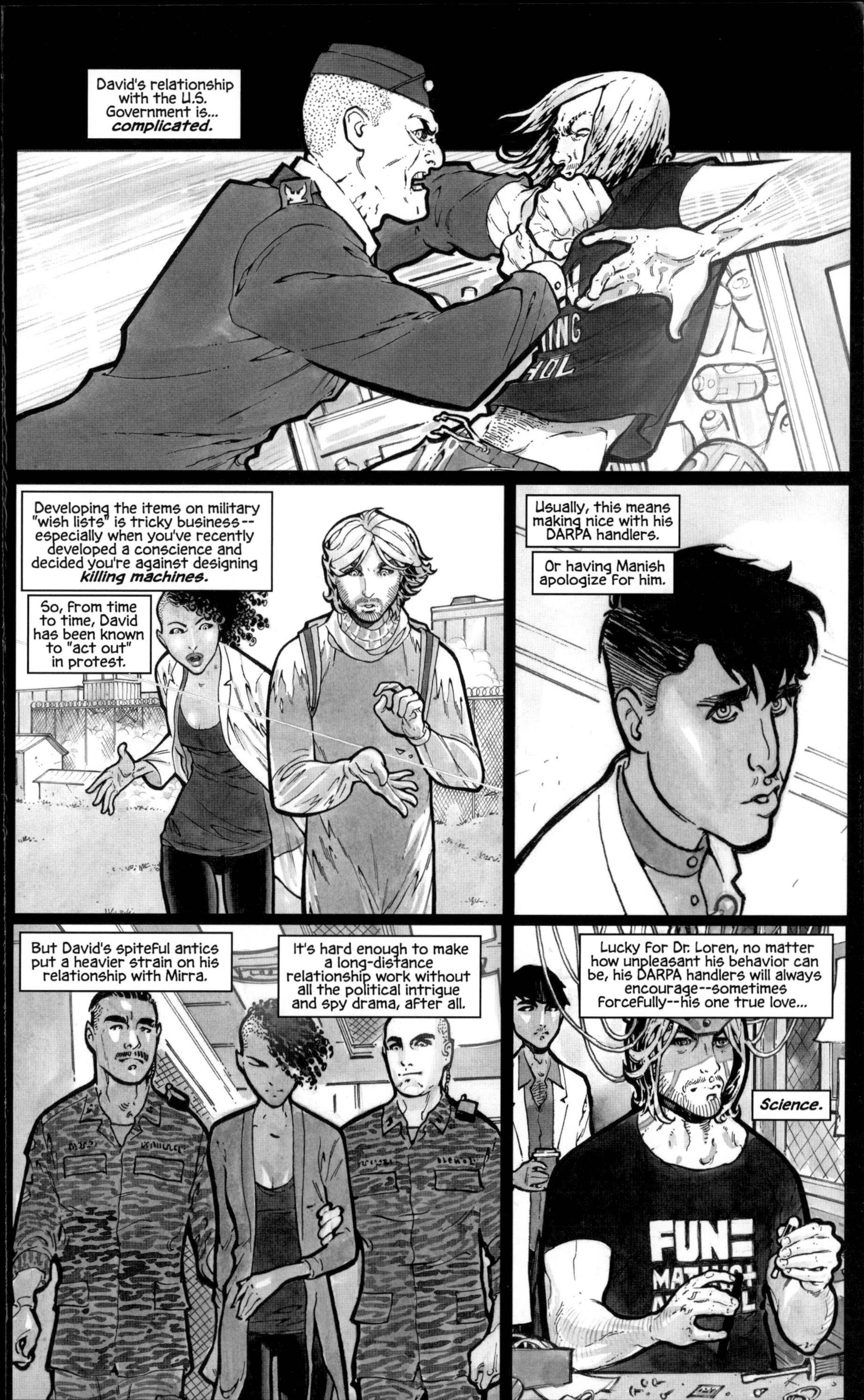

David's relationship with the U.S. Government is... *complicated.*
Developing the items on military "wish lists" is tricky business--especially when you've recently developed a conscience and decided you're against designing *killing machines.*
So, from time to time, David has been known to "act out" in protest.
Usually, this means making nice with his DARPA handlers.
Or having Manish apologize for him.
But David's spiteful antics put a heavier strain on his relationship with Mirra.
It's hard enough to make a long-distance relationship work without all the political intrigue and spy drama, after all.
Lucky for Dr. Loren, no matter how unpleasant his behavior can be, his DARPA handlers will always encourage--sometimes forcefully--his one true love...
Science.
FUN

BREAKING: MANHAT
MILLIONS WITHOUT POW
VECTOR THIS

CHAPTER ONE

THINK TANK

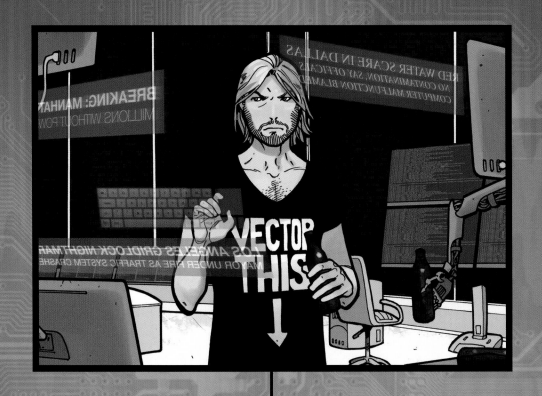

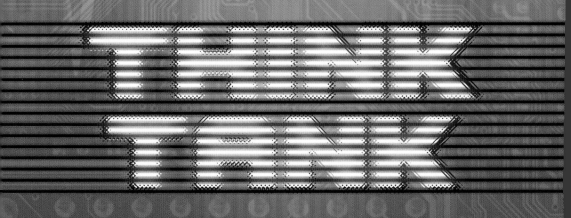

In the councils
of GOVERNMENT, we
must guard against
the ACQUISITION of
unwarranted influence,
whether sought or unsought,
by the MILITARY INDUSTRIAL
COMPLEX. The potential for
the disastrous rise of
misplaced power exists
and will persist.

President Dwight Eisenhower 1961

Eisenhower was a lifelong
military man, commanding the
D-Day invasion while serving
as Supreme Allied Commander
in Europe during World War 2.

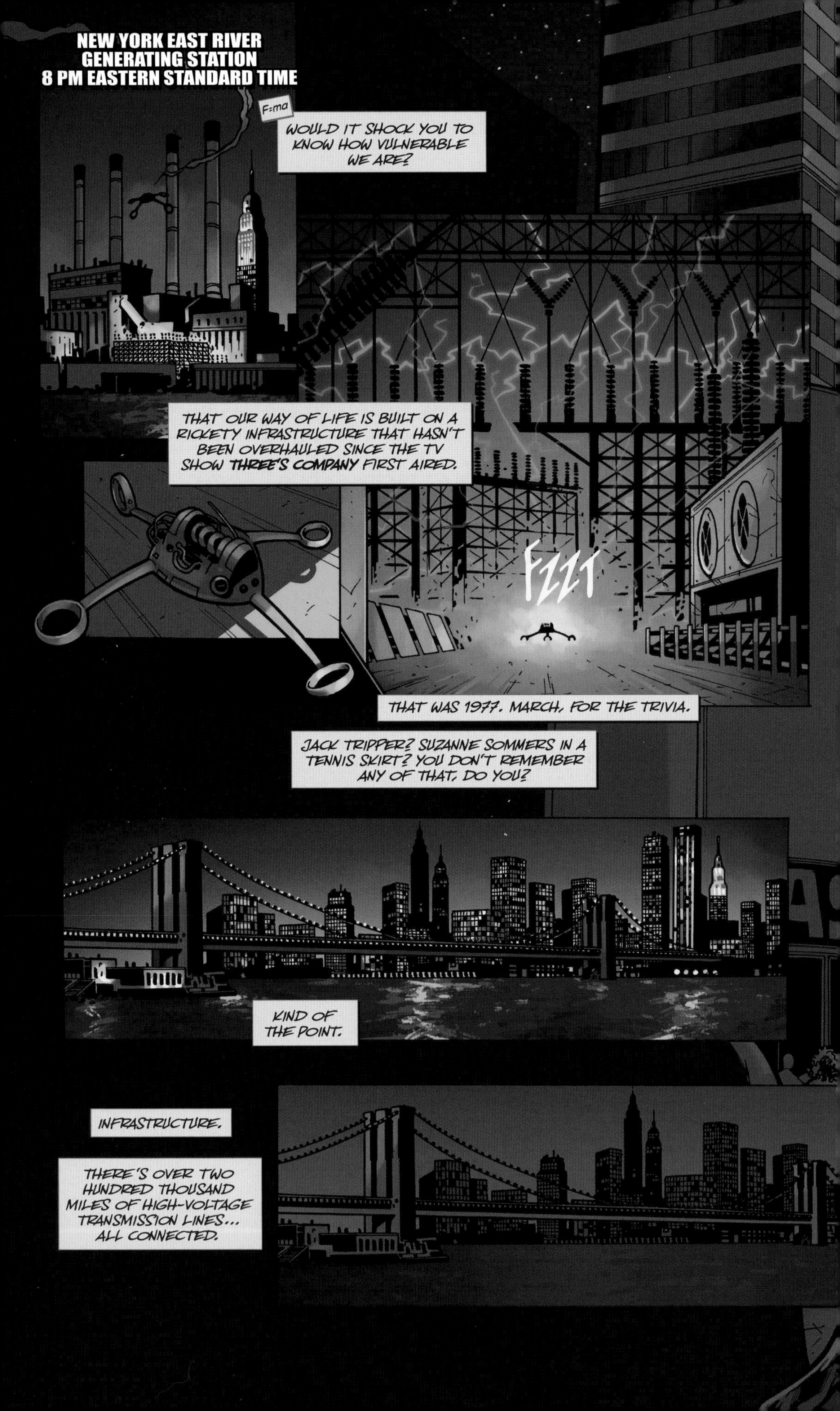
NEW YORK EAST RIVER GENERATING STATION 8 PM EASTERN STANDARD TIME
F=ma
WOULD IT SHOCK YOU TO KNOW HOW VULNERABLE WE ARE?
THAT OUR WAY OF LIFE IS BUILT ON A RICKETY INFRASTRUCTURE THAT HASN'T BEEN OVERHAULED SINCE THE TV SHOW THREE'S COMPANY FIRST AIRED.
FZZT
THAT WAS 1977. MARCH, FOR THE TRIVIA.
JACK TRIPPER? SUZANNE SOMMERS IN A TENNIS SKIRT? YOU DON'T REMEMBER ANY OF THAT, DO YOU?
KIND OF THE POINT.
INFRASTRUCTURE.
THERE'S OVER TWO HUNDRED THOUSAND MILES OF HIGH-VOLTAGE TRANSMISSION LINES... ALL CONNECTED.

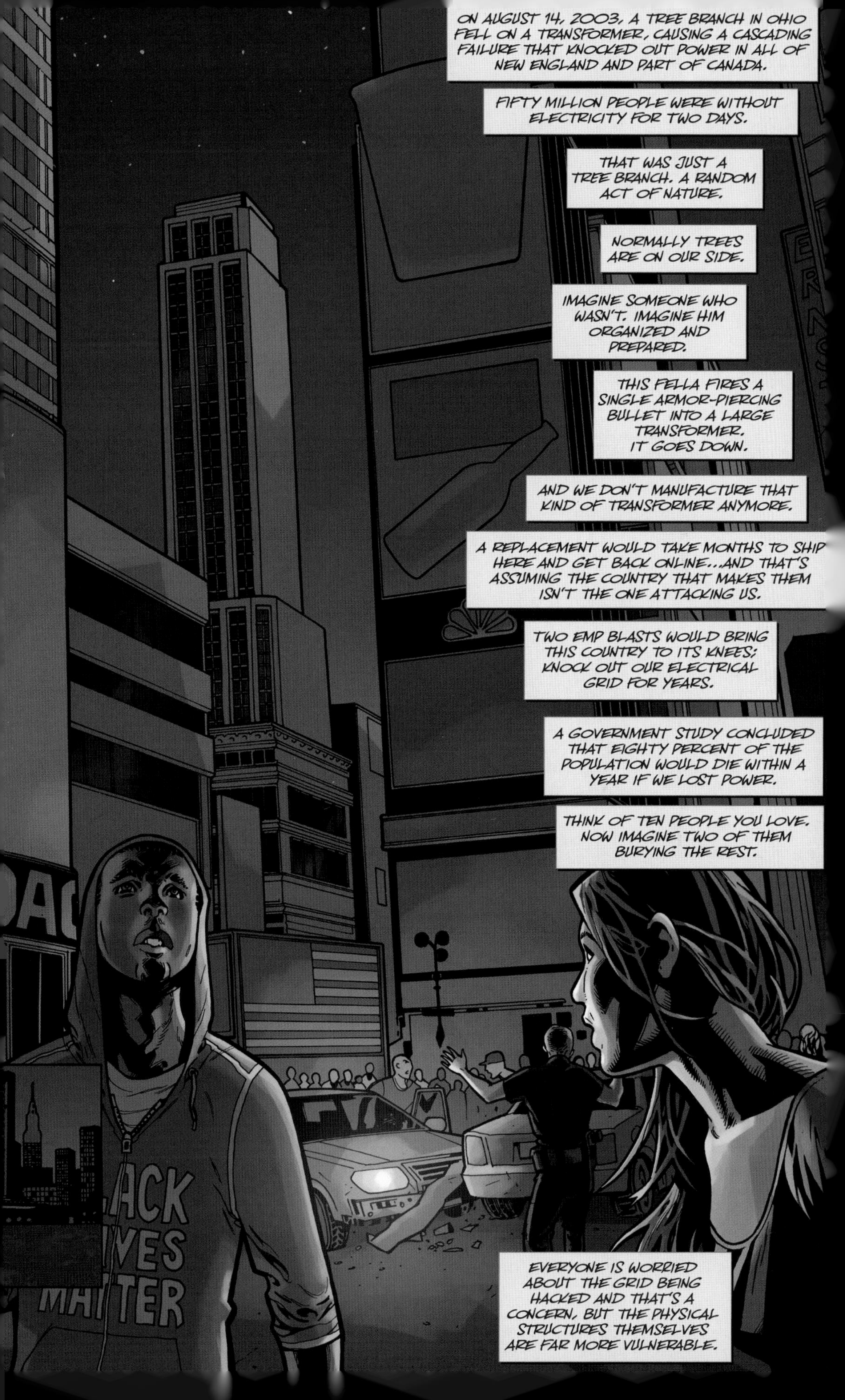
ON AUGUST 14, 2003, A TREE BRANCH IN OHIO FELL ON A TRANSFORMER, CAUSING A CASCADING FAILURE THAT KNOCKED OUT POWER IN ALL OF NEW ENGLAND AND PART OF CANADA.
FIFTY MILLION PEOPLE WERE WITHOUT ELECTRICITY FOR TWO DAYS.
THAT WAS JUST A TREE BRANCH. A RANDOM ACT OF NATURE.
NORMALLY TREES ARE ON OUR SIDE.
IMAGINE SOMEONE WHO WASN'T. IMAGINE HIM ORGANIZED AND PREPARED.
THIS FELLA FIRES A SINGLE ARMOR-PIERCING BULLET INTO A LARGE TRANSFORMER. IT GOES DOWN.
AND WE DON'T MANUFACTURE THAT KIND OF TRANSFORMER ANYMORE.
A REPLACEMENT WOULD TAKE MONTHS TO SHIP HERE AND GET BACK ONLINE...AND THAT'S ASSUMING THE COUNTRY THAT MAKES THEM ISN'T THE ONE ATTACKING US.
TWO EMP BLASTS WOULD BRING THIS COUNTRY TO ITS KNEES; KNOCK OUT OUR ELECTRICAL GRID FOR YEARS.
A GOVERNMENT STUDY CONCLUDED THAT EIGHTY PERCENT OF THE POPULATION WOULD DIE WITHIN A YEAR IF WE LOST POWER.
THINK OF TEN PEOPLE YOU LOVE. NOW IMAGINE TWO OF THEM BURYING THE REST.
EVERYONE IS WORRIED ABOUT THE GRID BEING HACKED AND THAT'S A CONCERN, BUT THE PHYSICAL STRUCTURES THEMSELVES ARE FAR MORE VULNERABLE.

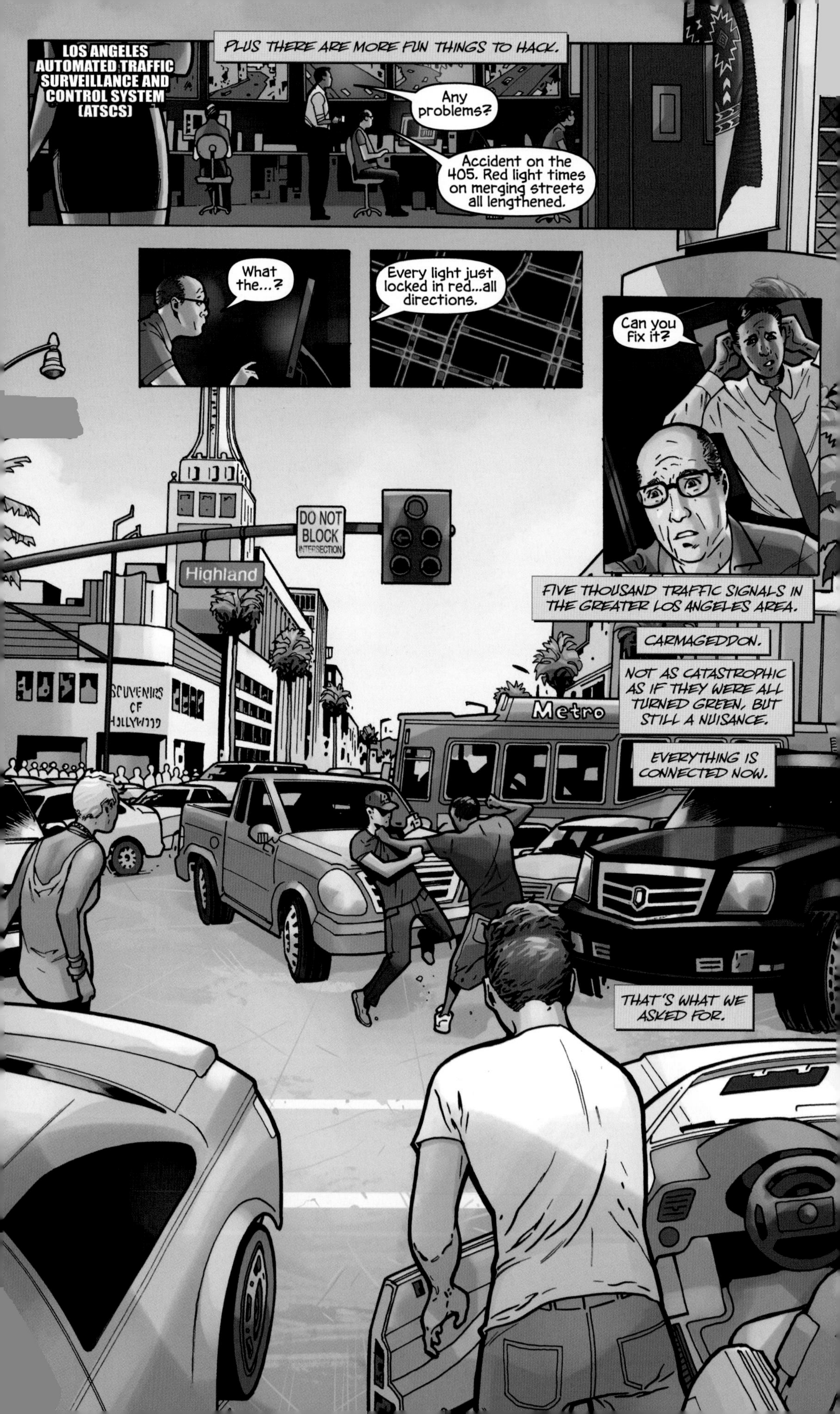
LOS ANGELES AUTOMATED TRAFFIC SURVEILLANCE AND CONTROL SYSTEM (ATSCS)
PLUS THERE ARE MORE FUN THINGS TO HACK.
Any problems?
Accident on the 405. Red light times on merging streets all lengthened.
What the...?
Every light just locked in red...all directions.
Can you fix it?
DO NOT BLOCK INTERSECTION
Highland
SOUVENIRS OF HOLLYWOOD
Metro
FIVE THOUSAND TRAFFIC SIGNALS IN THE GREATER LOS ANGELES AREA.
CARMAGEDDON.
NOT AS CATASTROPHIC AS IF THEY WERE ALL TURNED GREEN, BUT STILL A NUISANCE.
EVERYTHING IS CONNECTED NOW.
THAT'S WHAT WE ASKED FOR.

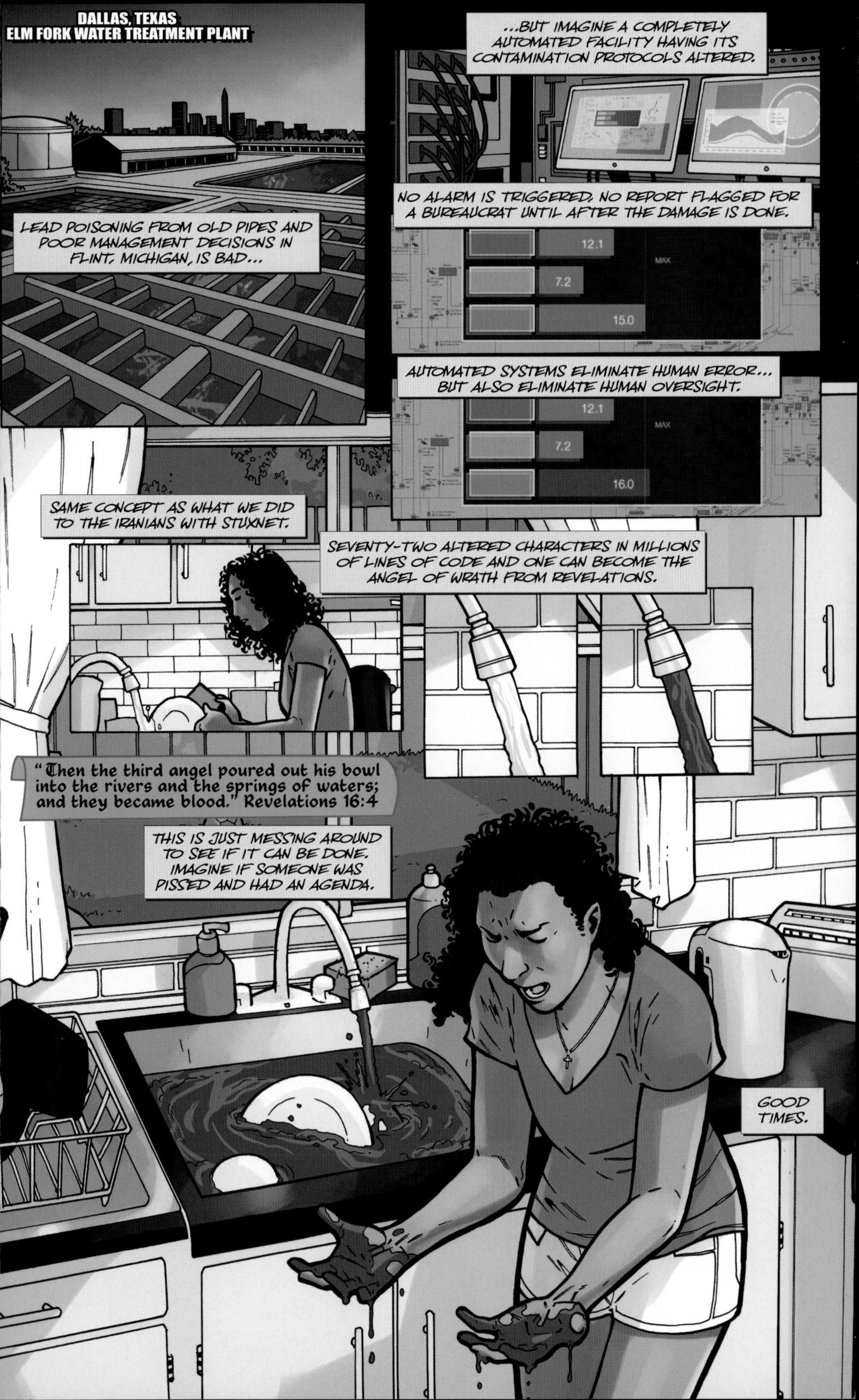
DALLAS, TEXAS
ELM FORK WATER TREATMENT PLANT
LEAD POISONING FROM OLD PIPES AND POOR MANAGEMENT DECISIONS IN FLINT, MICHIGAN, IS BAD...
...BUT IMAGINE A COMPLETELY AUTOMATED FACILITY HAVING ITS CONTAMINATION PROTOCOLS ALTERED.
NO ALARM IS TRIGGERED, NO REPORT FLAGGED FOR A BUREAUCRAT UNTIL AFTER THE DAMAGE IS DONE.
12.1
MAX
7.2
15.0
AUTOMATED SYSTEMS ELIMINATE HUMAN ERROR... BUT ALSO ELIMINATE HUMAN OVERSIGHT.
12.1
MAX
7.2
16.0
SAME CONCEPT AS WHAT WE DID TO THE IRANIANS WITH STUXNET.
SEVENTY-TWO ALTERED CHARACTERS IN MILLIONS OF LINES OF CODE AND ONE CAN BECOME THE ANGEL OF WRATH FROM REVELATIONS.
"Then the third angel poured out his bowl into the rivers and the springs of waters; and they became blood." Revelations 16:4
THIS IS JUST MESSING AROUND TO SEE IF IT CAN BE DONE. IMAGINE IF SOMEONE WAS PISSED AND HAD AN AGENDA.
GOOD TIMES.

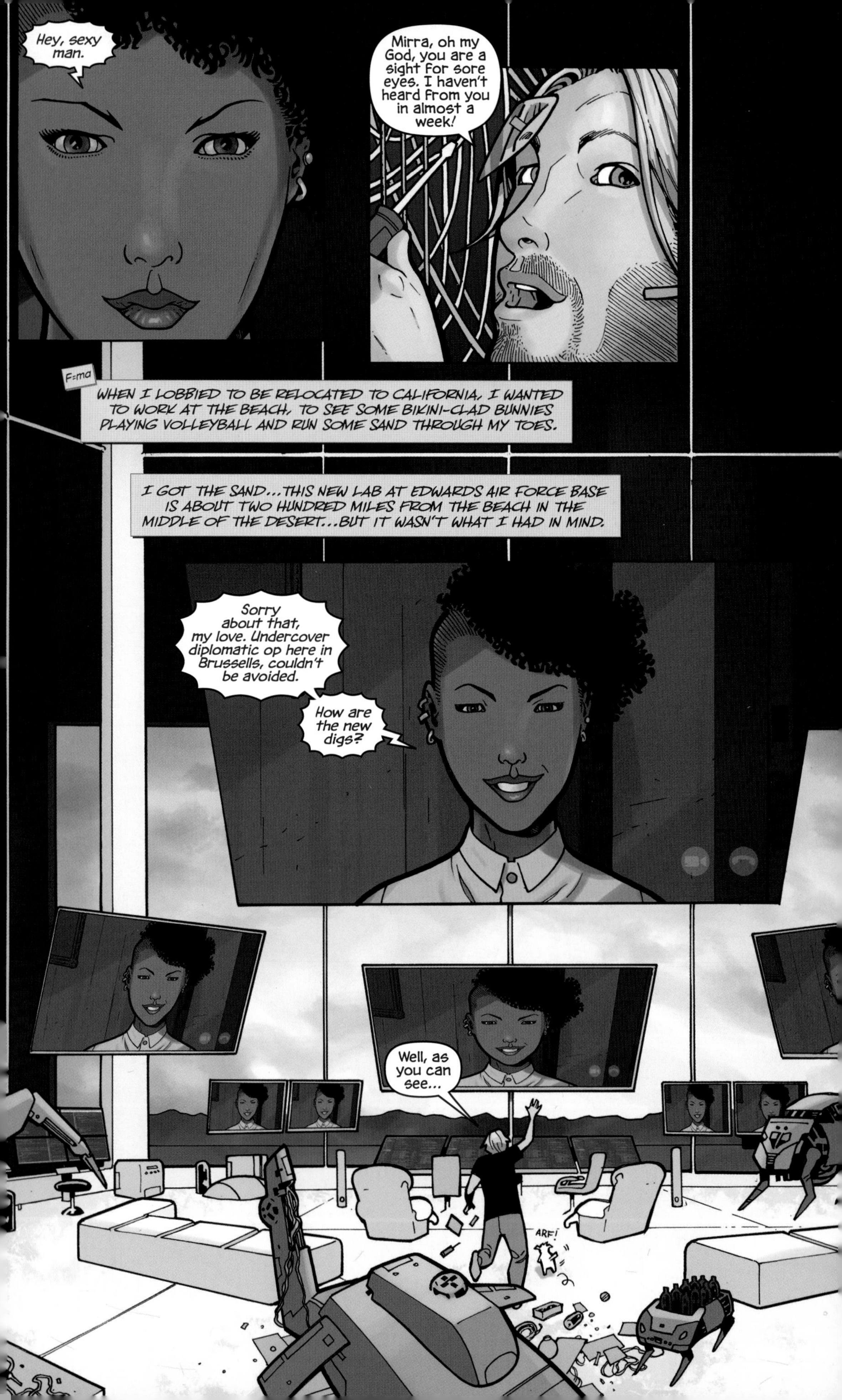

Hey, sexy man.
Mirra, oh my God, you are a sight for sore eyes. I haven't heard from you in almost a week!
F=ma
WHEN I LOBBIED TO BE RELOCATED TO CALIFORNIA, I WANTED TO WORK AT THE BEACH, TO SEE SOME BIKINI-CLAD BUNNIES PLAYING VOLLEYBALL AND RUN SOME SAND THROUGH MY TOES.
I GOT THE SAND...THIS NEW LAB AT EDWARDS AIR FORCE BASE IS ABOUT TWO HUNDRED MILES FROM THE BEACH IN THE MIDDLE OF THE DESERT...BUT IT WASN'T WHAT I HAD IN MIND.
Sorry about that, my love. Undercover diplomatic op here in Brussells, couldn't be avoided.
How are the new digs?
Well, as you can see...
ARF!

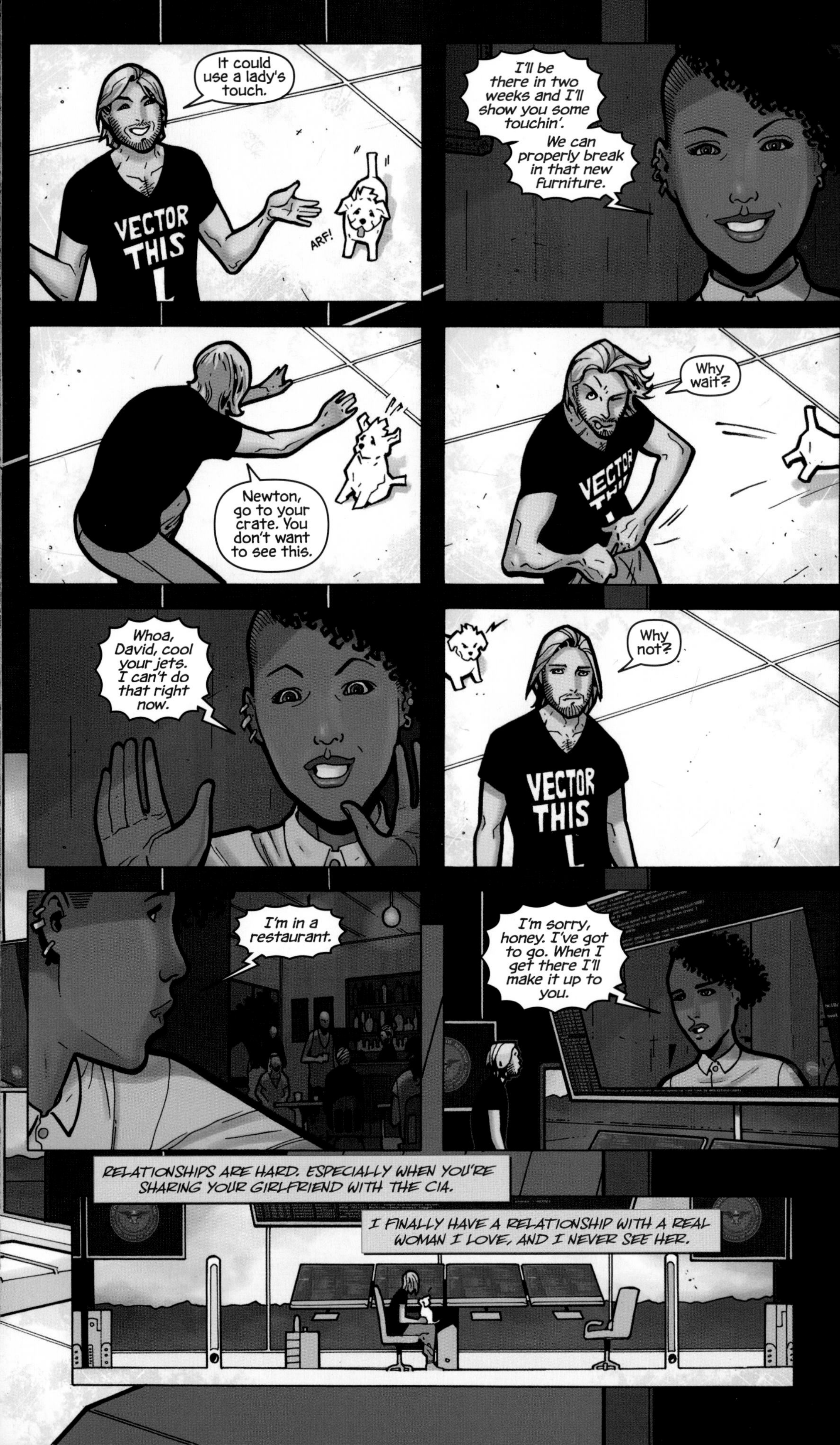
It could use a lady's touch.
ARF!
I'll be there in two weeks and I'll show you some touchin'.
We can properly break in that new furniture.
Newton, go to your crate. You don't want to see this.
Why wait?
Whoa, David, cool your jets. I can't do that right now.
Why not?
I'm in a restaurant.
I'm sorry, honey. I've got to go. When I get there I'll make it up to you.
RELATIONSHIPS ARE HARD. ESPECIALLY WHEN YOU'RE SHARING YOUR GIRLFRIEND WITH THE CIA.
I FINALLY HAVE A RELATIONSHIP WITH A REAL WOMAN I LOVE, AND I NEVER SEE HER.

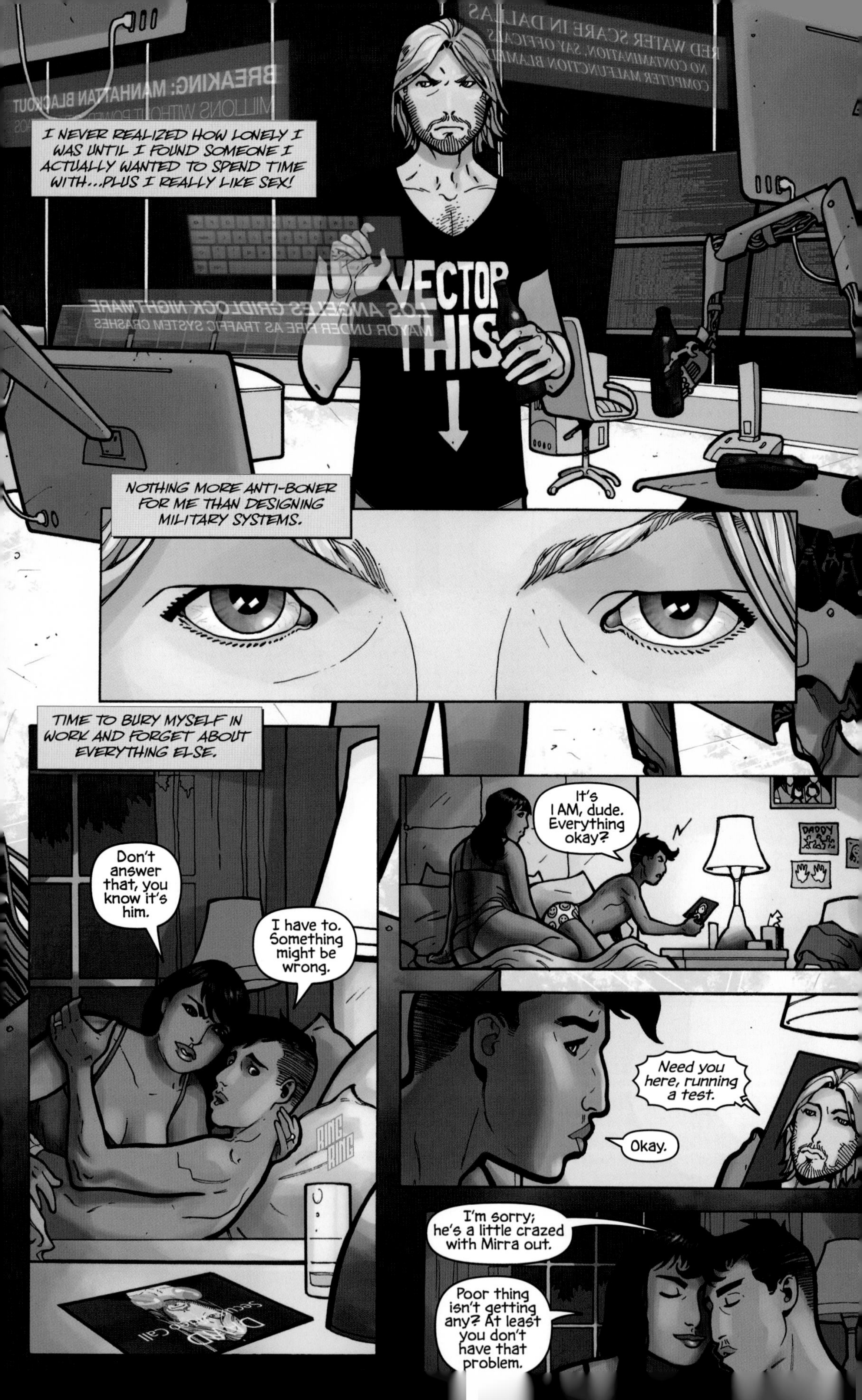
BREAKING: MANHATTAN BLACKOUT
RED WATER SCARE IN DALLAS
I NEVER REALIZED HOW LONELY I WAS UNTIL I FOUND SOMEONE I ACTUALLY WANTED TO SPEND TIME WITH...PLUS I REALLY LIKE SEX!
VECTOR THIS
LOS ANGELES GRIDLOCK NIGHTMARE
MAYOR UNDER FIRE AS TRAFFIC SYSTEM CRASHES
NOTHING MORE ANTI-BONER FOR ME THAN DESIGNING MILITARY SYSTEMS.
TIME TO BURY MYSELF IN WORK AND FORGET ABOUT EVERYTHING ELSE.
Don't answer that, you know it's him.
I have to. Something might be wrong.
RING RING
It's I AM, dude. Everything okay?
Need you here, running a test.
Okay.
I'm sorry; he's a little crazed with Mirra out.
Poor thing isn't getting any? At least you don't have that problem.

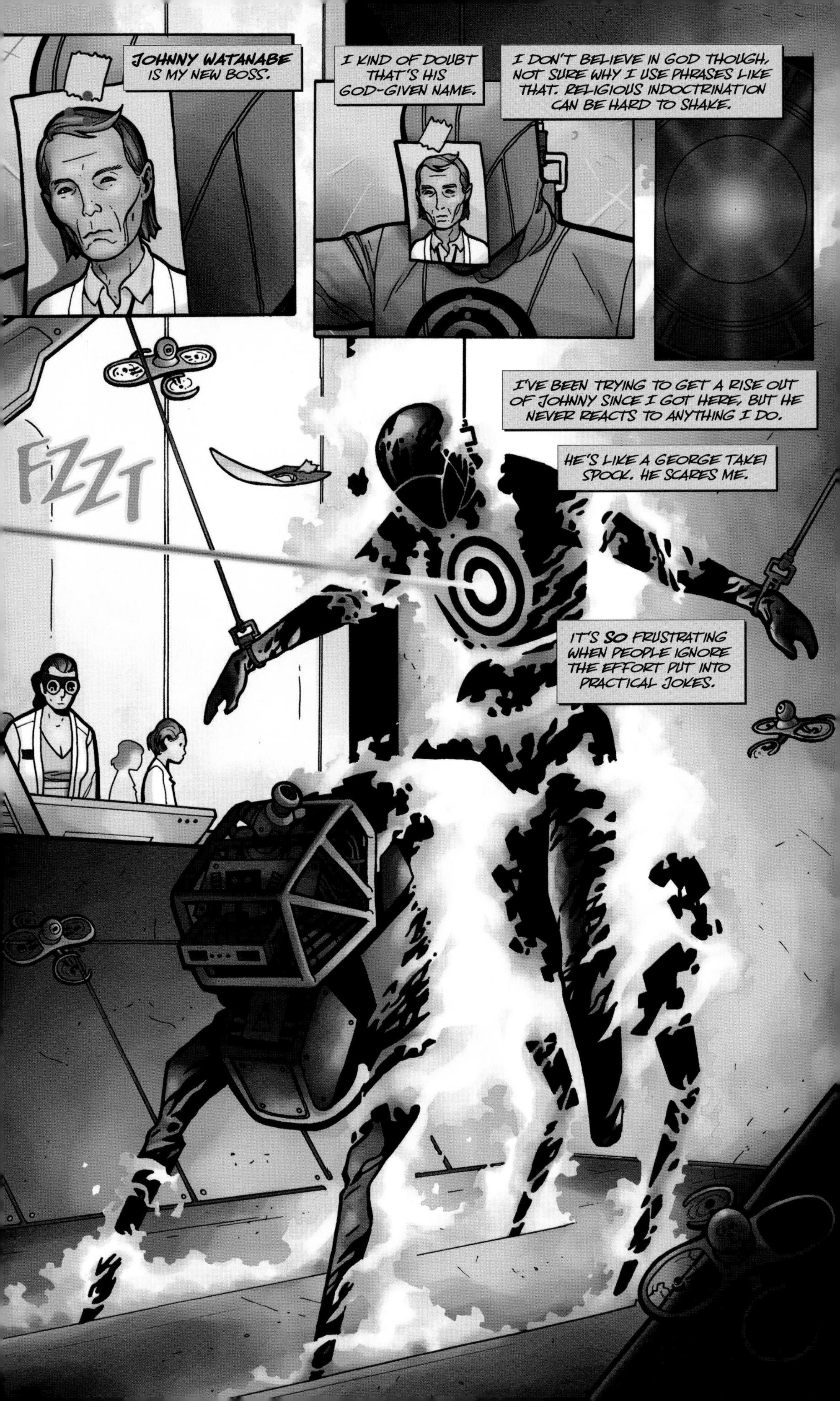
JOHNNY WATANABE IS MY NEW BOSS.
I KIND OF DOUBT THAT'S HIS GOD-GIVEN NAME.
I DON'T BELIEVE IN GOD THOUGH, NOT SURE WHY I USE PHRASES LIKE THAT. RELIGIOUS INDOCTRINATION CAN BE HARD TO SHAKE.
FZZT
I'VE BEEN TRYING TO GET A RISE OUT OF JOHNNY SINCE I GOT HERE, BUT HE NEVER REACTS TO ANYTHING I DO.
HE'S LIKE A GEORGE TAKEI SPOCK. HE SCARES ME.
IT'S SO FRUSTRATING WHEN PEOPLE IGNORE THE EFFORT PUT INTO PRACTICAL JOKES.

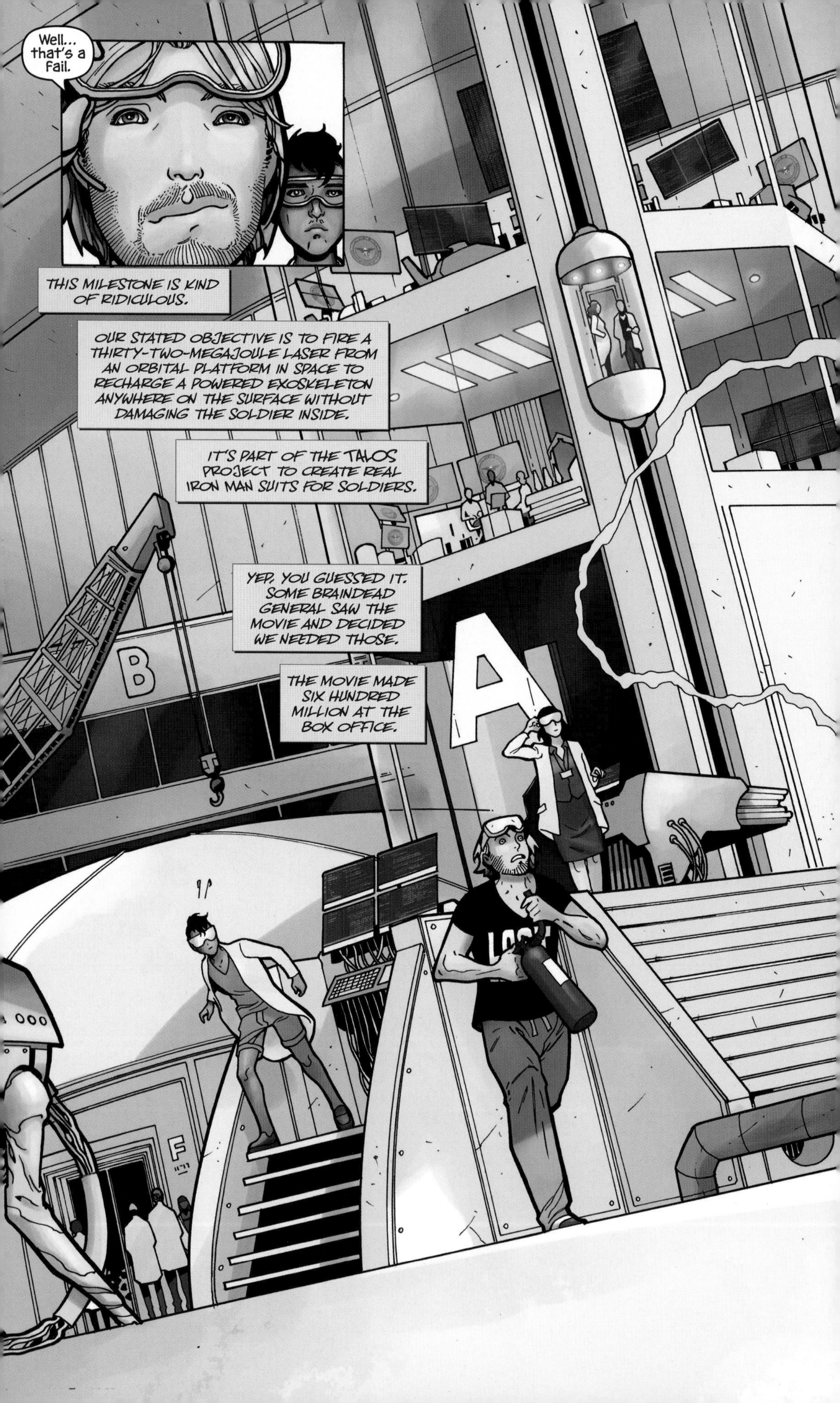
Well... that's a Fail.
THIS MILESTONE IS KIND OF RIDICULOUS.
OUR STATED OBJECTIVE IS TO FIRE A THIRTY-TWO-MEGAJOULE LASER FROM AN ORBITAL PLATFORM IN SPACE TO RECHARGE A POWERED EXOSKELETON ANYWHERE ON THE SURFACE WITHOUT DAMAGING THE SOLDIER INSIDE.
IT'S PART OF THE TALOS PROJECT TO CREATE REAL IRON MAN SUITS FOR SOLDIERS.
YEP, YOU GUESSED IT. SOME BRAINDEAD GENERAL SAW THE MOVIE AND DECIDED WE NEEDED THOSE.
THE MOVIE MADE SIX HUNDRED MILLION AT THE BOX OFFICE.
B
A
F

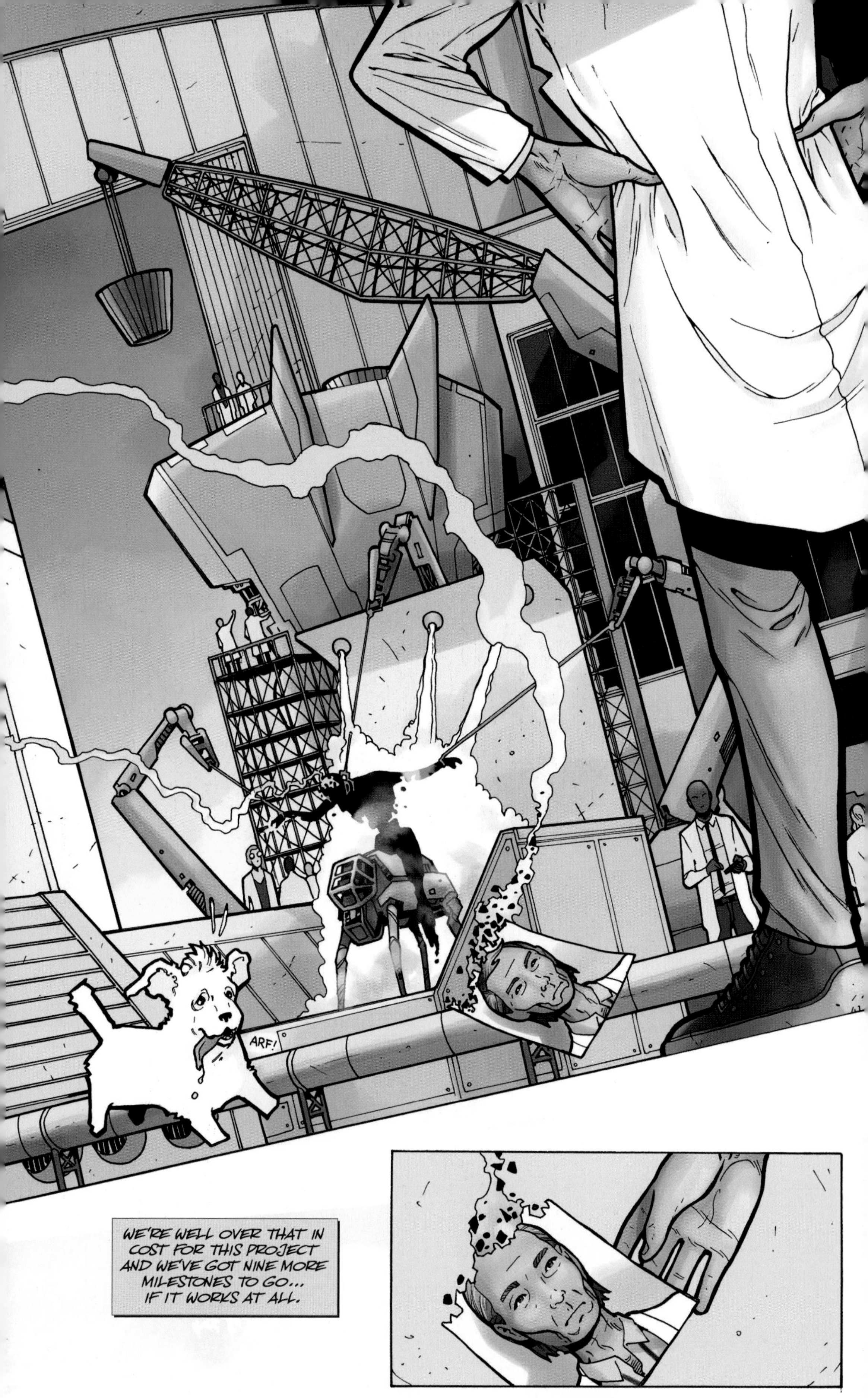
ARF!
WE'RE WELL OVER THAT IN COST FOR THIS PROJECT AND WE'VE GOT NINE MORE MILESTONES TO GO... IF IT WORKS AT ALL.

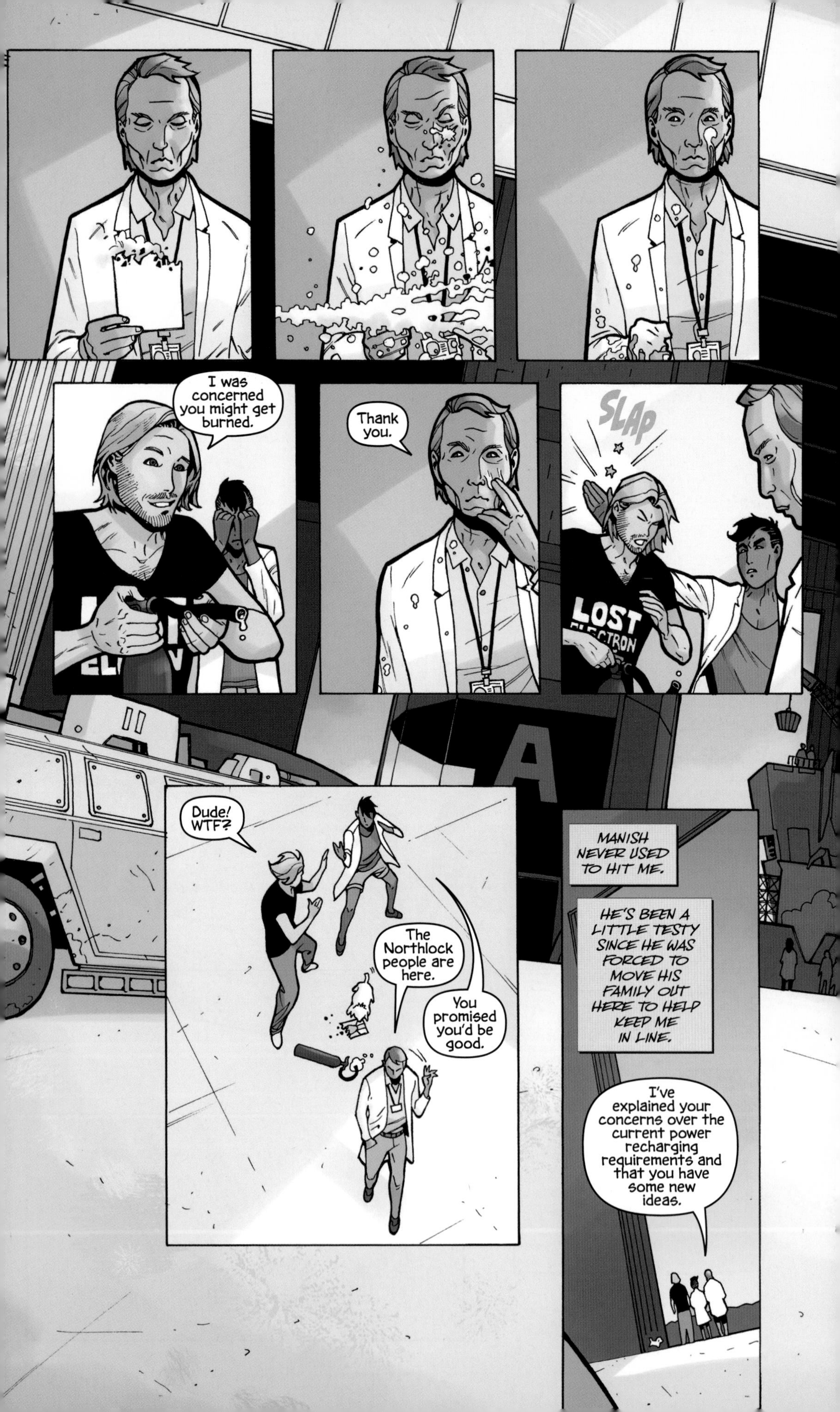
I was concerned you might get burned.
LOST ELECTRON
Thank you.
SLAP
LOST ELECTRON
Dude! WTF?
The Northlock people are here.
You promised you'd be good.
MANISH NEVER USED TO HIT ME.
HE'S BEEN A LITTLE TESTY SINCE HE WAS FORCED TO MOVE HIS FAMILY OUT HERE TO HELP KEEP ME IN LINE.
I've explained your concerns over the current power recharging requirements and that you have some new ideas.

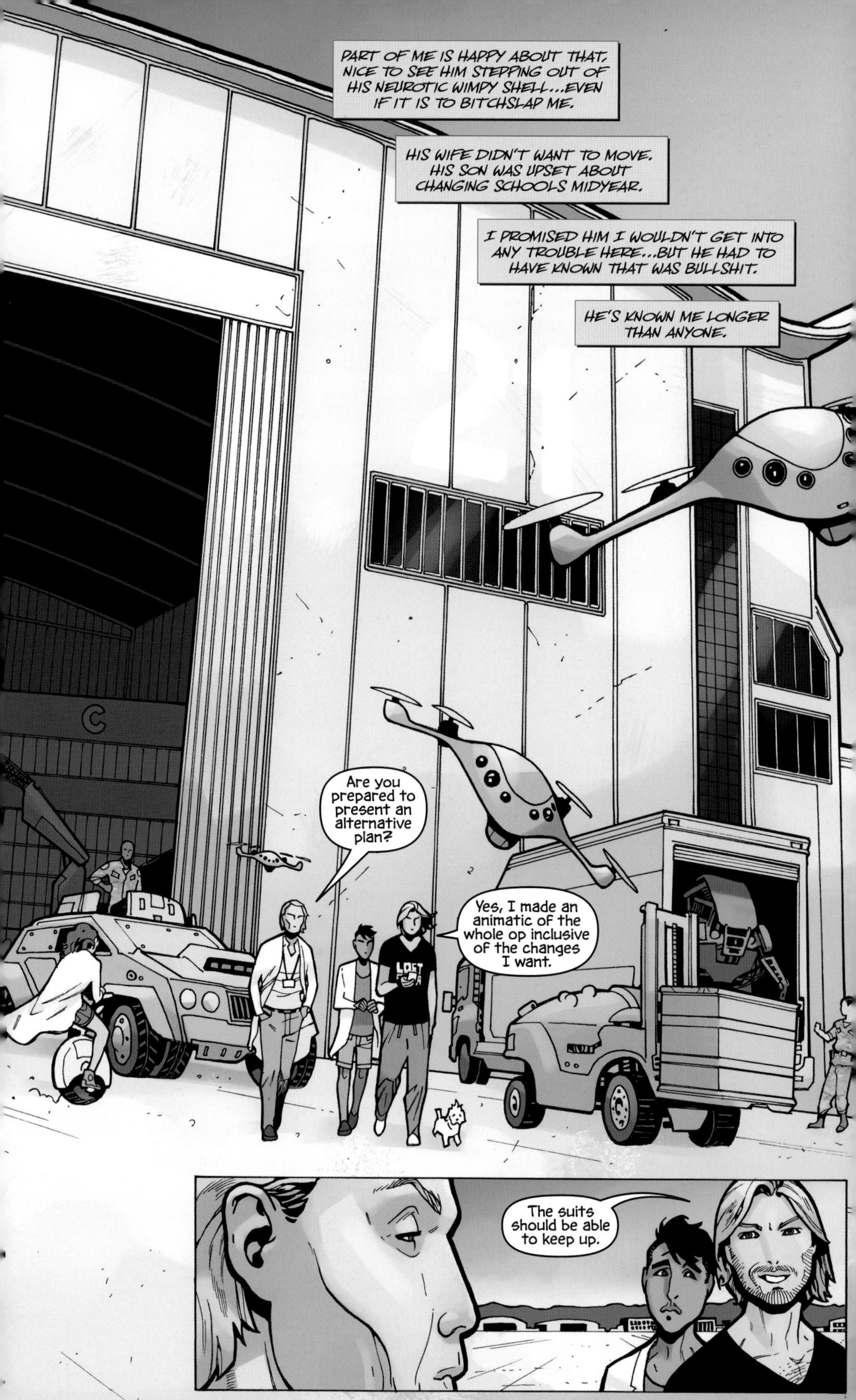
PART OF ME IS HAPPY ABOUT THAT. NICE TO SEE HIM STEPPING OUT OF HIS NEUROTIC WIMPY SHELL...EVEN IF IT IS TO BITCHSLAP ME.
HIS WIFE DIDN'T WANT TO MOVE. HIS SON WAS UPSET ABOUT CHANGING SCHOOLS MIDYEAR.
I PROMISED HIM I WOULDN'T GET INTO ANY TROUBLE HERE...BUT HE HAD TO HAVE KNOWN THAT WAS BULLSHIT.
HE'S KNOWN ME LONGER THAN ANYONE.
Are you prepared to present an alternative plan?
Yes, I made an animatic of the whole op inclusive of the changes I want.
The suits should be able to keep up.

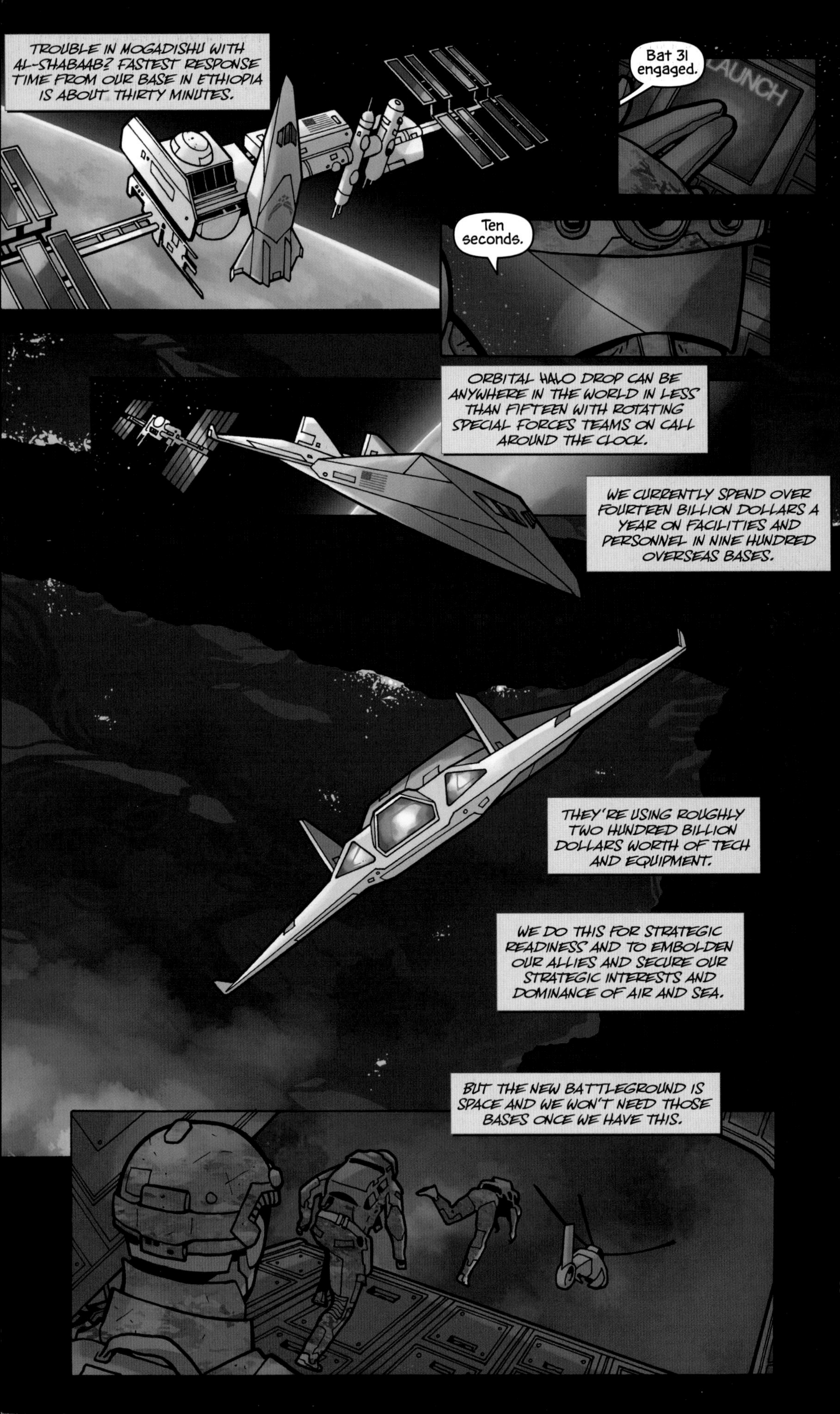
TROUBLE IN MOGADISHU WITH AL-SHABAAB? FASTEST RESPONSE TIME FROM OUR BASE IN ETHIOPIA IS ABOUT THIRTY MINUTES.
Bat 31 engaged.
LAUNCH
Ten seconds.
ORBITAL HALO DROP CAN BE ANYWHERE IN THE WORLD IN LESS THAN FIFTEEN WITH ROTATING SPECIAL FORCES TEAMS ON CALL AROUND THE CLOCK.
WE CURRENTLY SPEND OVER FOURTEEN BILLION DOLLARS A YEAR ON FACILITIES AND PERSONNEL IN NINE HUNDRED OVERSEAS BASES.
THEY'RE USING ROUGHLY TWO HUNDRED BILLION DOLLARS WORTH OF TECH AND EQUIPMENT.
WE DO THIS FOR STRATEGIC READINESS AND TO EMBOLDEN OUR ALLIES AND SECURE OUR STRATEGIC INTERESTS AND DOMINANCE OF AIR AND SEA.
BUT THE NEW BATTLEGROUND IS SPACE AND WE WON'T NEED THOSE BASES ONCE WE HAVE THIS.

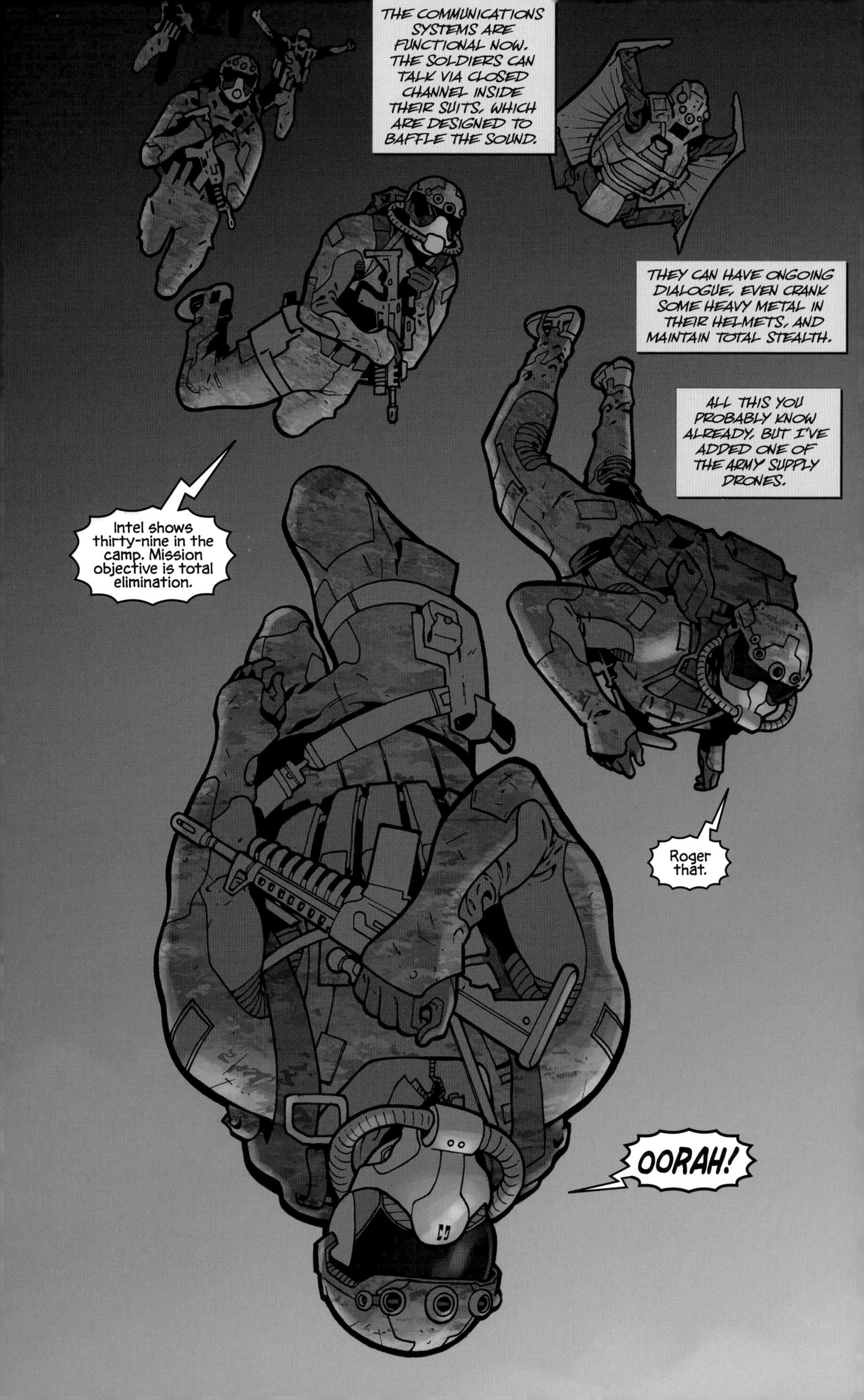
THE COMMUNICATIONS SYSTEMS ARE FUNCTIONAL NOW. THE SOLDIERS CAN TALK VIA CLOSED CHANNEL INSIDE THEIR SUITS, WHICH ARE DESIGNED TO BAFFLE THE SOUND.
THEY CAN HAVE ONGOING DIALOGUE, EVEN CRANK SOME HEAVY METAL IN THEIR HELMETS, AND MAINTAIN TOTAL STEALTH.
ALL THIS YOU PROBABLY KNOW ALREADY, BUT I'VE ADDED ONE OF THE ARMY SUPPLY DRONES.
Intel shows thirty-nine in the camp. Mission objective is total elimination.
Roger that.
OORAH!

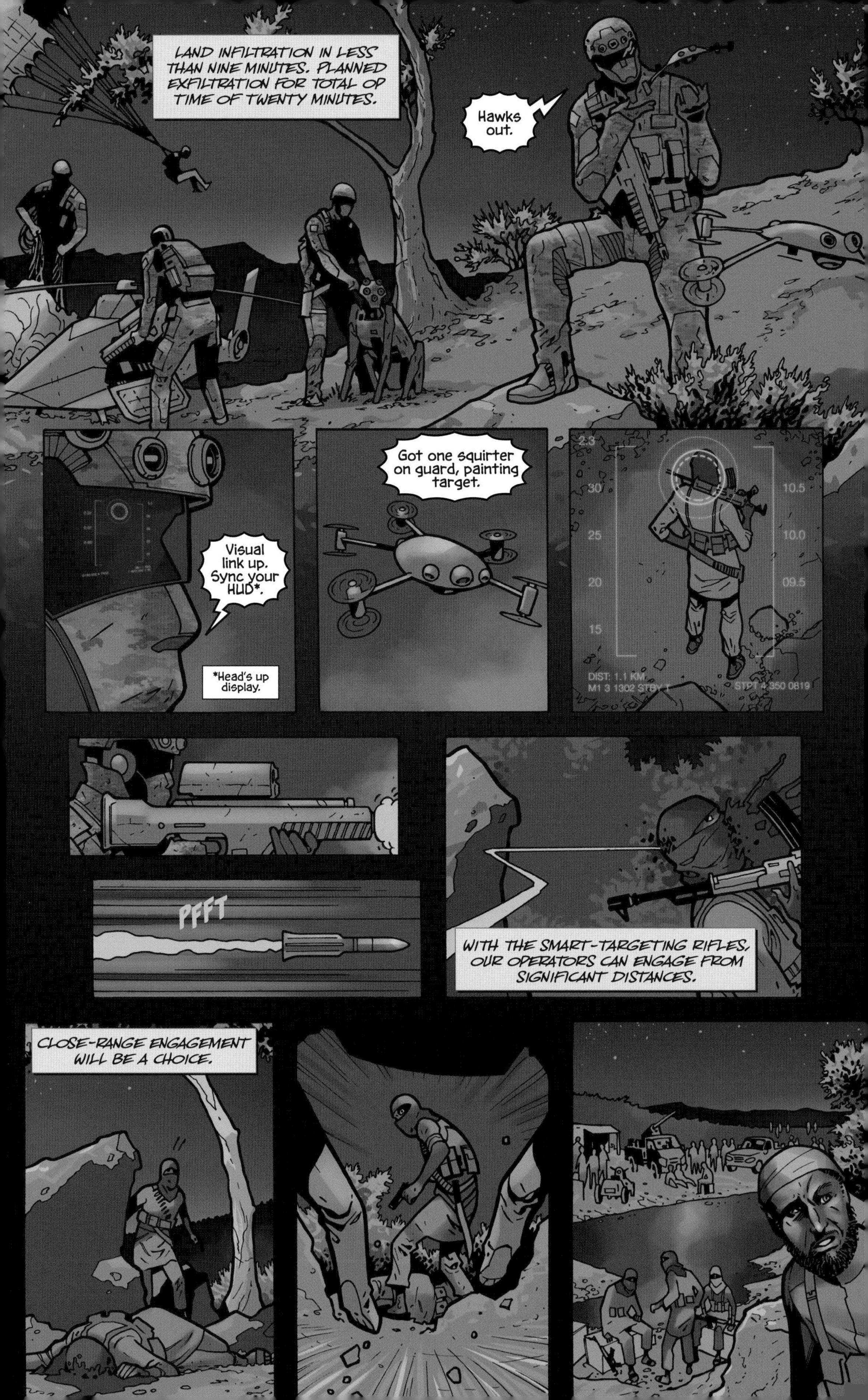
LAND INFILTRATION IN LESS THAN NINE MINUTES. PLANNED EXFILTRATION FOR TOTAL OP TIME OF TWENTY MINUTES.
Hawks out.
Visual link up. Sync your HUD*.
*Head's up display.
Got one squirter on guard, painting target.
2.3
30
25
20
15
10.5
10.0
09.5
DIST: 1.1 KM
M1 3 1302 STBY I
STPT 4 350 0819
PFFT
WITH THE SMART-TARGETING RIFLES, OUR OPERATORS CAN ENGAGE FROM SIGNIFICANT DISTANCES.
CLOSE-RANGE ENGAGEMENT WILL BE A CHOICE.

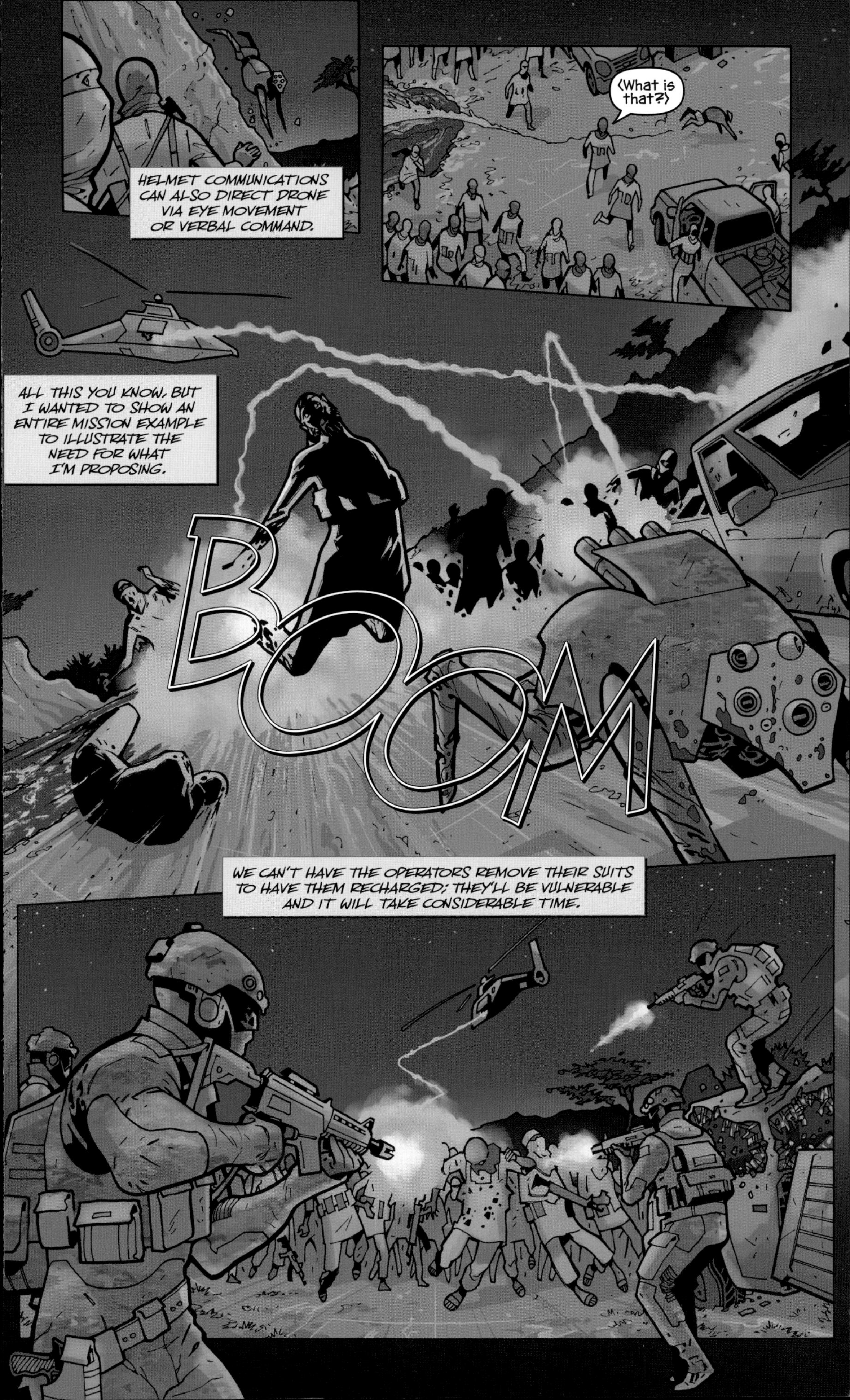
HELMET COMMUNICATIONS CAN ALSO DIRECT DRONE VIA EYE MOVEMENT OR VERBAL COMMAND.
‹What is that?›
ALL THIS YOU KNOW, BUT I WANTED TO SHOW AN ENTIRE MISSION EXAMPLE TO ILLUSTRATE THE NEED FOR WHAT I'M PROPOSING.
BOOOM
WE CAN'T HAVE THE OPERATORS REMOVE THEIR SUITS TO HAVE THEM RECHARGED; THEY'LL BE VULNERABLE AND IT WILL TAKE CONSIDERABLE TIME.

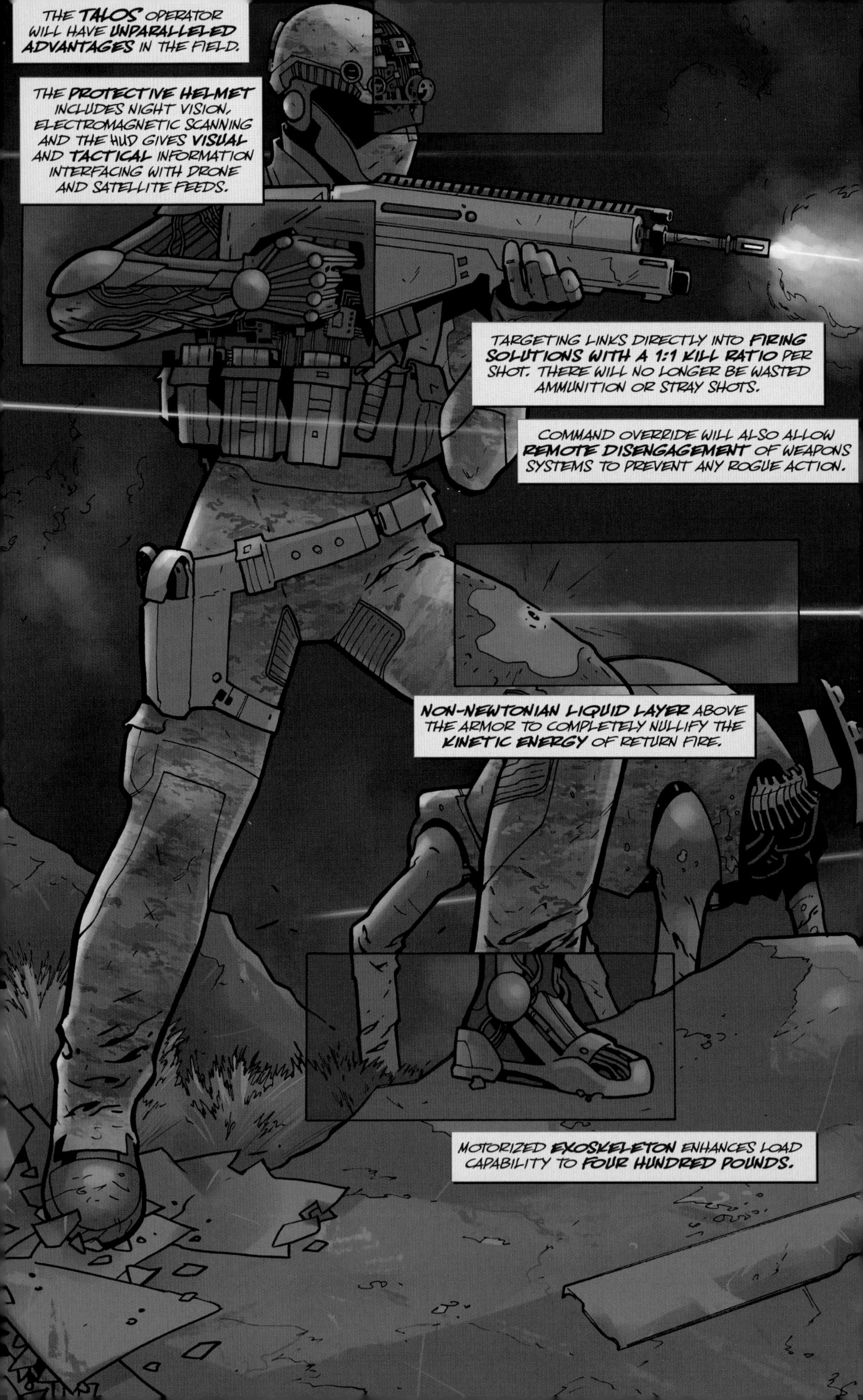
THE TALOS OPERATOR WILL HAVE UNPARALLELED ADVANTAGES IN THE FIELD.
THE PROTECTIVE HELMET INCLUDES NIGHT VISION, ELECTROMAGNETIC SCANNING AND THE HUD GIVES VISUAL AND TACTICAL INFORMATION INTERFACING WITH DRONE AND SATELLITE FEEDS.
TARGETING LINKS DIRECTLY INTO FIRING SOLUTIONS WITH A 1:1 KILL RATIO PER SHOT. THERE WILL NO LONGER BE WASTED AMMUNITION OR STRAY SHOTS.
COMMAND OVERRIDE WILL ALSO ALLOW REMOTE DISENGAGEMENT OF WEAPONS SYSTEMS TO PREVENT ANY ROGUE ACTION.
NON-NEWTONIAN LIQUID LAYER ABOVE THE ARMOR TO COMPLETELY NULLIFY THE KINETIC ENERGY OF RETURN FIRE.
MOTORIZED EXOSKELETON ENHANCES LOAD CAPABILITY TO FOUR HUNDRED POUNDS.

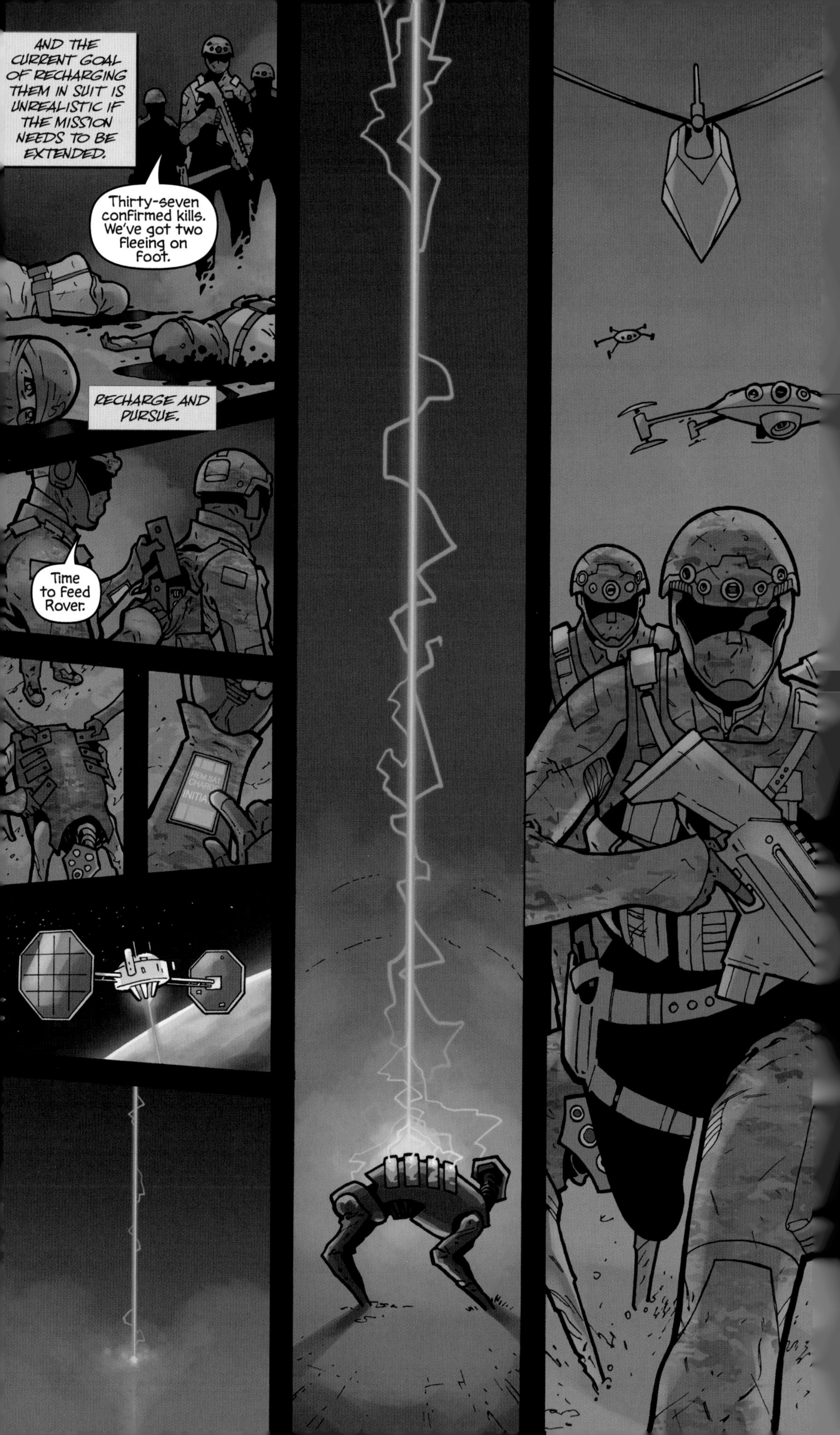

AND THE CURRENT GOAL OF RECHARGING THEM IN SUIT IS UNREALISTIC IF THE MISSION NEEDS TO BE EXTENDED.
Thirty-seven confirmed kills. We've got two fleeing on foot.
RECHARGE AND PURSUE.
Time to Feed Rover.

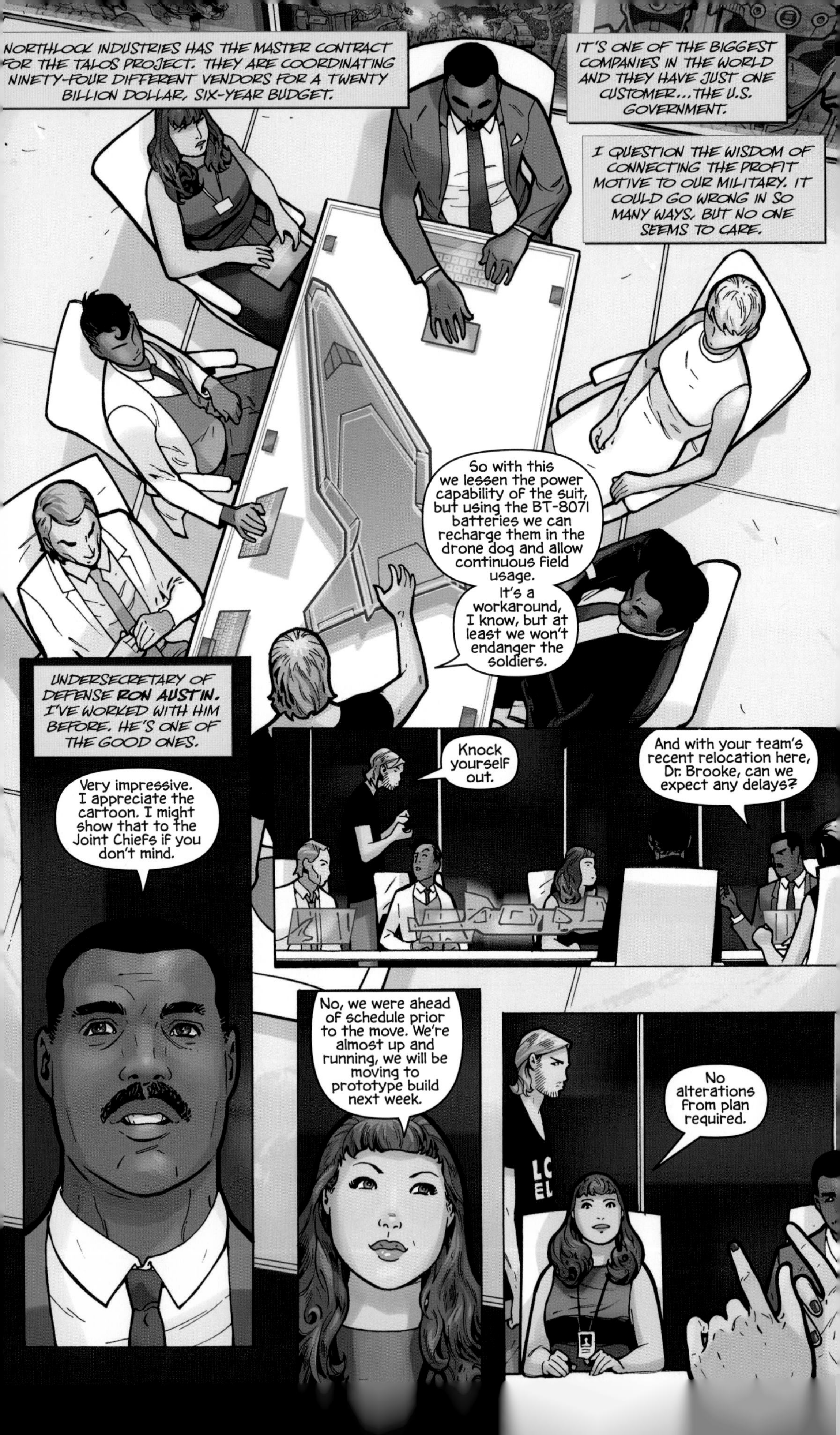
NORTHLOCK INDUSTRIES HAS THE MASTER CONTRACT FOR THE TALOS PROJECT. THEY ARE COORDINATING NINETY-FOUR DIFFERENT VENDORS FOR A TWENTY BILLION DOLLAR, SIX-YEAR BUDGET.
IT'S ONE OF THE BIGGEST COMPANIES IN THE WORLD AND THEY HAVE JUST ONE CUSTOMER... THE U.S. GOVERNMENT.
I QUESTION THE WISDOM OF CONNECTING THE PROFIT MOTIVE TO OUR MILITARY. IT COULD GO WRONG IN SO MANY WAYS, BUT NO ONE SEEMS TO CARE.
So with this we lessen the power capability of the suit, but using the BT-8071 batteries we can recharge them in the drone dog and allow continuous field usage.
It's a workaround, I know, but at least we won't endanger the soldiers.
UNDERSECRETARY OF DEFENSE RON AUSTIN. I'VE WORKED WITH HIM BEFORE. HE'S ONE OF THE GOOD ONES.
Very impressive. I appreciate the cartoon. I might show that to the Joint Chiefs if you don't mind.
Knock yourself out.
And with your team's recent relocation here, Dr. Brooke, can we expect any delays?
No, we were ahead of schedule prior to the move. We're almost up and running, we will be moving to prototype build next week.
No alterations from plan required.

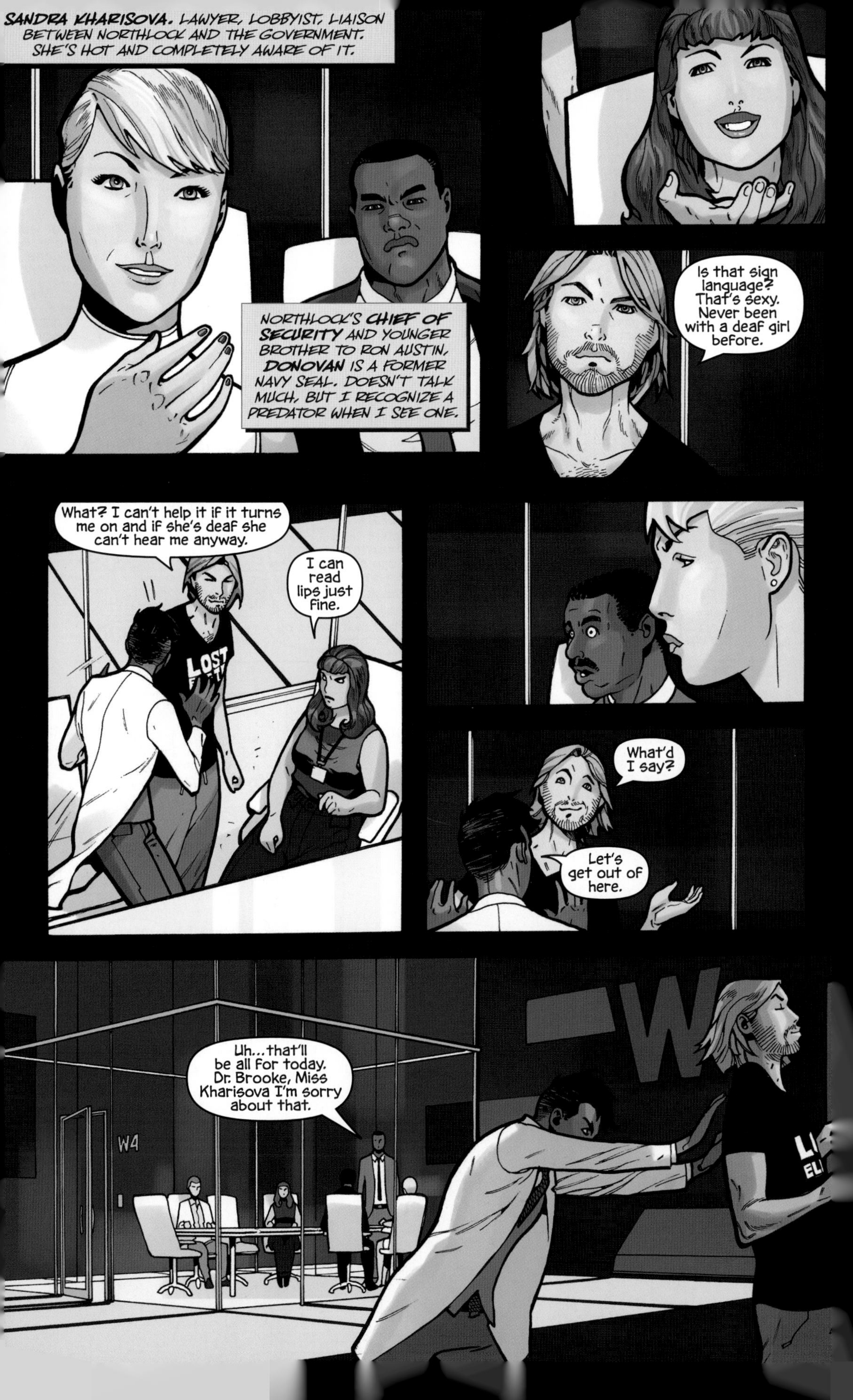
SANDRA KHARISOVA. LAWYER, LOBBYIST, LIAISON BETWEEN NORTHLOCK AND THE GOVERNMENT. SHE'S HOT AND COMPLETELY AWARE OF IT.
NORTHLOCK'S CHIEF OF SECURITY AND YOUNGER BROTHER TO RON AUSTIN, DONOVAN IS A FORMER NAVY SEAL. DOESN'T TALK MUCH, BUT I RECOGNIZE A PREDATOR WHEN I SEE ONE.
Is that sign language? That's sexy. Never been with a deaf girl before.
What? I can't help it if it turns me on and if she's deaf she can't hear me anyway.
I can read lips just fine.
LOST
What'd I say?
Let's get out of here.
Uh...that'll be all for today. Dr. Brooke, Miss Kharisova I'm sorry about that.
W4
W

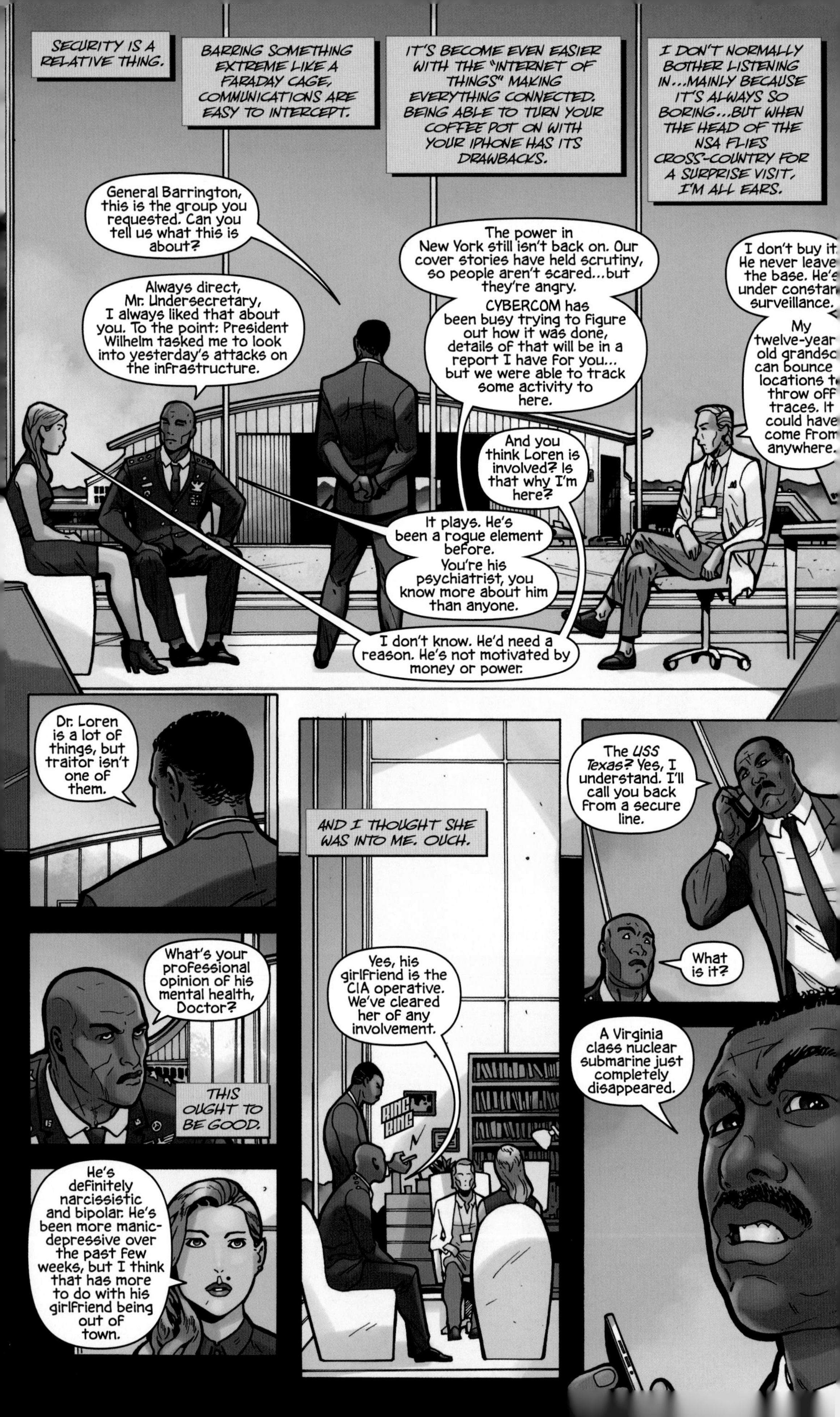

SECURITY IS A RELATIVE THING.
BARRING SOMETHING EXTREME LIKE A FARADAY CAGE, COMMUNICATIONS ARE EASY TO INTERCEPT.
IT'S BECOME EVEN EASIER WITH THE "INTERNET OF THINGS" MAKING EVERYTHING CONNECTED. BEING ABLE TO TURN YOUR COFFEE POT ON WITH YOUR IPHONE HAS ITS DRAWBACKS.
I DON'T NORMALLY BOTHER LISTENING IN...MAINLY BECAUSE IT'S ALWAYS SO BORING...BUT WHEN THE HEAD OF THE NSA FLIES CROSS-COUNTRY FOR A SURPRISE VISIT, I'M ALL EARS.
General Barrington, this is the group you requested. Can you tell us what this is about?
Always direct, Mr. Undersecretary, I always liked that about you. To the point: President Wilhelm tasked me to look into yesterday's attacks on the infrastructure.
The power in New York still isn't back on. Our cover stories have held scrutiny, so people aren't scared...but they're angry.
CYBERCOM has been busy trying to figure out how it was done, details of that will be in a report I have for you... but we were able to track some activity to here.
I don't buy it He never leave the base. He's under constar surveillance.
My twelve-year old grandsc can bounce locations t throw off traces. It could have come from anywhere.
And you think Loren is involved? Is that why I'm here?
It plays. He's been a rogue element before.
You're his psychiatrist, you know more about him than anyone.
I don't know. He'd need a reason. He's not motivated by money or power.
Dr. Loren is a lot of things, but traitor isn't one of them.
What's your professional opinion of his mental health, Doctor?
THIS OUGHT TO BE GOOD.
He's definitely narcissistic and bipolar. He's been more manic-depressive over the past few weeks, but I think that has more to do with his girlfriend being out of town.
AND I THOUGHT SHE WAS INTO ME. OUCH.
Yes, his girlfriend is the CIA operative. We've cleared her of any involvement.
RING RING
The USS Texas? Yes, I understand. I'll call you back from a secure line.
What is it?
A Virginia class nuclear submarine just completely disappeared.

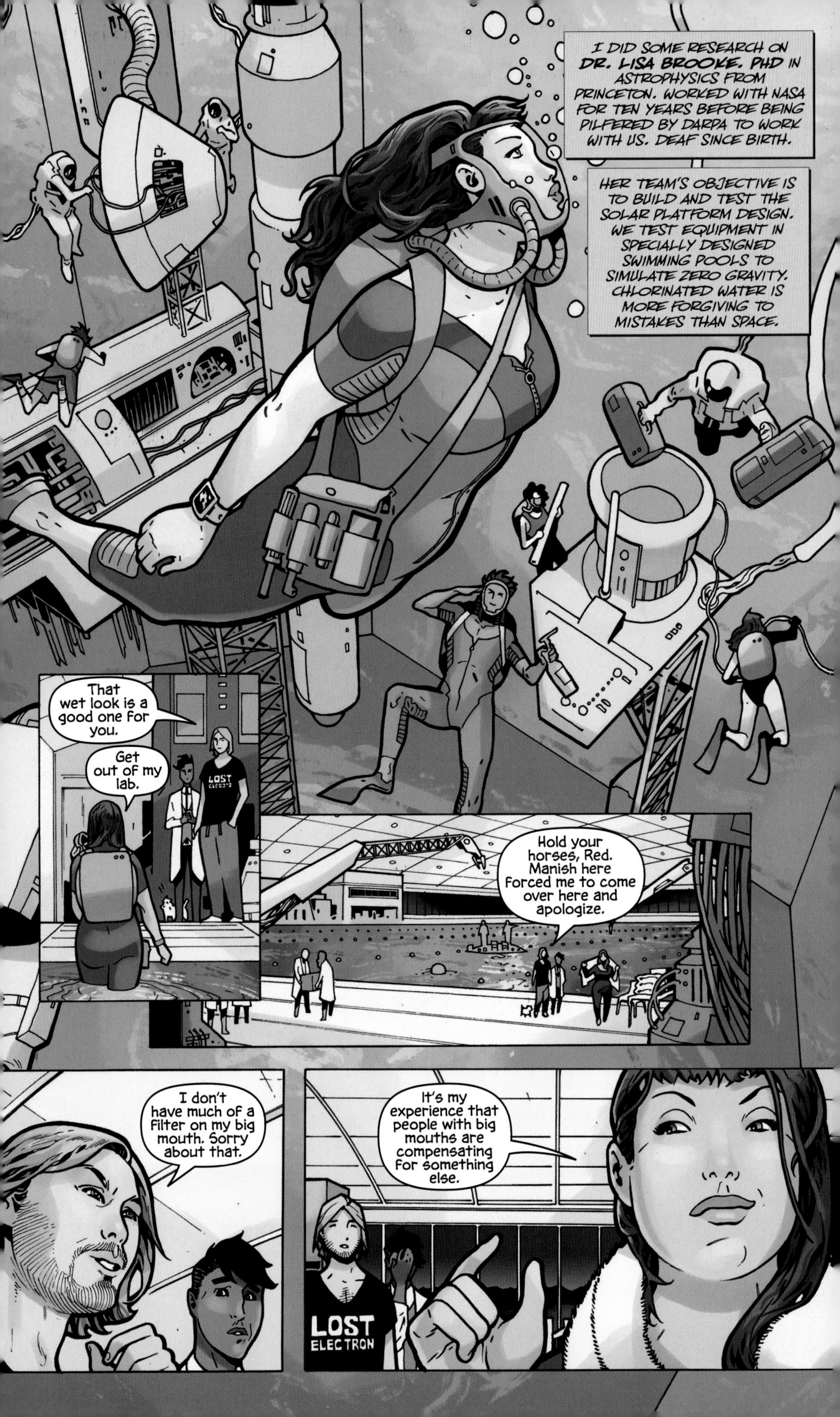
I DID SOME RESEARCH ON DR. LISA BROOKE. PHD IN ASTROPHYSICS FROM PRINCETON. WORKED WITH NASA FOR TEN YEARS BEFORE BEING PILFERED BY DARPA TO WORK WITH US. DEAF SINCE BIRTH.
HER TEAM'S OBJECTIVE IS TO BUILD AND TEST THE SOLAR PLATFORM DESIGN. WE TEST EQUIPMENT IN SPECIALLY DESIGNED SWIMMING POOLS TO SIMULATE ZERO GRAVITY. CHLORINATED WATER IS MORE FORGIVING TO MISTAKES THAN SPACE.
That wet look is a good one for you.
Get out of my lab.
LOST
Hold your horses, Red. Manish here forced me to come over here and apologize.
I don't have much of a filter on my big mouth. Sorry about that.
It's my experience that people with big mouths are compensating for something else.
LOST ELECTRON

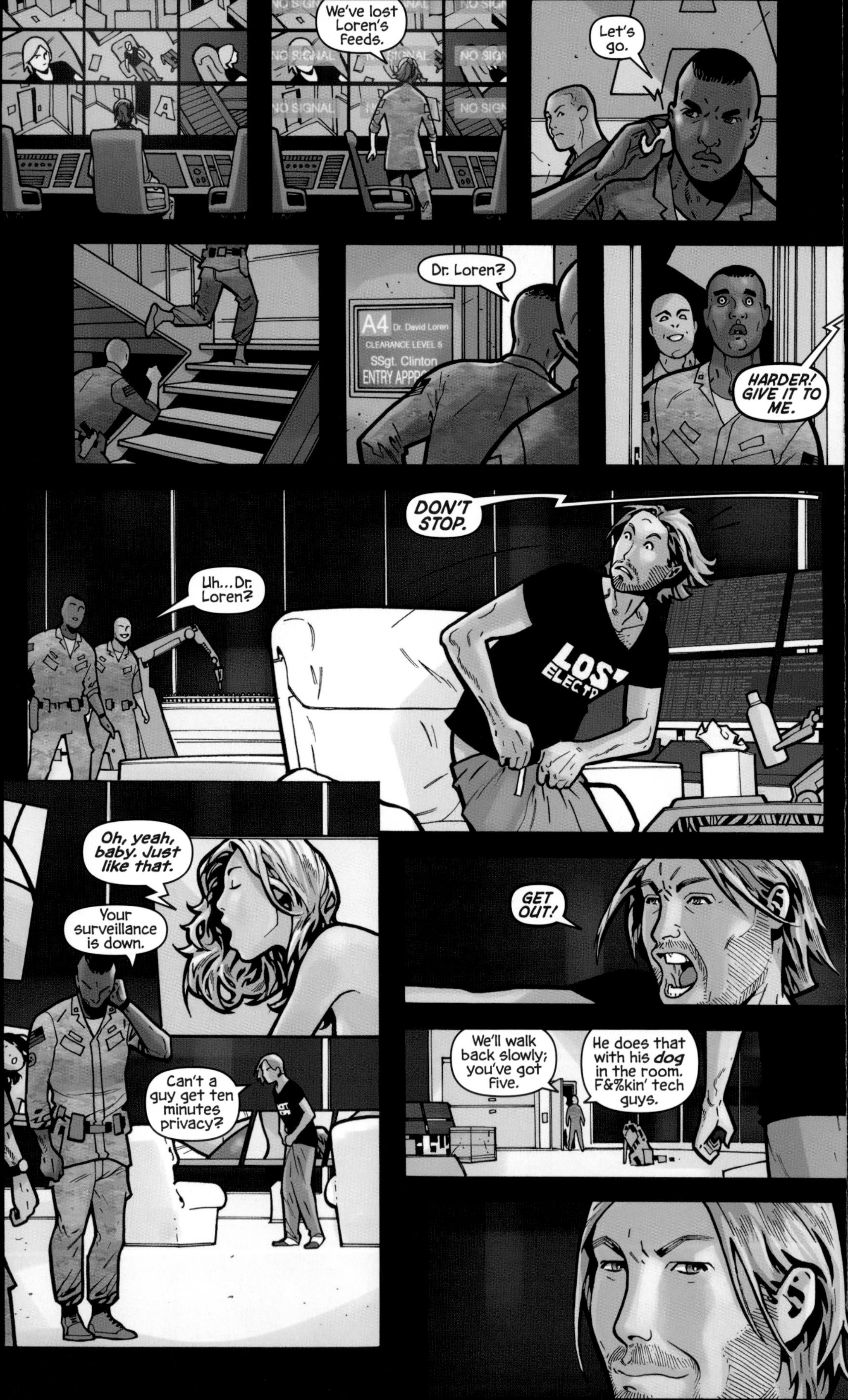
NO SIGNAL
We've lost Loren's feeds.
Let's go.
A4 Dr. David Loren
CLEARANCE LEVEL 5
SSgt. Clinton
Dr. Loren?
HARDER! GIVE IT TO ME.
DON'T STOP.
Uh...Dr. Loren?
Oh, yeah, baby. Just like that.
Your surveillance is down.
GET OUT!
Can't a guy get ten minutes privacy?
We'll walk back slowly; you've got five.
He does that with his dog in the room. F&%kin' tech guys.

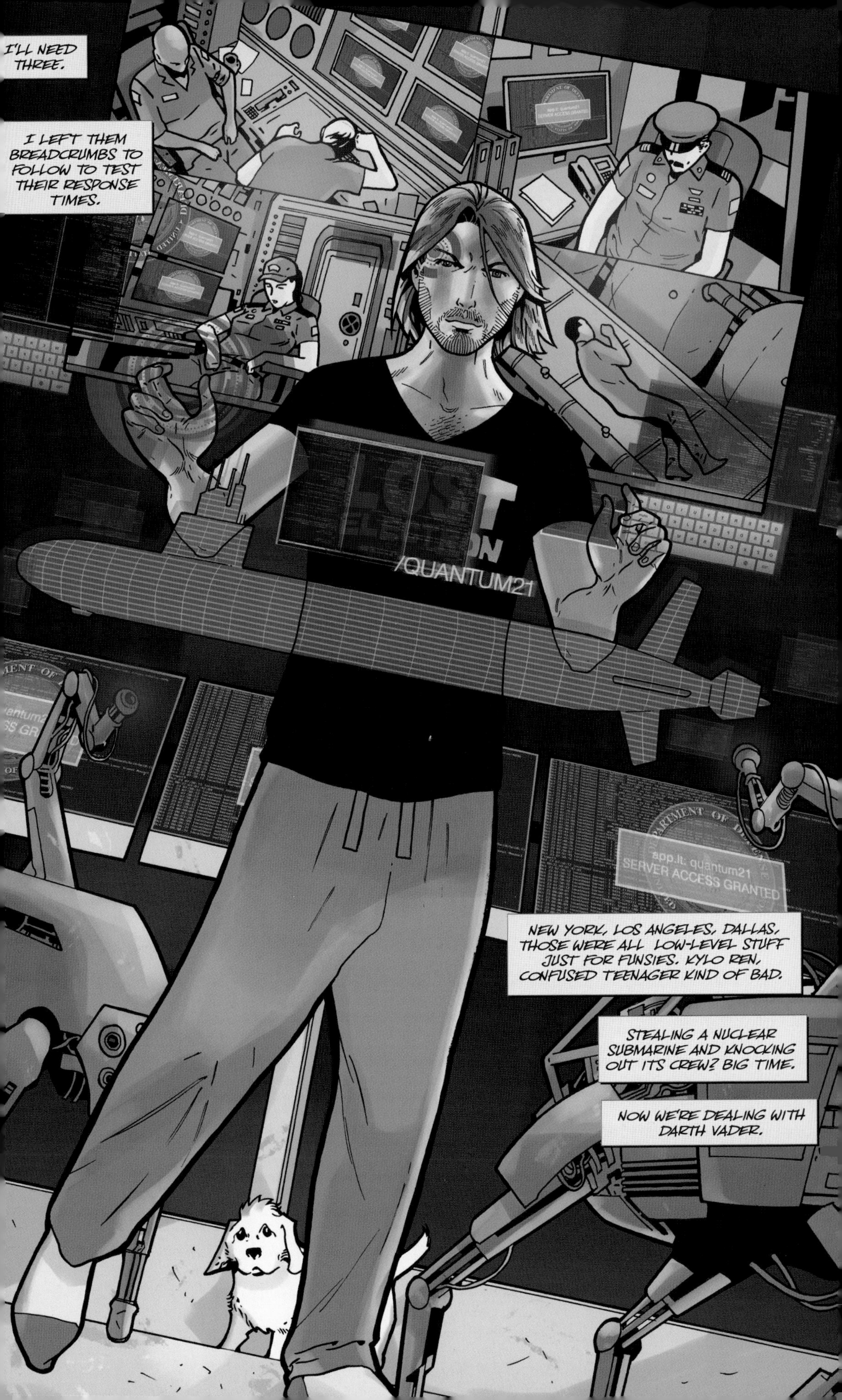

I'LL NEED THREE.
I LEFT THEM BREADCRUMBS TO FOLLOW TO TEST THEIR RESPONSE TIMES.
/QUANTUM21
app.it. quantum21
SERVER ACCESS GRANTED
NEW YORK, LOS ANGELES, DALLAS, THOSE WERE ALL LOW-LEVEL STUFF JUST FOR FUNSIES. KYLO REN, CONFUSED TEENAGER KIND OF BAD.
STEALING A NUCLEAR SUBMARINE AND KNOCKING OUT ITS CREW? BIG TIME.
NOW WE'RE DEALING WITH DARTH VADER.

CHAPTER TWO

THINK TANK

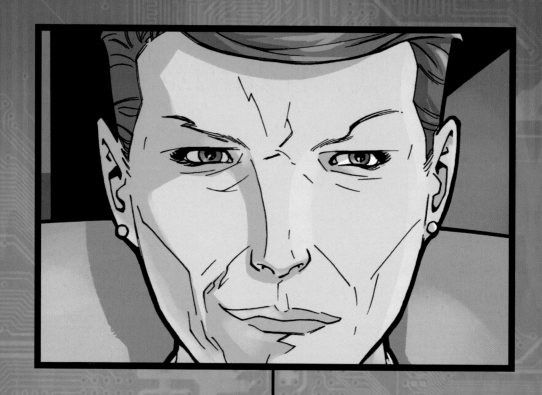

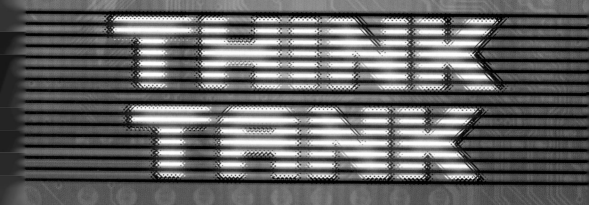

$$\oint d\vec{A} = \frac{1}{\varepsilon_0} q_{in} \qquad \oint B \, dA = 0 \qquad \oint E \, d\lambda = -\frac{d}{dt} \int B \, dA$$

$$\oint d\vec{l} = \mu_0 I_{in} \qquad \vec{F} = q(\vec{v} \times \vec{B} + \vec{E}) \qquad i = \frac{dq}{dt}$$

charge $\qquad E = \frac{1}{4\pi\varepsilon_0} \frac{q}{r^2} \qquad V = \frac{1}{4\pi\varepsilon_0} \frac{q}{r} \qquad p = qd$

$-V_i = -\int$

$\vec{\tau} = \vec{p} \times \vec{E}$

If you want a vision of the future, imagine a boot stamping on a human face. Forever.

George Orwell

$\frac{Q}{V} \qquad U_E = \frac{1}{2} QV = \frac{1}{2} CV^2 = \frac{1}{2} \frac{Q^2}{C}$

$C = \varepsilon_0 \frac{A}{d}$

$\frac{V}{i} \qquad P = Vi \qquad P = i^2 R = \frac{V^2}{R} \qquad R = \rho \frac{L}{A}$

$q = R_1 + R_2 + \cdots \qquad C_{eq} = C_1 + C_2 + \cdots$

$= \frac{1}{R_1} + \frac{1}{R_2} + \cdots \qquad \frac{1}{C_{eq}} = \frac{1}{C_1} + \frac{1}{C_2} + \cdots$

$= \frac{\mu_0}{4\pi} \frac{i \, d\vec{s} \times \hat{r}}{r^2} \qquad B = \frac{\mu_0}{2\pi} \frac{i}{r} \qquad B = \mu_0 n i \qquad \vec{\tau} = \vec{\mu} \times \vec{B}$

$-\frac{d\Phi}{dt} \qquad \varepsilon = -N \frac{d\phi}{dt} \qquad L = \frac{|\varepsilon|}{\left|\frac{di}{dt}\right|} = \frac{N\Phi}{i}$

$u_E = \frac{1}{2} \varepsilon_0 E^2 \qquad u_B = \frac{1}{2} \frac{B^2}{\mu_0} \qquad U_B = \frac{1}{2} L i^2$

$e^{-t/\tau_c} \qquad q = C\varepsilon(1 - e^{-t/\tau_c}) \qquad i = i_0 e^{-t/\tau_L} \qquad i = \frac{\varepsilon}{R}(1 - e^{-t/\tau_L})$

$\tau_c = RC \qquad \mu = N i A \qquad \frac{1}{4\pi\varepsilon_0} = 9 \times 10^9 \qquad \frac{\mu_0}{4\pi} = 10^{-7}$

means $10^6 \qquad \mu$ means 10^{-6}

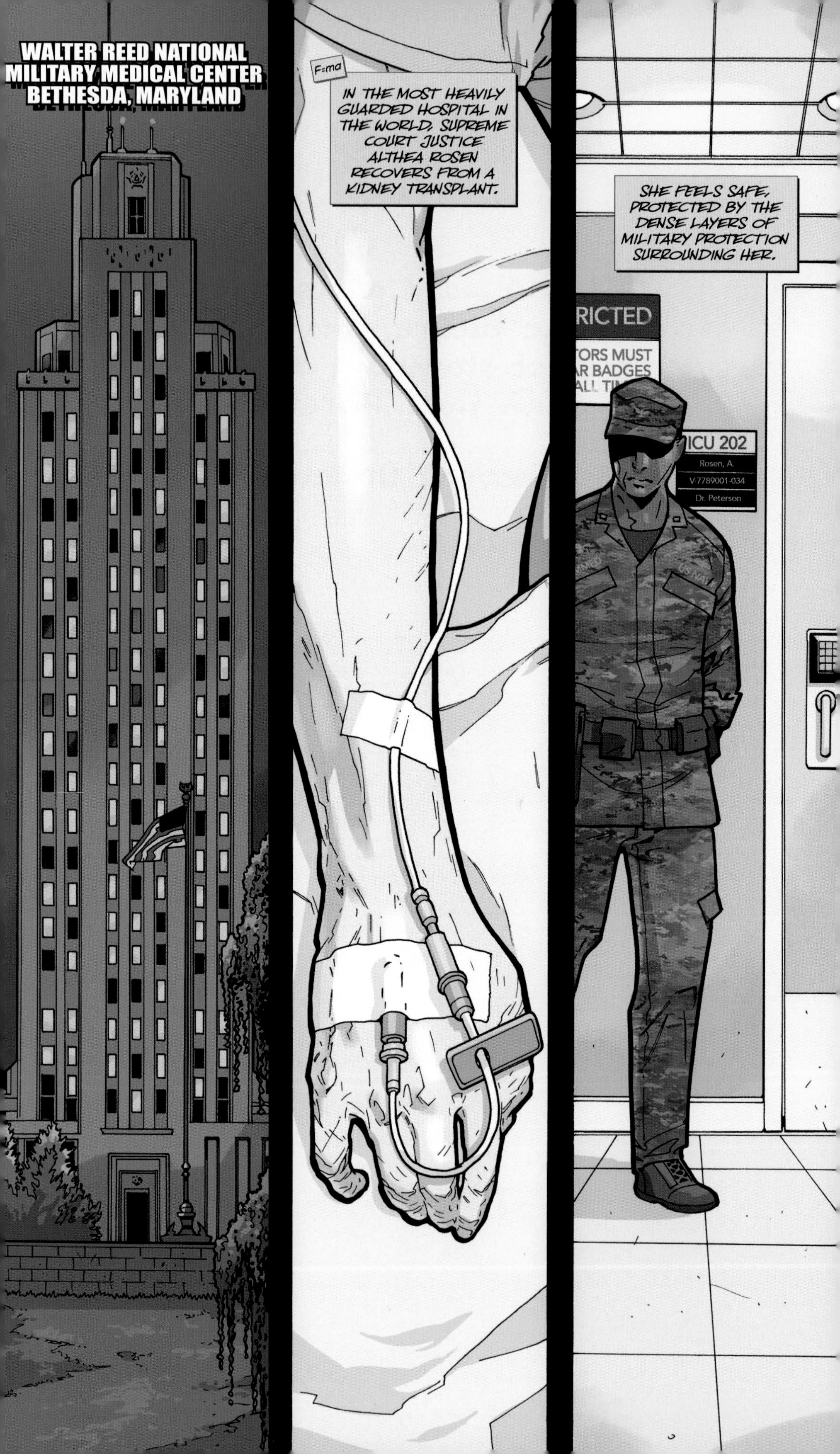
WALTER REED NATIONAL MILITARY MEDICAL CENTER BETHESDA, MARYLAND
F=ma
IN THE MOST HEAVILY GUARDED HOSPITAL IN THE WORLD, SUPREME COURT JUSTICE ALTHEA ROSEN RECOVERS FROM A KIDNEY TRANSPLANT.
SHE FEELS SAFE, PROTECTED BY THE DENSE LAYERS OF MILITARY PROTECTION SURROUNDING HER.
RICTED
TORS MUST
AR BADGES
ICU 202
Rosen, A.
V-7789001-034
Dr. Peterson

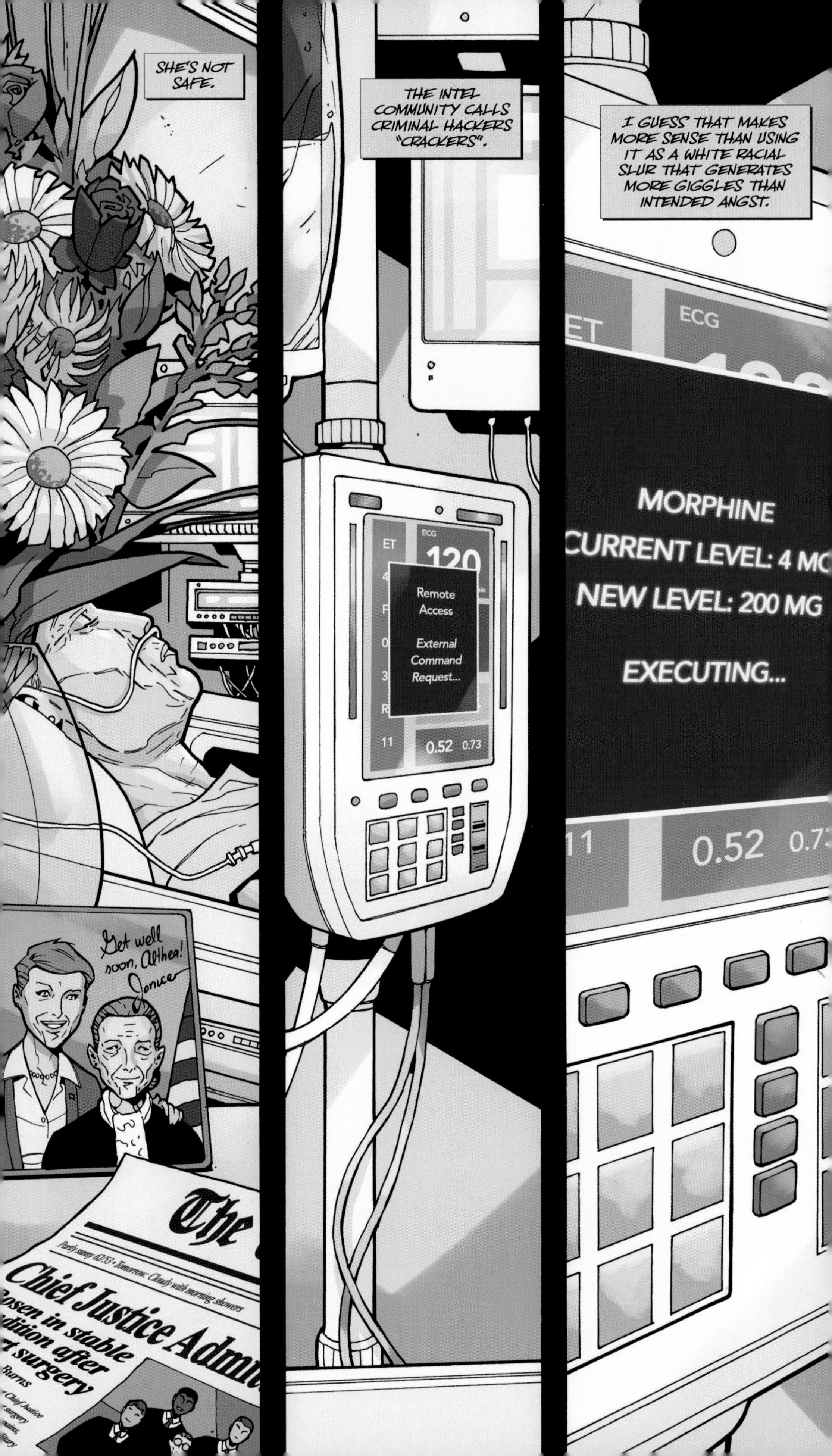
SHE'S NOT SAFE.
THE INTEL COMMUNITY CALLS CRIMINAL HACKERS "CRACKERS".
I GUESS THAT MAKES MORE SENSE THAN USING IT AS A WHITE RACIAL SLUR THAT GENERATES MORE GIGGLES THAN INTENDED ANGST.
Remote Access
External Command Request...
MORPHINE
URRENT LEVEL: 4 M
NEW LEVEL: 200 MG
EXECUTING...
0.52
Get well soon, Althea! Janice
Chief Justice Adm
in stable
dition after
surgery

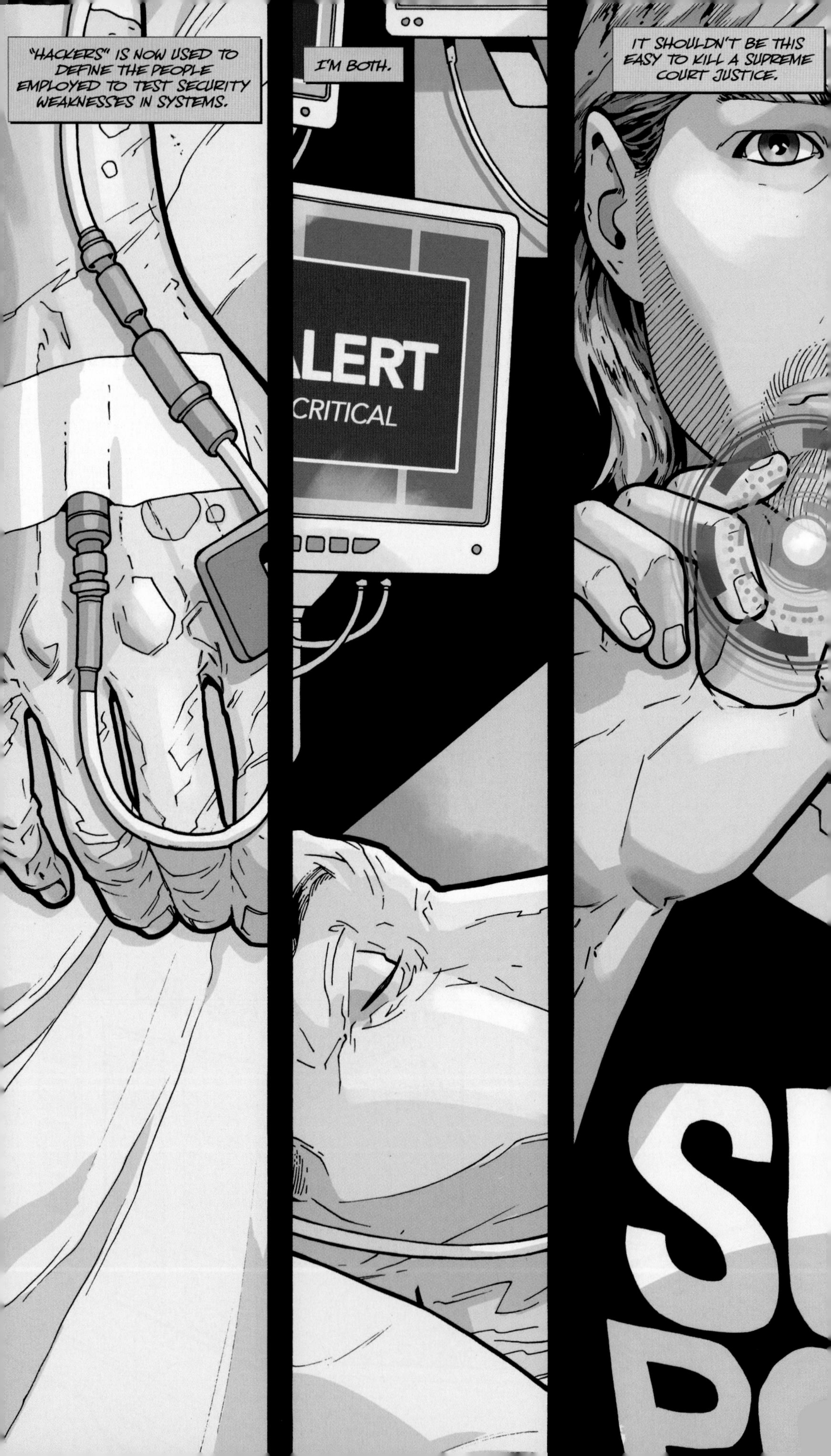
"HACKERS" IS NOW USED TO DEFINE THE PEOPLE EMPLOYED TO TEST SECURITY WEAKNESSES IN SYSTEMS.
I'M BOTH.
ALERT
CRITICAL
IT SHOULDN'T BE THIS EASY TO KILL A SUPREME COURT JUSTICE.

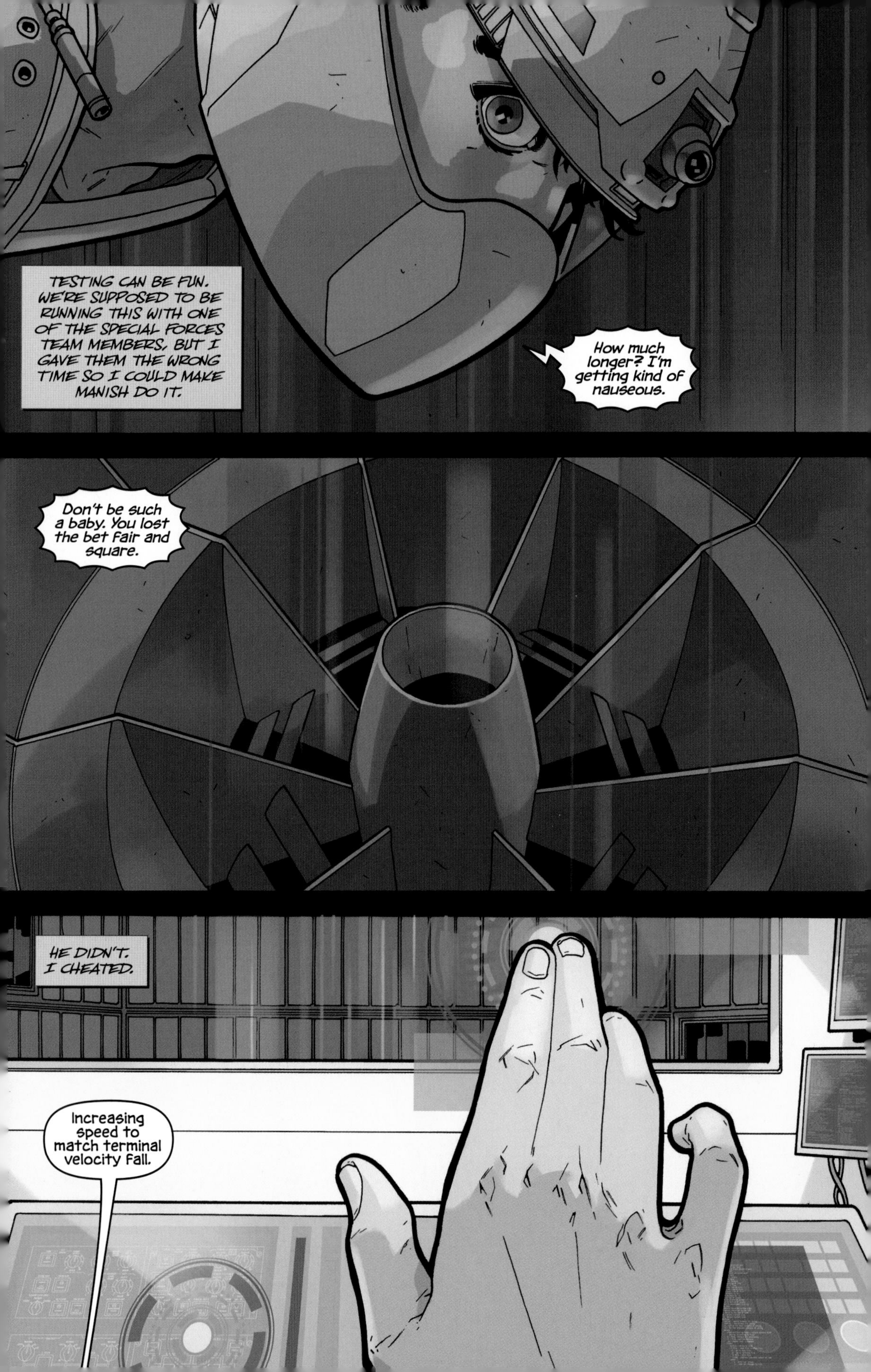
TESTING CAN BE FUN. WE'RE SUPPOSED TO BE RUNNING THIS WITH ONE OF THE SPECIAL FORCES TEAM MEMBERS, BUT I GAVE THEM THE WRONG TIME SO I COULD MAKE MANISH DO IT.
How much longer? I'm getting kind of nauseous.
Don't be such a baby. You lost the bet fair and square.
HE DIDN'T. I CHEATED.
Increasing speed to match terminal velocity fall.

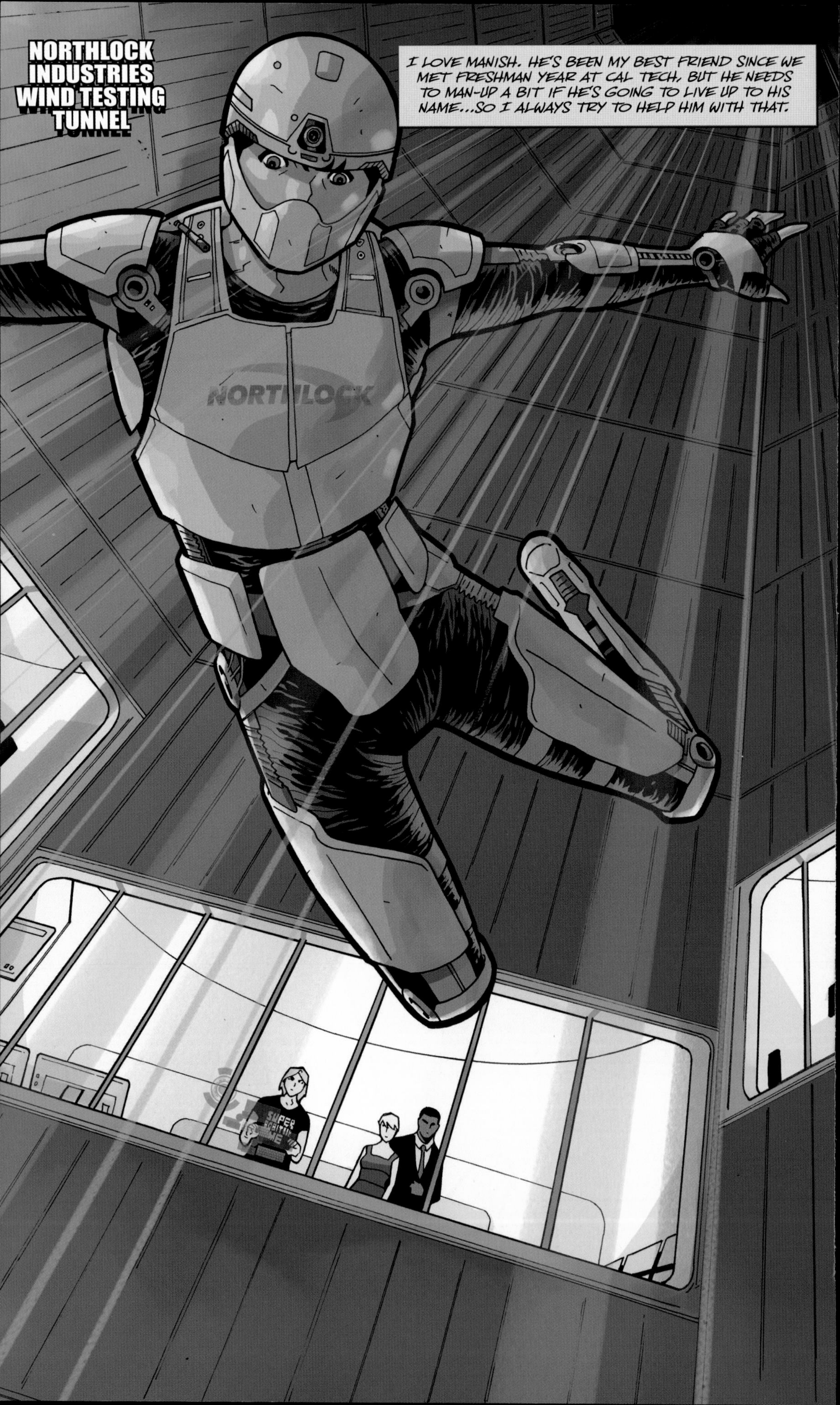
NORTHLOCK INDUSTRIES WIND TESTING TUNNEL
I LOVE MANISH. HE'S BEEN MY BEST FRIEND SINCE WE MET FRESHMAN YEAR AT CAL TECH, BUT HE NEEDS TO MAN-UP A BIT IF HE'S GOING TO LIVE UP TO HIS NAME...SO I ALWAYS TRY TO HELP HIM WITH THAT.
NORTHLOCK
SUPER

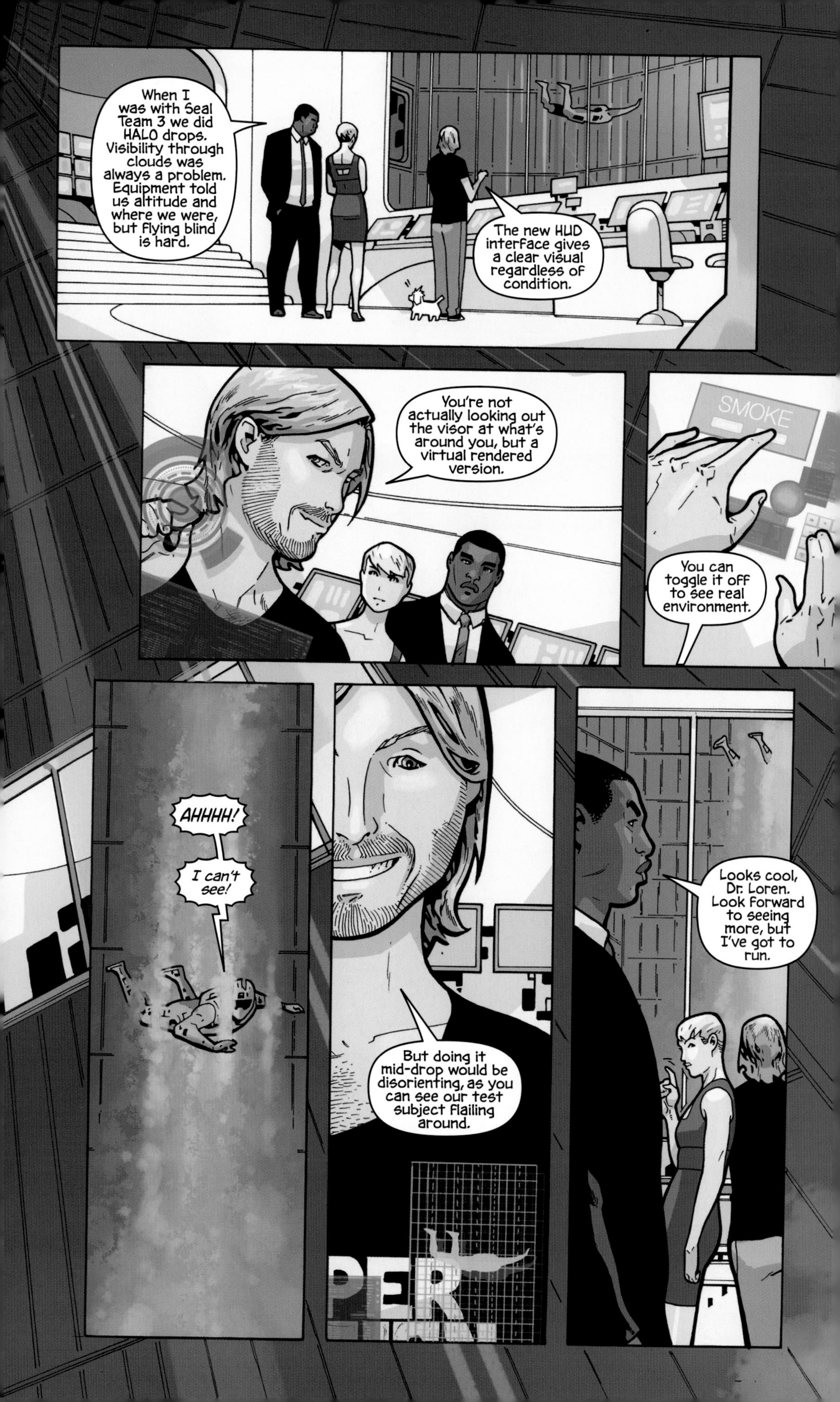

When I was with Seal Team 3 we did HALO drops. Visibility through clouds was always a problem. Equipment told us altitude and where we were, but flying blind is hard.
The new HUD interface gives a clear visual regardless of condition.
You're not actually looking out the visor at what's around you, but a virtual rendered version.
SMOKE
You can toggle it off to see real environment.
AHHHH!
I can't see!
But doing it mid-drop would be disorienting, as you can see our test subject flailing around.
Looks cool, Dr. Loren. Look forward to seeing more, but I've got to run.

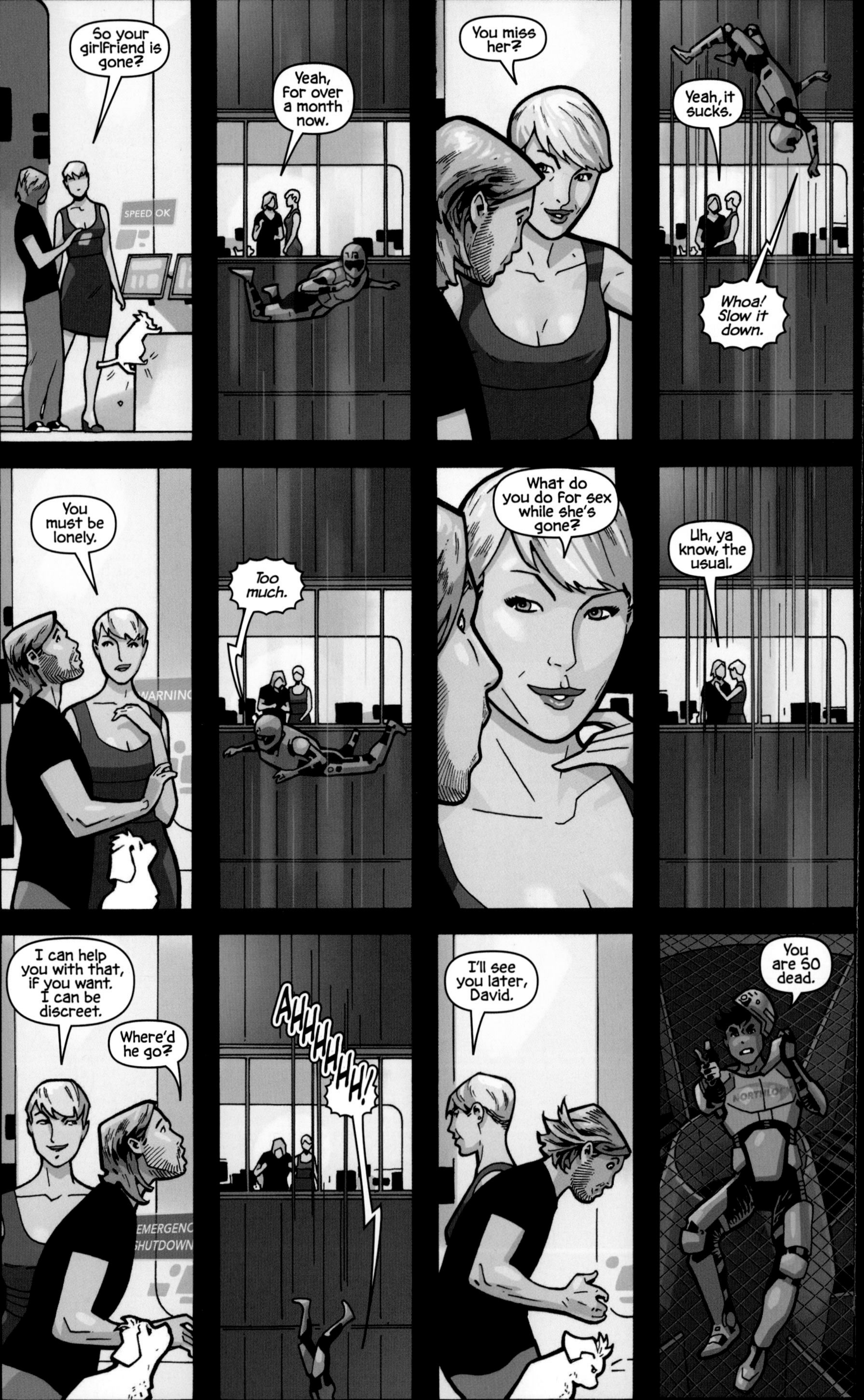
So your girlfriend is gone?
Yeah, for over a month now.
You miss her?
Yeah, it sucks.
Whoa! Slow it down.
SPEED OK
You must be lonely.
WARNING
Too much.
What do you do for sex while she's gone?
Uh, ya know, the usual.
I can help you with that, if you want. I can be discreet.
Where'd he go?
EMERGENC
SHUTDOWN
AHHHHHHH!
I'll see you later, David.
You are SO dead.

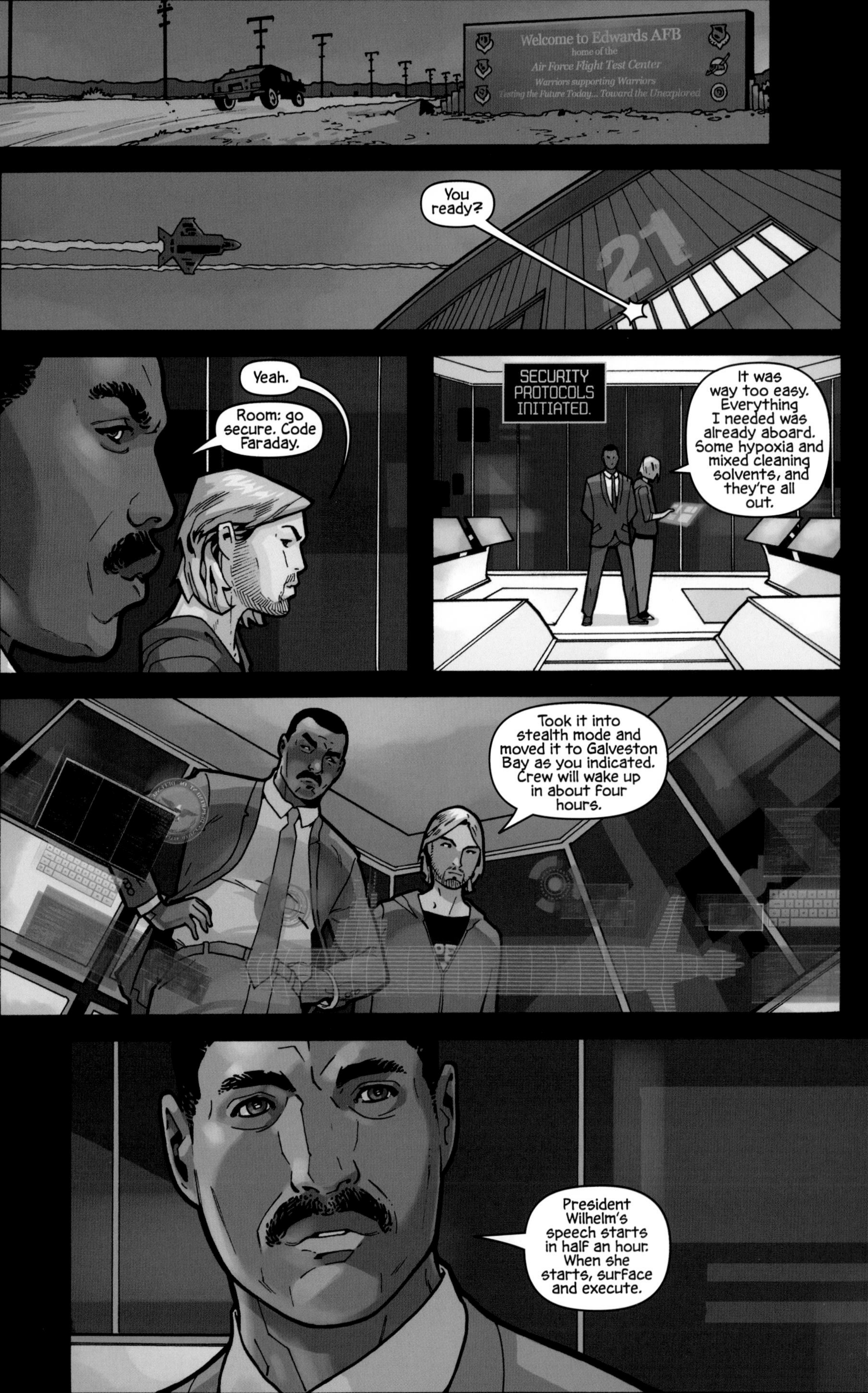

Welcome to Edwards AFB
home of the
Air Force Flight Test Center
Warriors supporting Warriors
Testing the Future Today... Toward the Unexplored
You ready?
21
Yeah.
Room: go secure. Code Faraday.
SECURITY PROTOCOLS INITIATED.
It was way too easy. Everything I needed was already aboard. Some hypoxia and mixed cleaning solvents, and they're all out.
Took it into stealth mode and moved it to Galveston Bay as you indicated. Crew will wake up in about four hours.
President Wilhelm's speech starts in half an hour. When she starts, surface and execute.

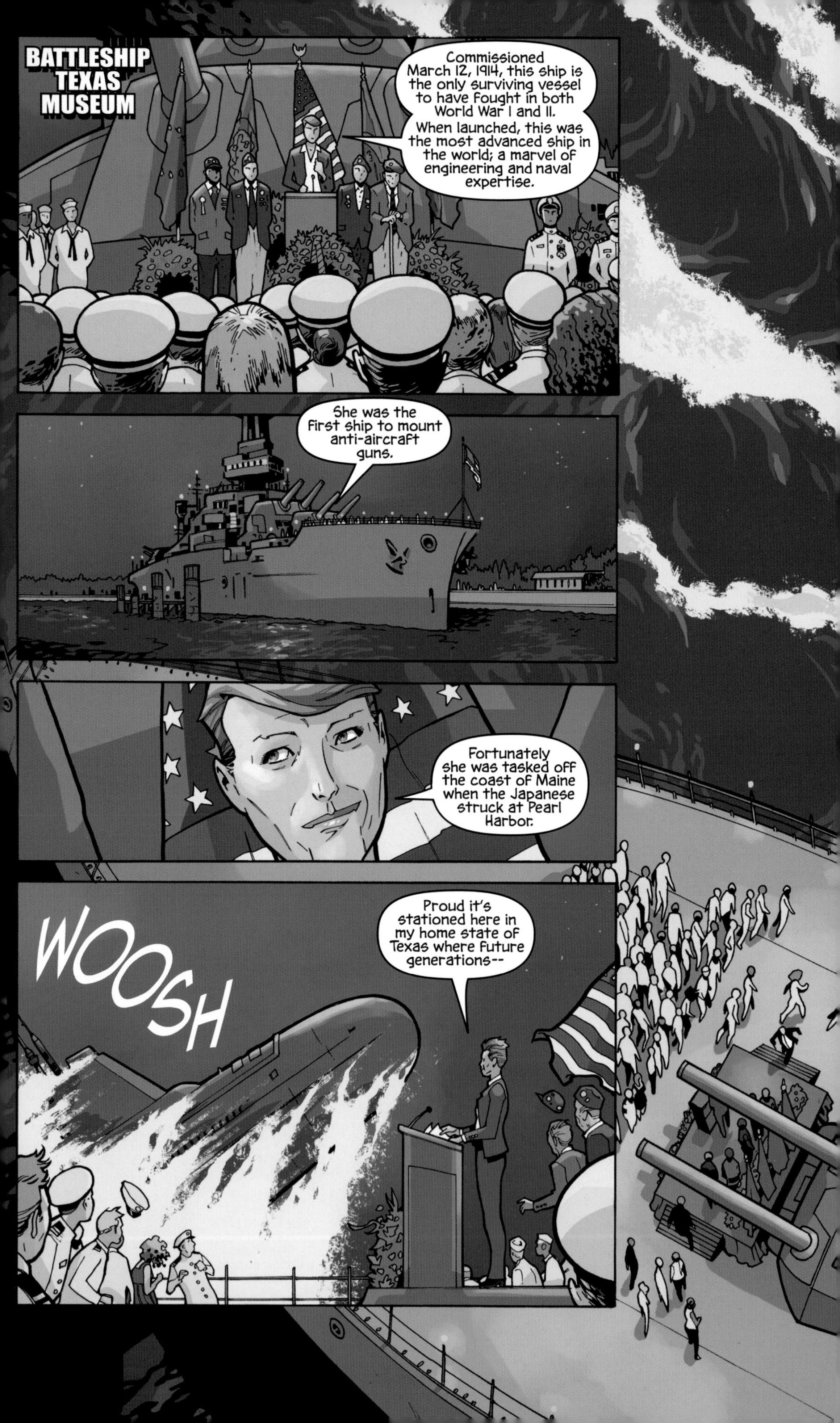
BATTLESHIP TEXAS MUSEUM
Commissioned March 12, 1914, this ship is the only surviving vessel to have fought in both World War I and II.
When launched, this was the most advanced ship in the world; a marvel of engineering and naval expertise.
She was the first ship to mount anti-aircraft guns.
Fortunately she was tasked off the coast of Maine when the Japanese struck at Pearl Harbor.
Proud it's stationed here in my home state of Texas where future generations--
WOOSH

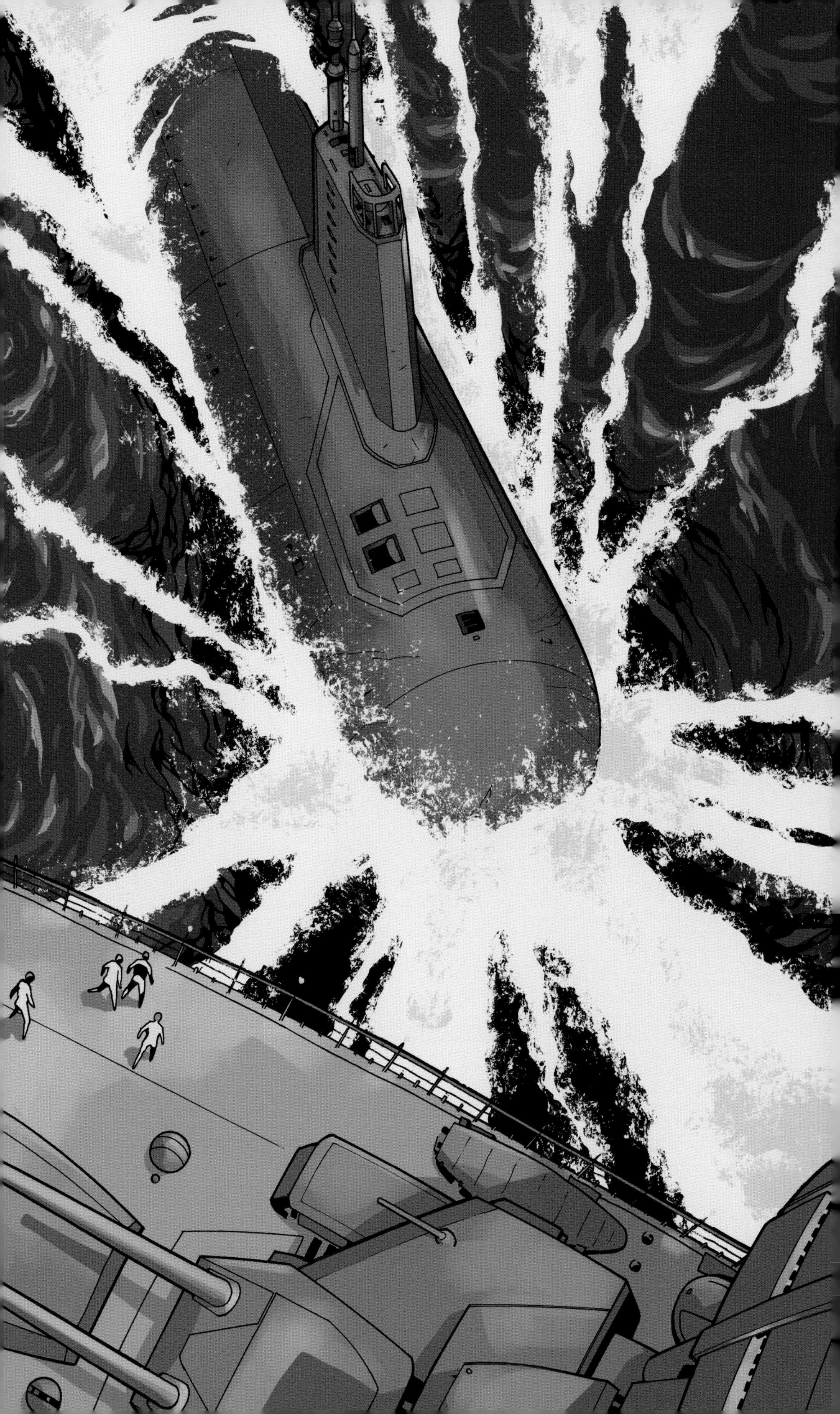

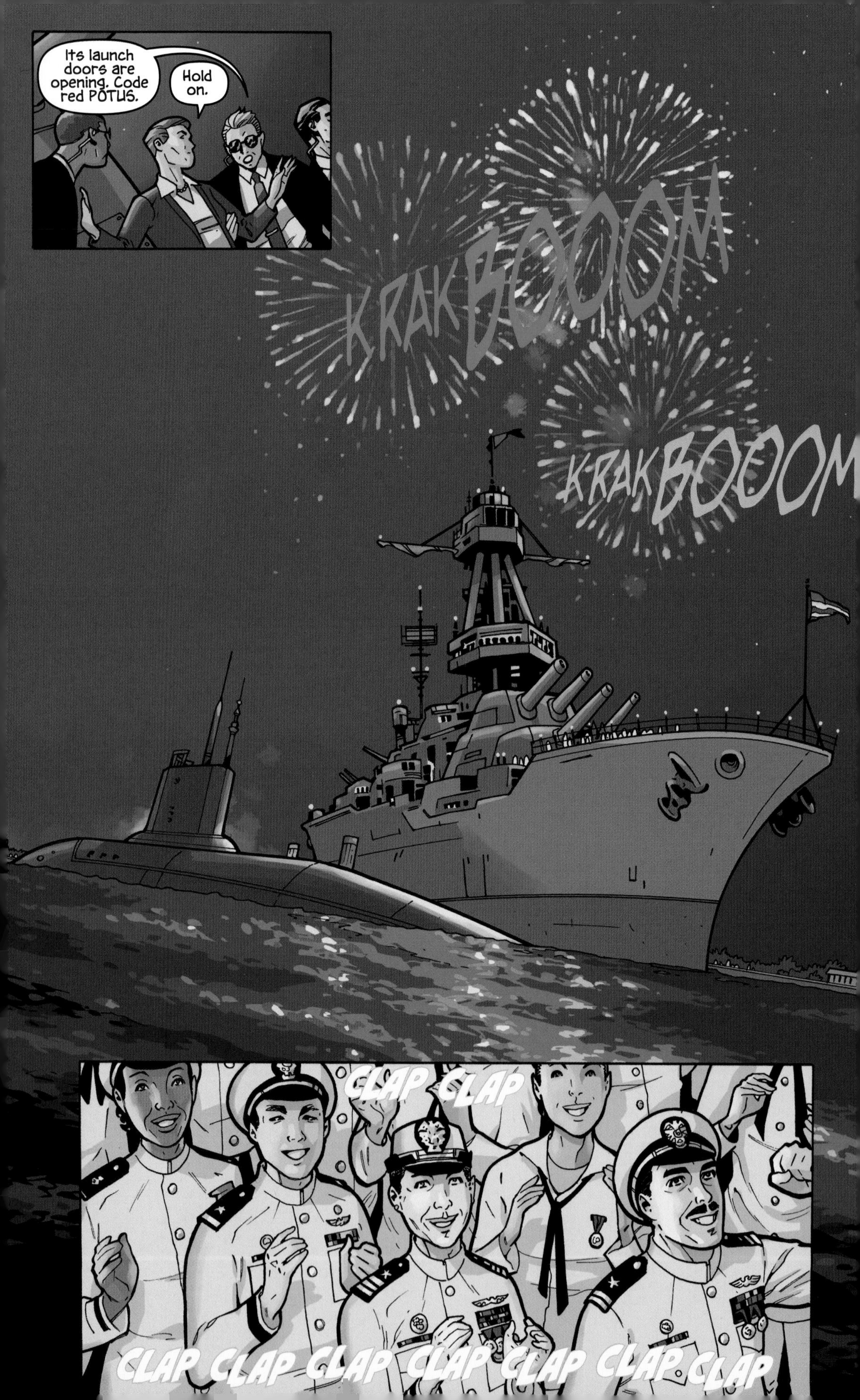
Its launch doors are opening. Code red POTUS.
Hold on.
KRAKBOOOM
KRAKBOOOM
CLAP CLAP
CLAP CLAP CLAP CLAP CLAP CLAP CLAP

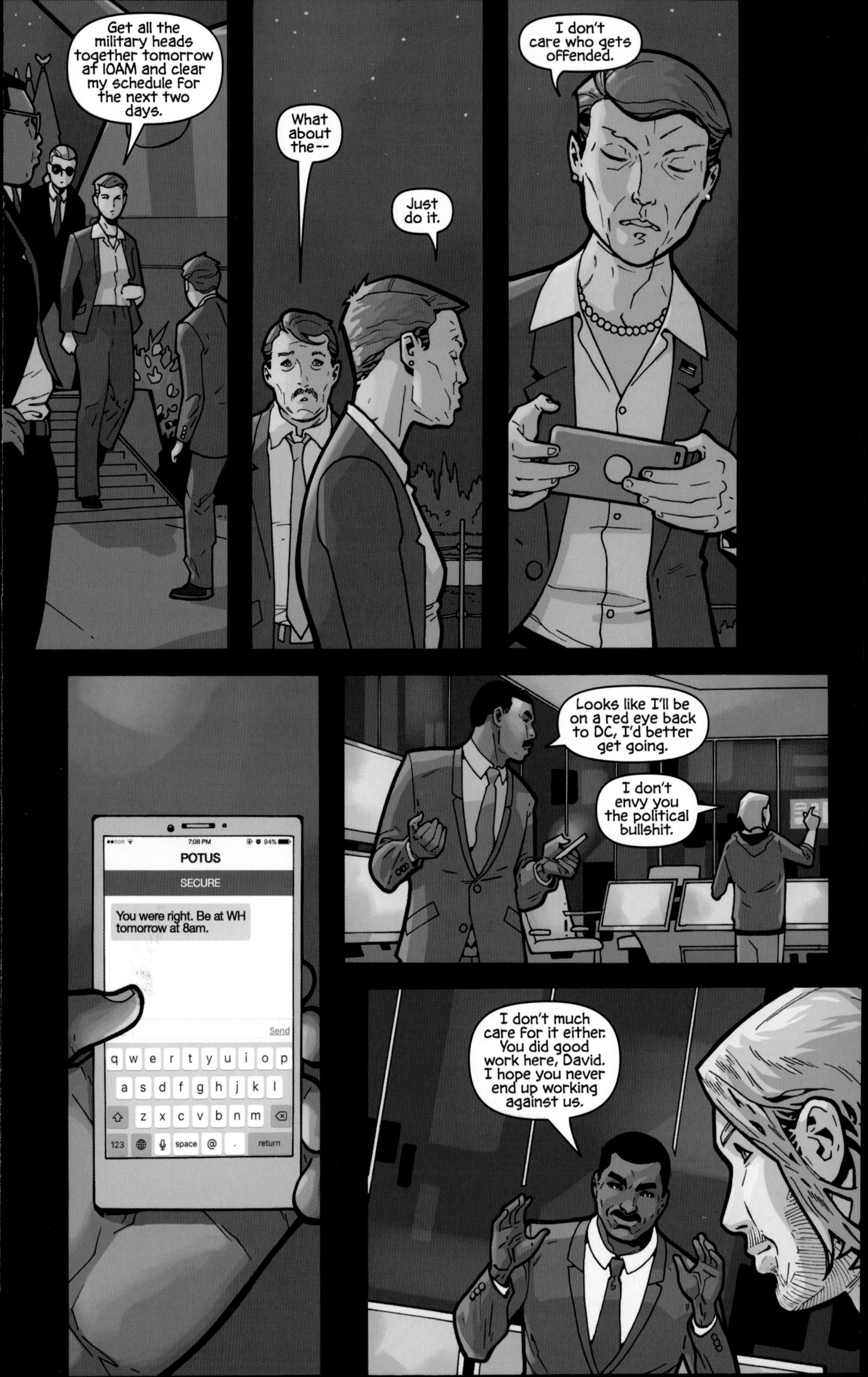
Get all the military heads together tomorrow at 10AM and clear my schedule for the next two days.
What about the--
Just do it.
I don't care who gets offended.
POTUS
SECURE
You were right. Be at WH tomorrow at 8am.
Looks like I'll be on a red eye back to DC, I'd better get going.
I don't envy you the political bullshit.
I don't much care for it either. You did good work here, David. I hope you never end up working against us.

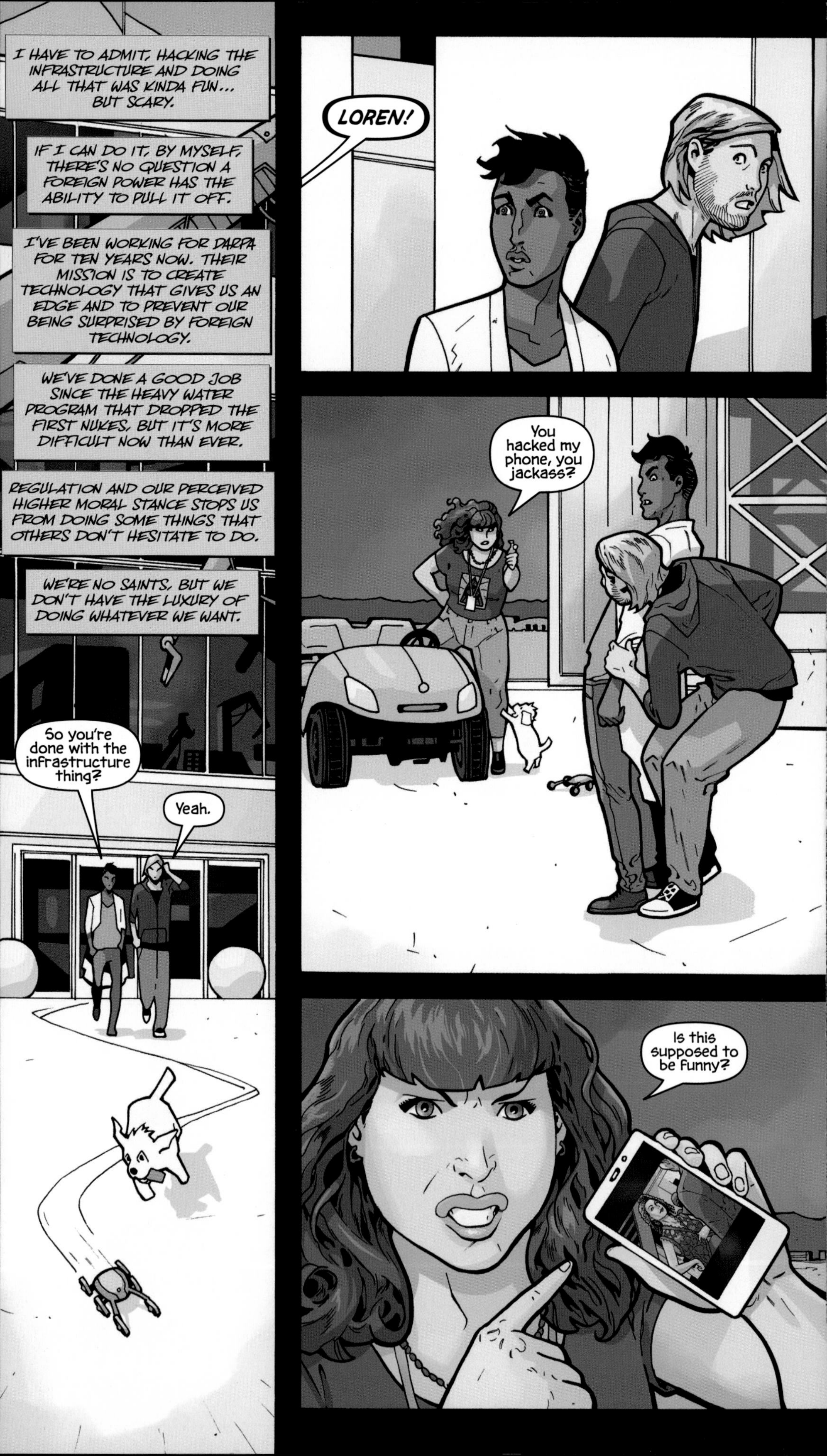

I HAVE TO ADMIT, HACKING THE INFRASTRUCTURE AND DOING ALL THAT WAS KINDA FUN... BUT SCARY.
IF I CAN DO IT, BY MYSELF, THERE'S NO QUESTION A FOREIGN POWER HAS THE ABILITY TO PULL IT OFF.
I'VE BEEN WORKING FOR DARPA FOR TEN YEARS NOW. THEIR MISSION IS TO CREATE TECHNOLOGY THAT GIVES US AN EDGE AND TO PREVENT OUR BEING SURPRISED BY FOREIGN TECHNOLOGY.
WE'VE DONE A GOOD JOB SINCE THE HEAVY WATER PROGRAM THAT DROPPED THE FIRST NUKES, BUT IT'S MORE DIFFICULT NOW THAN EVER.
REGULATION AND OUR PERCEIVED HIGHER MORAL STANCE STOPS US FROM DOING SOME THINGS THAT OTHERS DON'T HESITATE TO DO.
WE'RE NO SAINTS, BUT WE DON'T HAVE THE LUXURY OF DOING WHATEVER WE WANT.
So you're done with the infrastructure thing?
Yeah.
LOREN!
You hacked my phone, you jackass?
Is this supposed to be funny?

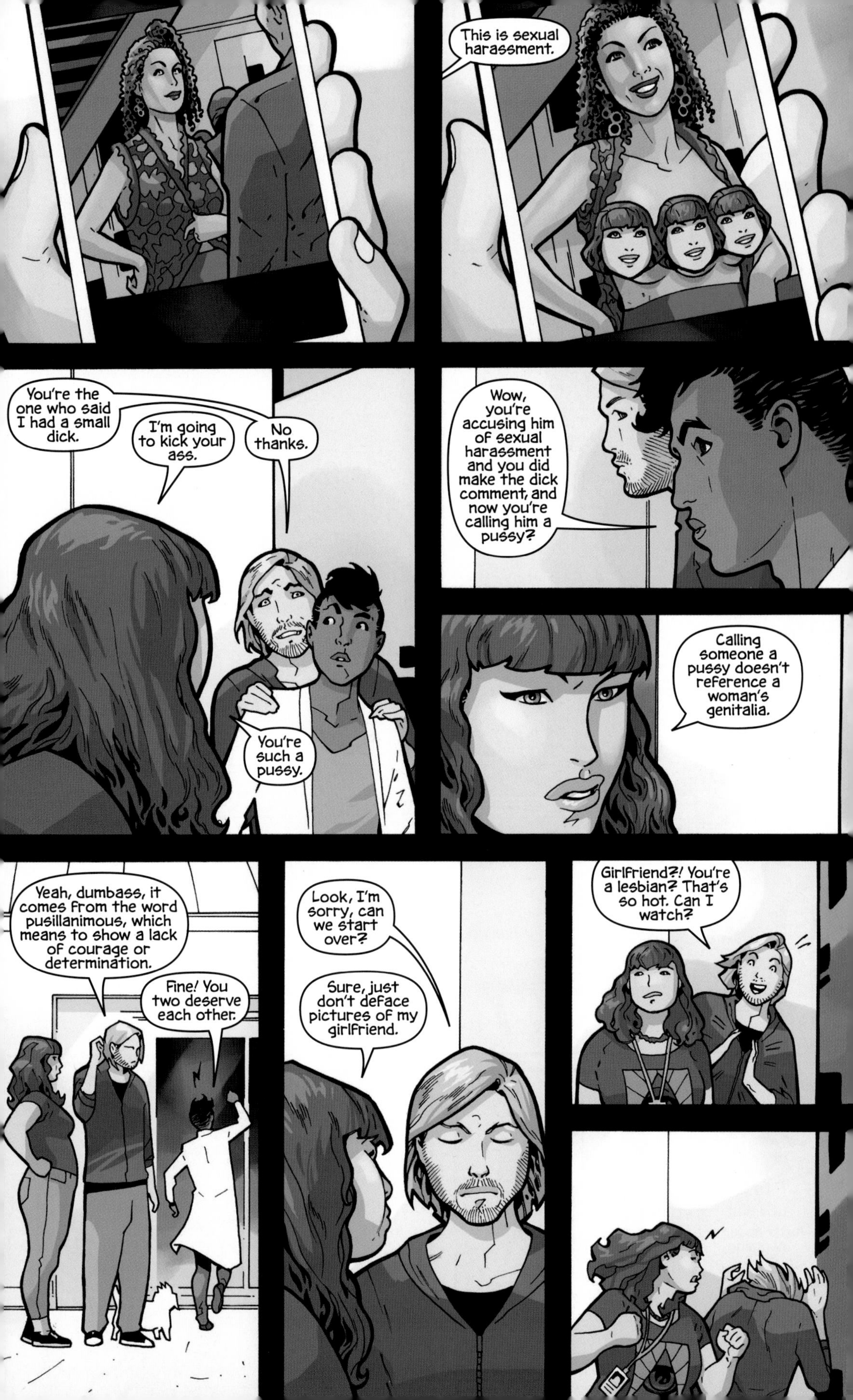
This is sexual harassment.
You're the one who said I had a small dick.
I'm going to kick your ass.
No thanks.
You're such a pussy.
Wow, you're accusing him of sexual harassment and you did make the dick comment, and now you're calling him a pussy?
Calling someone a pussy doesn't reference a woman's genitalia.
Yeah, dumbass, it comes from the word pusillanimous, which means to show a lack of courage or determination.
Fine! You two deserve each other.
Look, I'm sorry, can we start over?
Sure, just don't deface pictures of my girlfriend.
Girlfriend?! You're a lesbian? That's so hot. Can I watch?

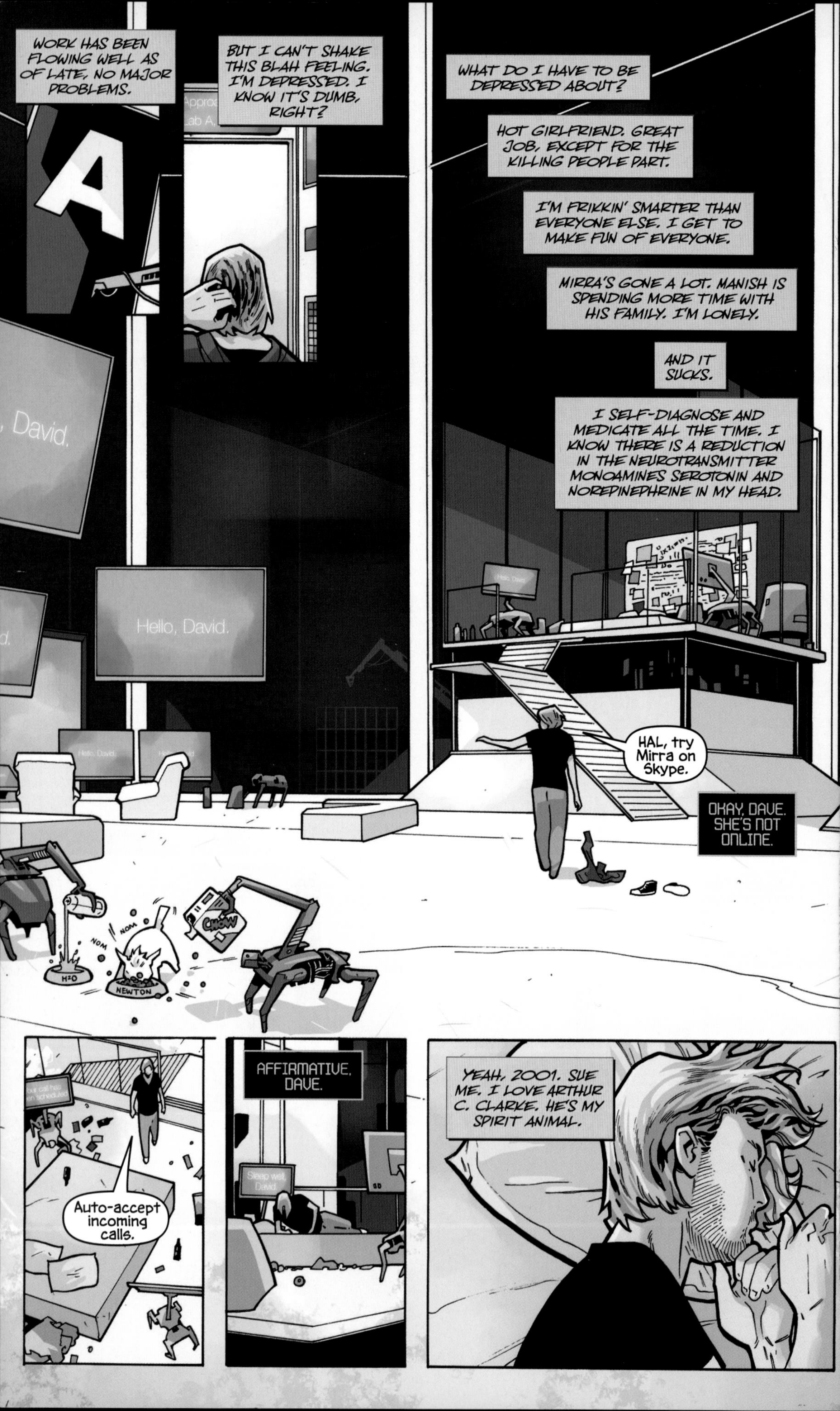
WORK HAS BEEN FLOWING WELL AS OF LATE. NO MAJOR PROBLEMS.
BUT I CAN'T SHAKE THIS BLAH FEELING. I'M DEPRESSED. I KNOW IT'S DUMB, RIGHT?
WHAT DO I HAVE TO BE DEPRESSED ABOUT?
HOT GIRLFRIEND. GREAT JOB, EXCEPT FOR THE KILLING PEOPLE PART.
I'M FRIKKIN' SMARTER THAN EVERYONE ELSE. I GET TO MAKE FUN OF EVERYONE.
MIRRA'S GONE A LOT. MANISH IS SPENDING MORE TIME WITH HIS FAMILY. I'M LONELY.
AND IT SUCKS.
I SELF-DIAGNOSE AND MEDICATE ALL THE TIME. I KNOW THERE IS A REDUCTION IN THE NEUROTRANSMITTER MONOAMINES SEROTONIN AND NOREPINEPHRINE IN MY HEAD.
Hello, David.
HAL, try Mirra on Skype.
OKAY, DAVE. SHE'S NOT ONLINE.
NOM
NOM
CHOW
H2O
NEWTON
Auto-accept incoming calls.
AFFIRMATIVE, DAVE.
Sleep well, David.
YEAH, 2001. SUE ME. I LOVE ARTHUR C. CLARKE. HE'S MY SPIRIT ANIMAL.

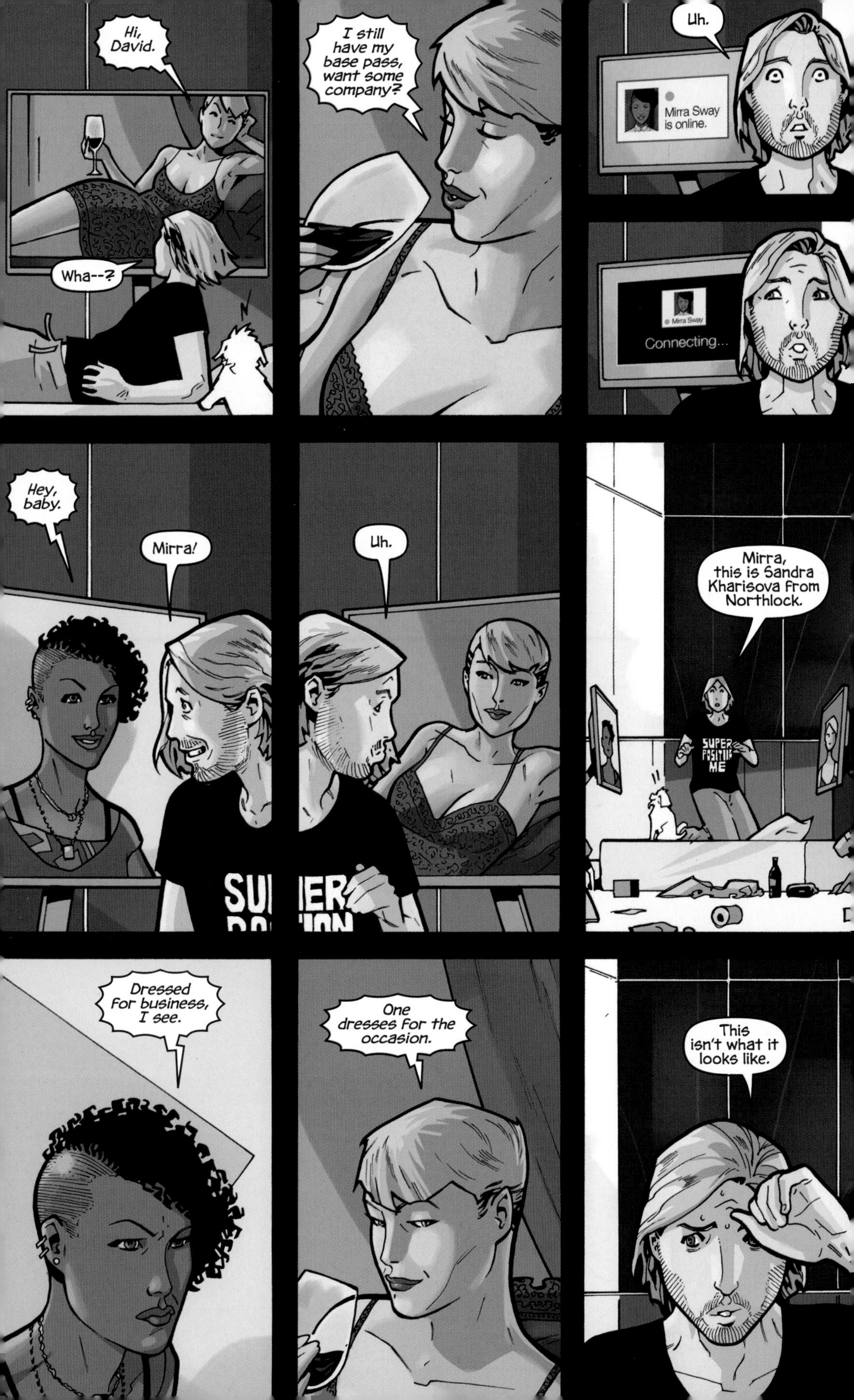
Hi, David.
Wha--?
I still have my base pass, want some company?
Uh.
Mirra Sway is online.
Mirra Sway
Connecting...
Hey, baby.
Mirra!
Uh.
Mirra, this is Sandra Kharisova from Northlock.
SUPER POSITIVE ME
Dressed for business, I see.
One dresses for the occasion.
This isn't what it looks like.

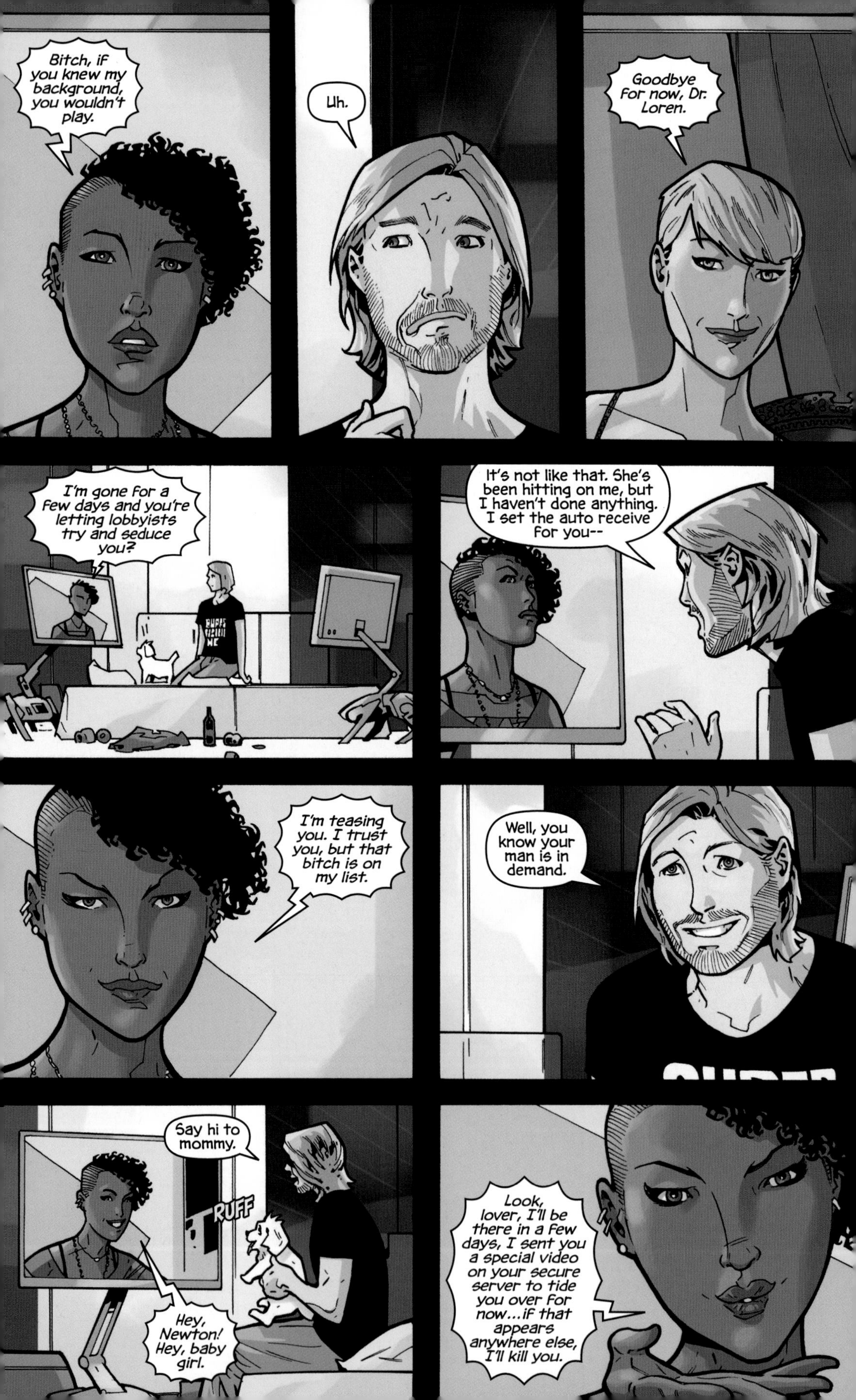
Bitch, if you knew my background, you wouldn't play.
Uh.
Goodbye for now, Dr. Loren.
I'm gone for a few days and you're letting lobbyists try and seduce you?
It's not like that. She's been hitting on me, but I haven't done anything. I set the auto receive for you--
I'm teasing you. I trust you, but that bitch is on my list.
Well, you know your man is in demand.
Say hi to mommy.
RUFF
Hey, Newton! Hey, baby girl.
Look, lover, I'll be there in a few days, I sent you a special video on your secure server to tide you over for now...if that appears anywhere else, I'll kill you.

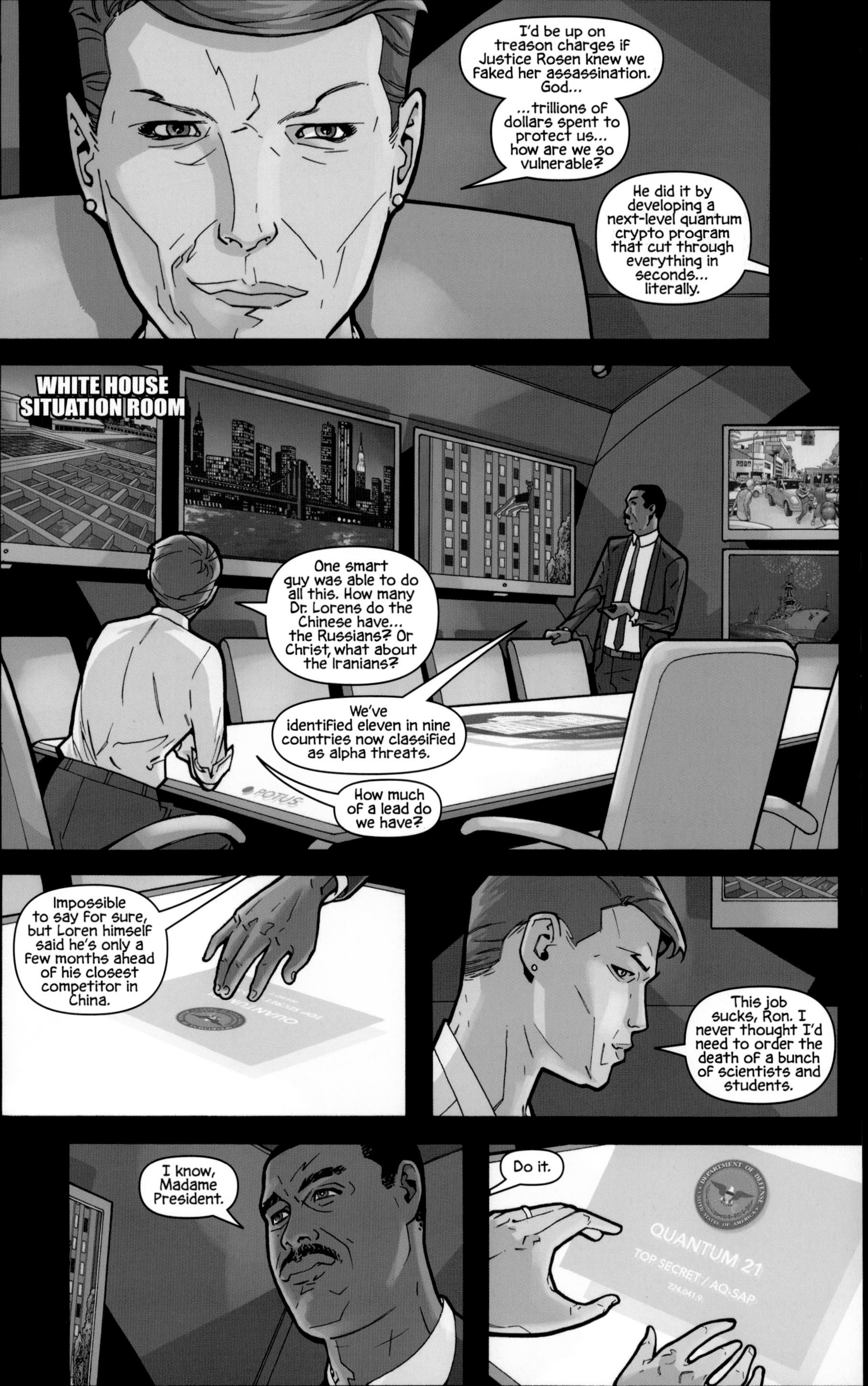
I'd be up on treason charges if Justice Rosen knew we faked her assassination. God...
...trillions of dollars spent to protect us... how are we so vulnerable?
He did it by developing a next-level quantum crypto program that cut through everything in seconds... literally.
WHITE HOUSE SITUATION ROOM
One smart guy was able to do all this. How many Dr. Lorens do the Chinese have... the Russians? Or Christ, what about the Iranians?
We've identified eleven in nine countries now classified as alpha threats.
POTUS
How much of a lead do we have?
Impossible to say for sure, but Loren himself said he's only a few months ahead of his closest competitor in China.
This job sucks, Ron. I never thought I'd need to order the death of a bunch of scientists and students.
I know, Madame President.
Do it.
DEPARTMENT OF DEFENSE
UNITED STATES OF AMERICA
QUANTUM 21
TOP SECRET / AQ-SAP
224.041.9

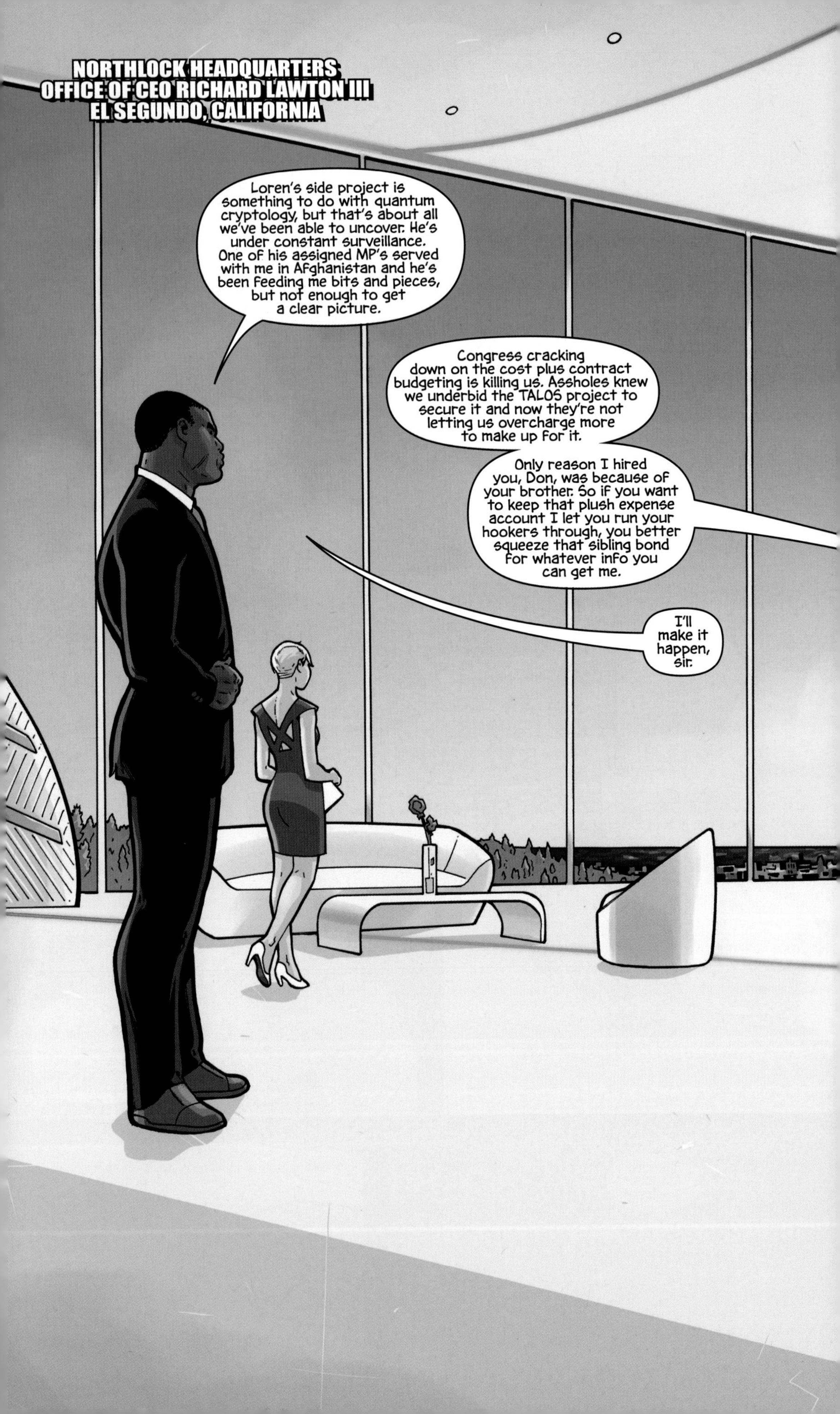
NORTHLOCK HEADQUARTERS OFFICE OF CEO RICHARD LAWTON III EL SEGUNDO, CALIFORNIA
Loren's side project is something to do with quantum cryptology, but that's about all we've been able to uncover. He's under constant surveillance. One of his assigned MP's served with me in Afghanistan and he's been feeding me bits and pieces, but not enough to get a clear picture.
Congress cracking down on the cost plus contract budgeting is killing us. Assholes knew we underbid the TALOS project to secure it and now they're not letting us overcharge more to make up for it.
Only reason I hired you, Don, was because of your brother. So if you want to keep that plush expense account I let you run your hookers through, you better squeeze that sibling bond for whatever info you can get me.
I'll make it happen, sir.

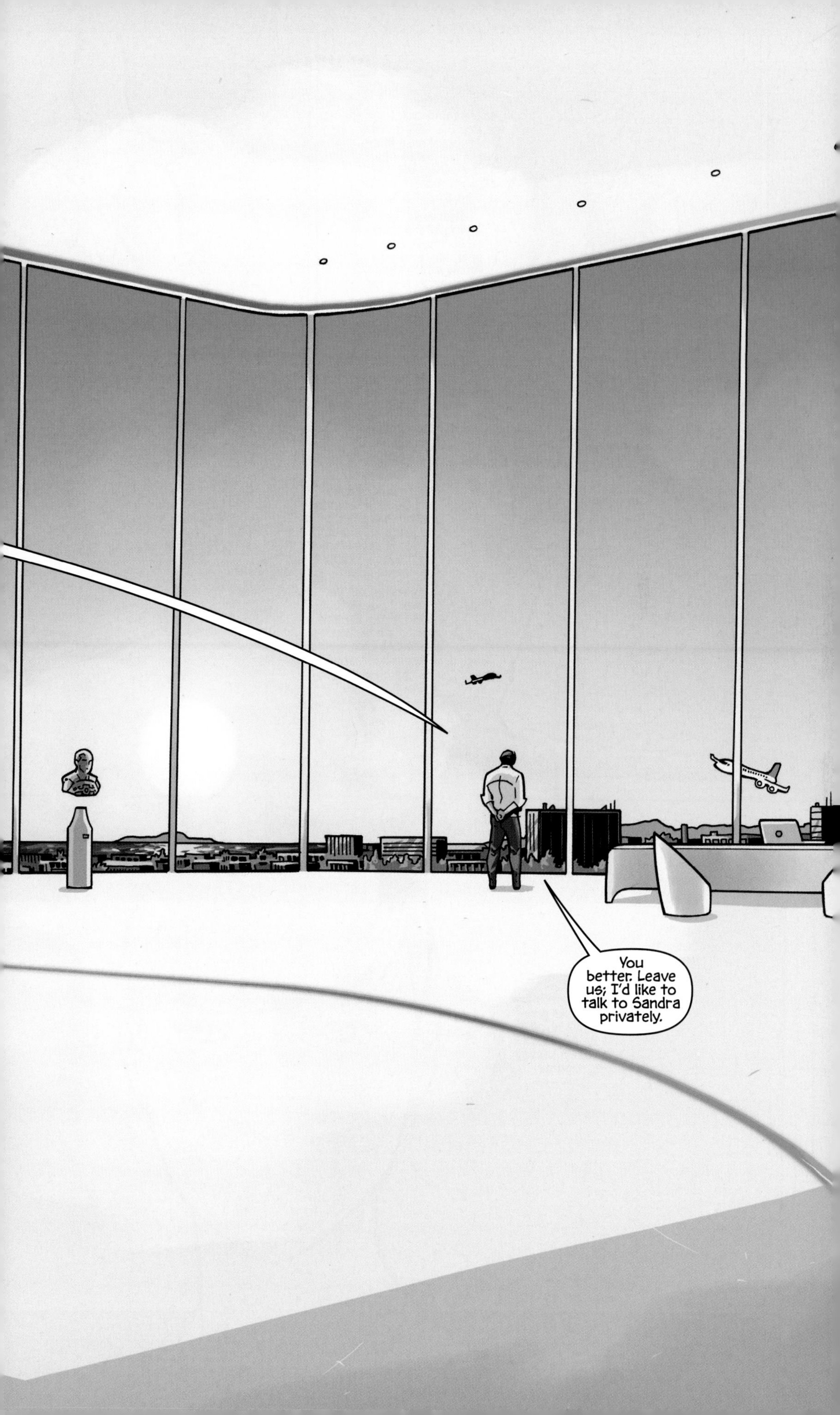
You better. Leave us; I'd like to talk to Sandra privately.

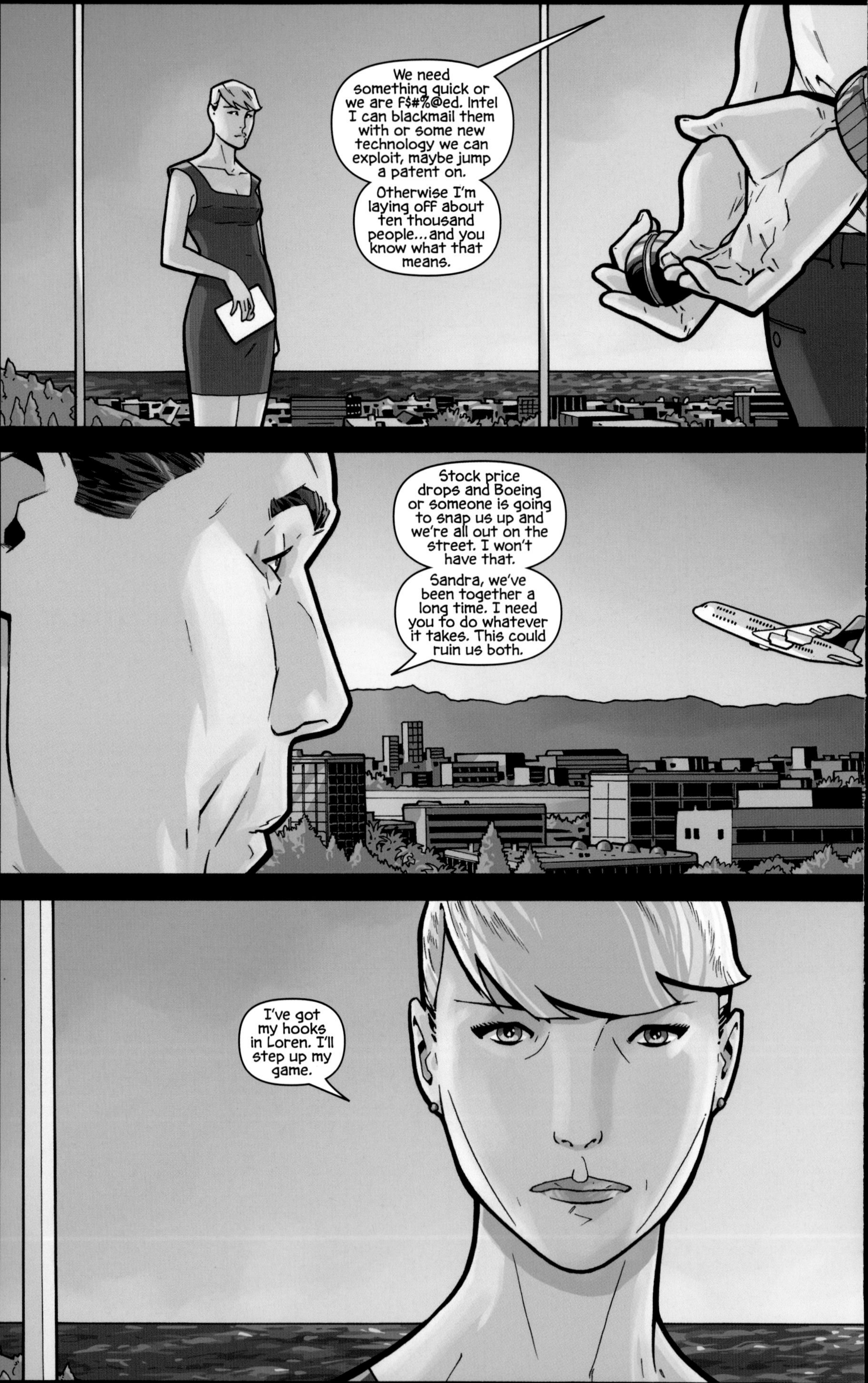
We need something quick or we are F$#%@ed. Intel I can blackmail them with or some new technology we can exploit, maybe jump a patent on.
Otherwise I'm laying off about ten thousand people...and you know what that means.
Stock price drops and Boeing or someone is going to snap us up and we're all out on the street. I won't have that.
Sandra, we've been together a long time. I need you to do whatever it takes. This could ruin us both.
I've got my hooks in Loren. I'll step up my game.

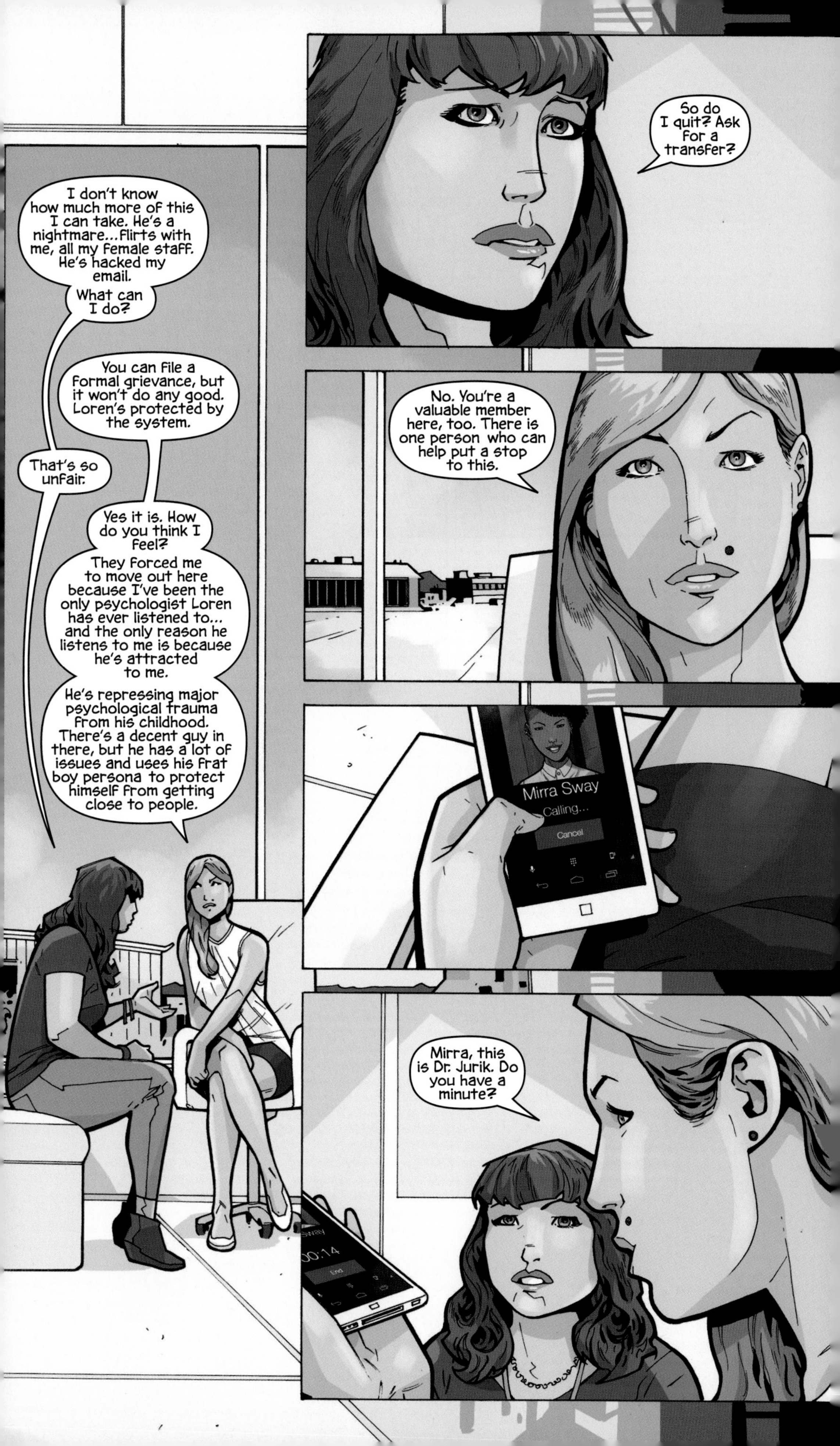
I don't know how much more of this I can take. He's a nightmare...flirts with me, all my female staff. He's hacked my email.
What can I do?
So do I quit? Ask for a transfer?
You can file a formal grievance, but it won't do any good. Loren's protected by the system.
That's so unfair.
No. You're a valuable member here, too. There is one person who can help put a stop to this.
Yes it is. How do you think I feel?
They forced me to move out here because I've been the only psychologist Loren has ever listened to... and the only reason he listens to me is because he's attracted to me.
He's repressing major psychological trauma from his childhood. There's a decent guy in there, but he has a lot of issues and uses his frat boy persona to protect himself from getting close to people.
Mirra Sway
Calling...
Cancel
Mirra, this is Dr. Jurik. Do you have a minute?
Sway
00:14
End

o you need help
something, David?

CHAPTER THREE

THINK TANK

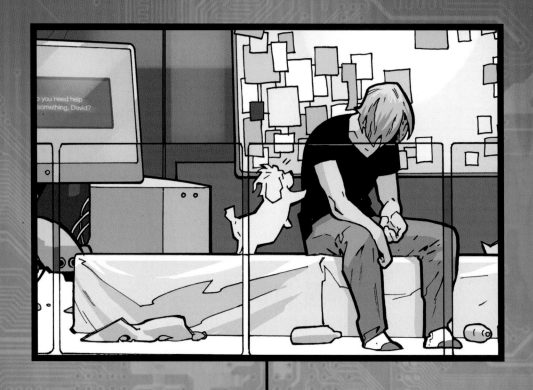

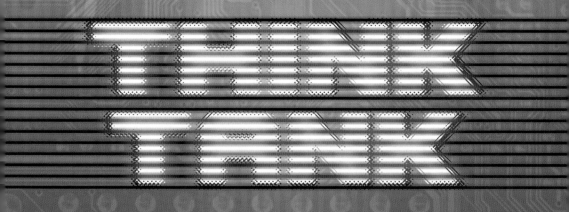

$$\oint \vec{E} \, d\vec{A} = \frac{1}{\varepsilon_0} q_{in} \qquad \oint \vec{B} \, d\vec{A} = 0 \qquad \oint \vec{E} \, d\vec{l} = -\frac{d}{dt} \int B \, dA$$

$$\oint \vec{B} \, d\vec{l} = \mu_0 I_{in} \qquad \vec{F} = q(\vec{v} \times \vec{B} + \vec{E}) \qquad i = \frac{dq}{dt}$$

int charge $\quad E = \frac{1}{4\pi\varepsilon_0} \frac{q}{r^2} \qquad V = \frac{1}{4\pi\varepsilon_0} \frac{q}{r} \qquad p = qd$

$$V_f - V_i = -\int_i^f \vec{E} \qquad \vec{\tau} = \vec{p} \times \vec{E}$$

Our Generation has had no Great war, no Great Depression. Our war is spiritual. Our depression is our lives.

Chuck Palahniuk

$$C = \frac{Q}{V} \qquad U_E = \frac{1}{2} \qquad C = \varepsilon_0 \frac{A}{d}$$

$$R = \frac{V}{i} \qquad P = Vi \qquad R = \rho \frac{L}{A}$$

$$R_{eq} = R_1 + R_2 + \cdots \qquad C_{eq} = C_1 + C_2 + \cdots$$

$$\frac{1}{R_{eq}} = \frac{1}{R_1} + \frac{1}{R_2} + \cdots \qquad \frac{1}{C_{eq}} = \frac{1}{C_1} + \frac{1}{C_2} + \cdots$$

$$d\vec{B} = \frac{\mu_0}{4\pi} \frac{i \, d\vec{s} \times \hat{r}}{r^2} \qquad B = \frac{\mu_0}{2\pi} \frac{i}{r} \qquad B = \mu_0 n i \qquad \vec{\tau} = \vec{\mu} \times$$

$$\mathcal{E} = -\frac{d\Phi}{dt} \qquad \mathcal{E} = -N \frac{d\Phi}{dt} \qquad L = \frac{|\mathcal{E}|}{\left|\frac{di}{dt}\right|} = \frac{N\Phi}{i}$$

$$u_E = \frac{1}{2} \varepsilon_0 E^2 \qquad u_B = \frac{1}{2} \frac{B^2}{\mu_0} \qquad U_B = \frac{1}{2} L i^2$$

$$q_0 e^{-t/\tau_c} \qquad q = C\mathcal{E}(1 - e^{-t/\tau_c}) \qquad i = i_0 e^{-t/\tau_L} \qquad i = \frac{\mathcal{E}}{R}(1 - e^{-t/\tau_L})$$

$$\frac{L}{R} \qquad \tau_c = RC \qquad \mu = NiA \qquad \frac{1}{4\pi\varepsilon_0} = 9 \times 10^9 \qquad \frac{\mu_0}{4\pi} = 10^{-7}$$

means $10^6 \qquad \mu$ means 10^{-6}

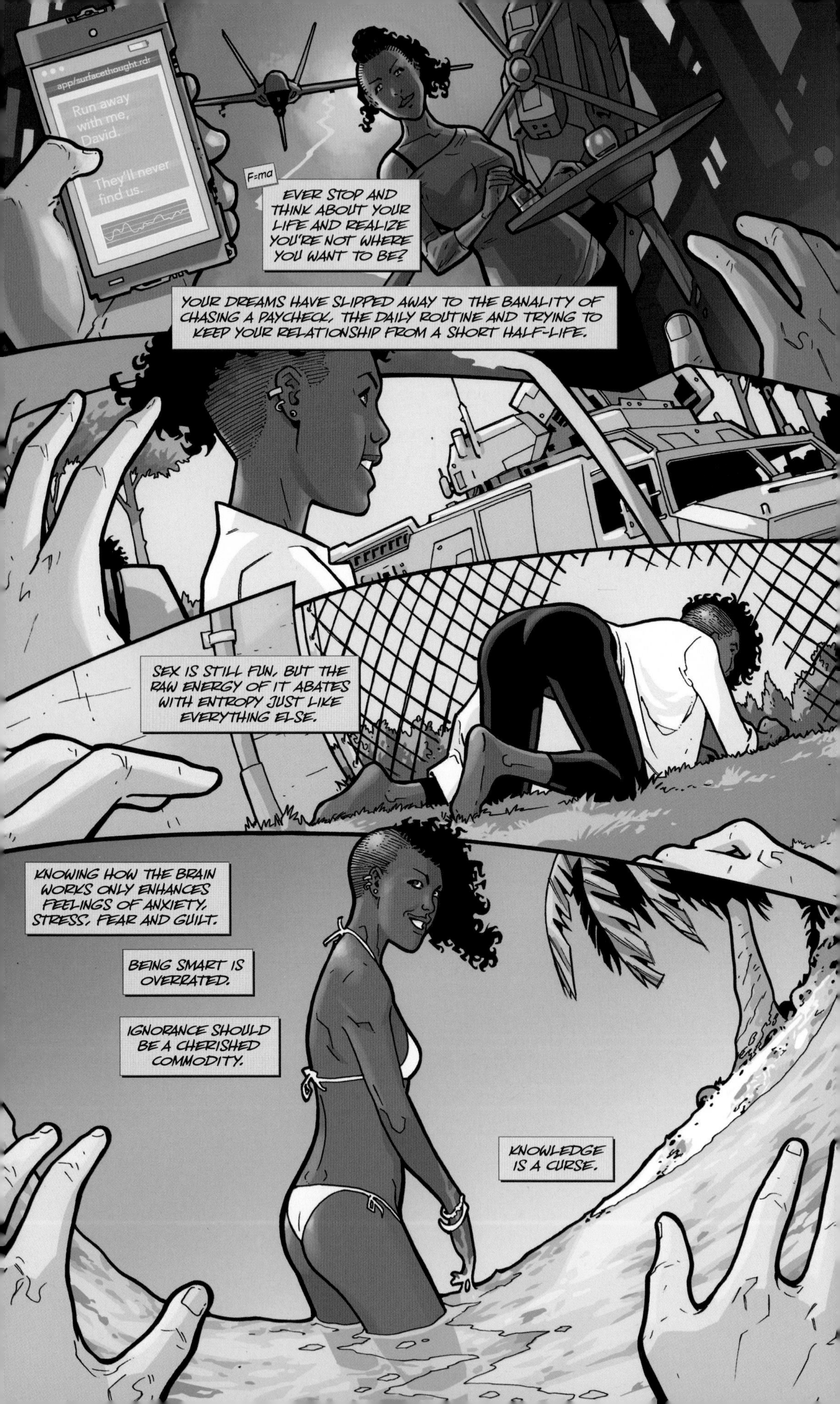
app/surfacethought.rdr
Run away with me, David.
They'll never find us.
F=ma
EVER STOP AND THINK ABOUT YOUR LIFE AND REALIZE YOU'RE NOT WHERE YOU WANT TO BE?
YOUR DREAMS HAVE SLIPPED AWAY TO THE BANALITY OF CHASING A PAYCHECK, THE DAILY ROUTINE AND TRYING TO KEEP YOUR RELATIONSHIP FROM A SHORT HALF-LIFE.
SEX IS STILL FUN, BUT THE RAW ENERGY OF IT ABATES WITH ENTROPY JUST LIKE EVERYTHING ELSE.
KNOWING HOW THE BRAIN WORKS ONLY ENHANCES FEELINGS OF ANXIETY, STRESS, FEAR AND GUILT.
BEING SMART IS OVERRATED.
IGNORANCE SHOULD BE A CHERISHED COMMODITY.
KNOWLEDGE IS A CURSE.

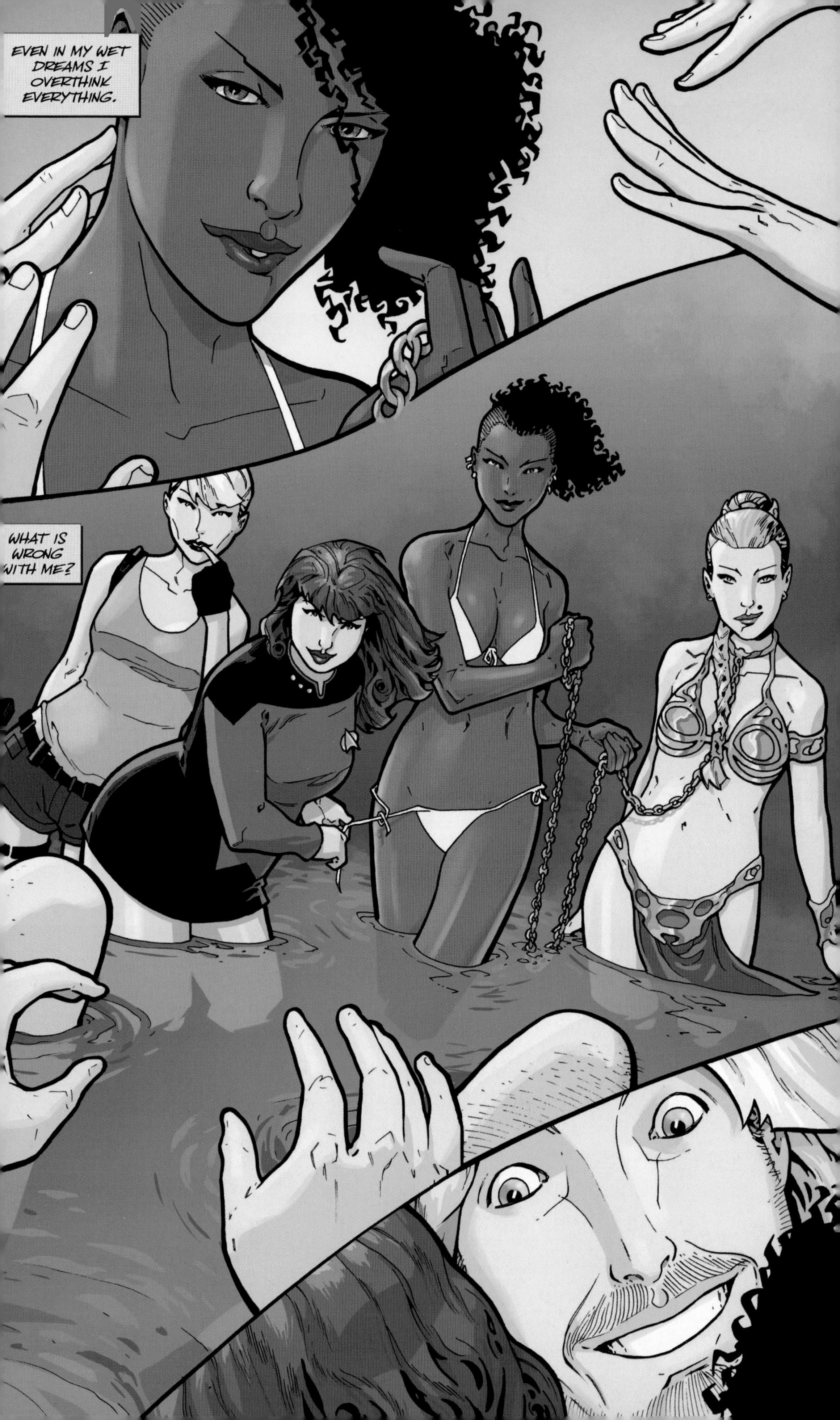

EVEN IN MY WET DREAMS I OVERTHINK EVERYTHING.
WHAT IS WRONG WITH ME?

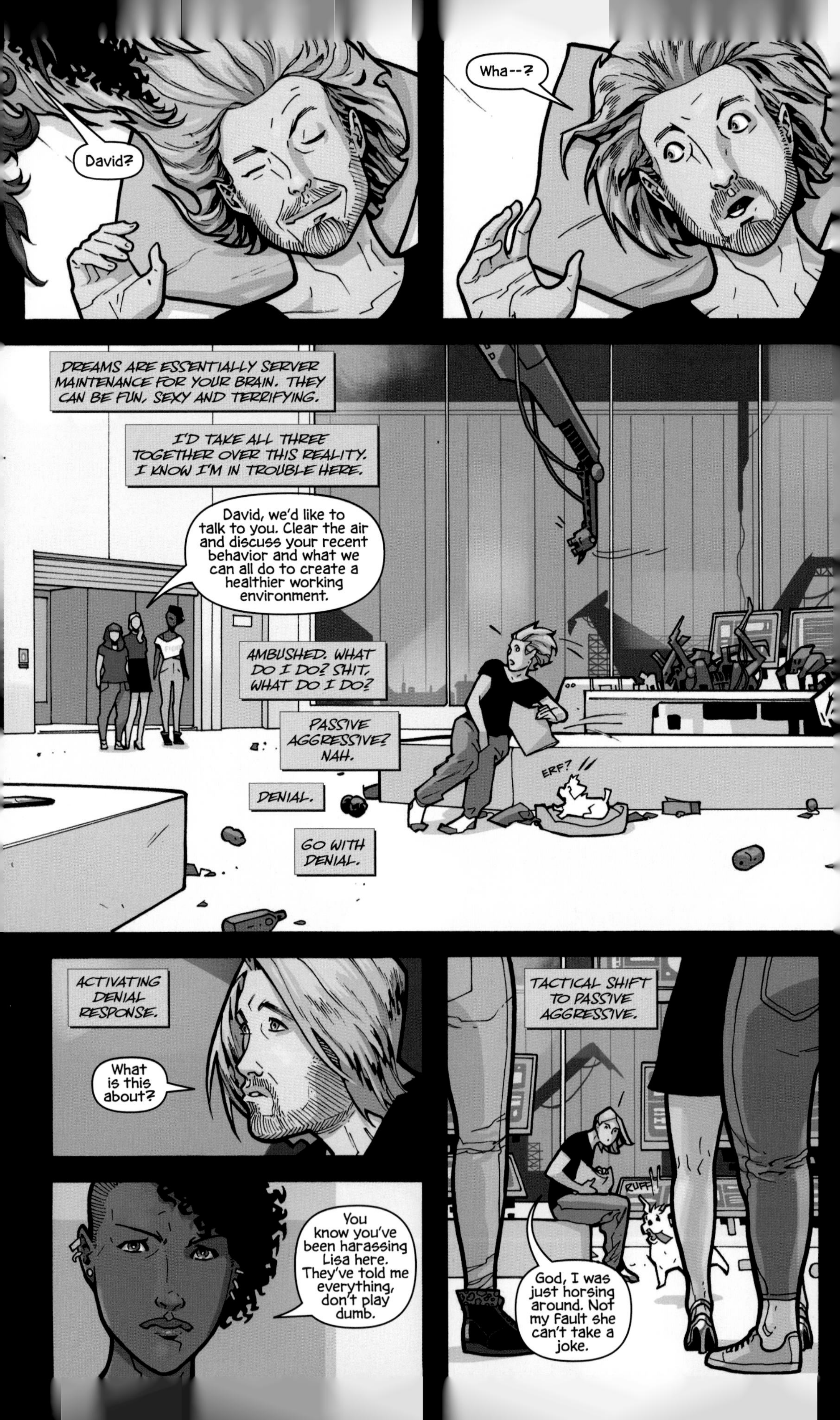

David?
Wha--?
DREAMS ARE ESSENTIALLY SERVER MAINTENANCE FOR YOUR BRAIN. THEY CAN BE FUN, SEXY AND TERRIFYING.
I'D TAKE ALL THREE TOGETHER OVER THIS REALITY. I KNOW I'M IN TROUBLE HERE.
David, we'd like to talk to you. Clear the air and discuss your recent behavior and what we can all do to create a healthier working environment.
AMBUSHED. WHAT DO I DO? SHIT, WHAT DO I DO?
PASSIVE AGGRESSIVE? NAH.
DENIAL.
GO WITH DENIAL.
ERF?
ACTIVATING DENIAL RESPONSE.
What is this about?
TACTICAL SHIFT TO PASSIVE AGGRESSIVE.
RUFF
You know you've been harassing Lisa here. They've told me everything, don't play dumb.
God, I was just horsing around. Not my fault she can't take a joke.

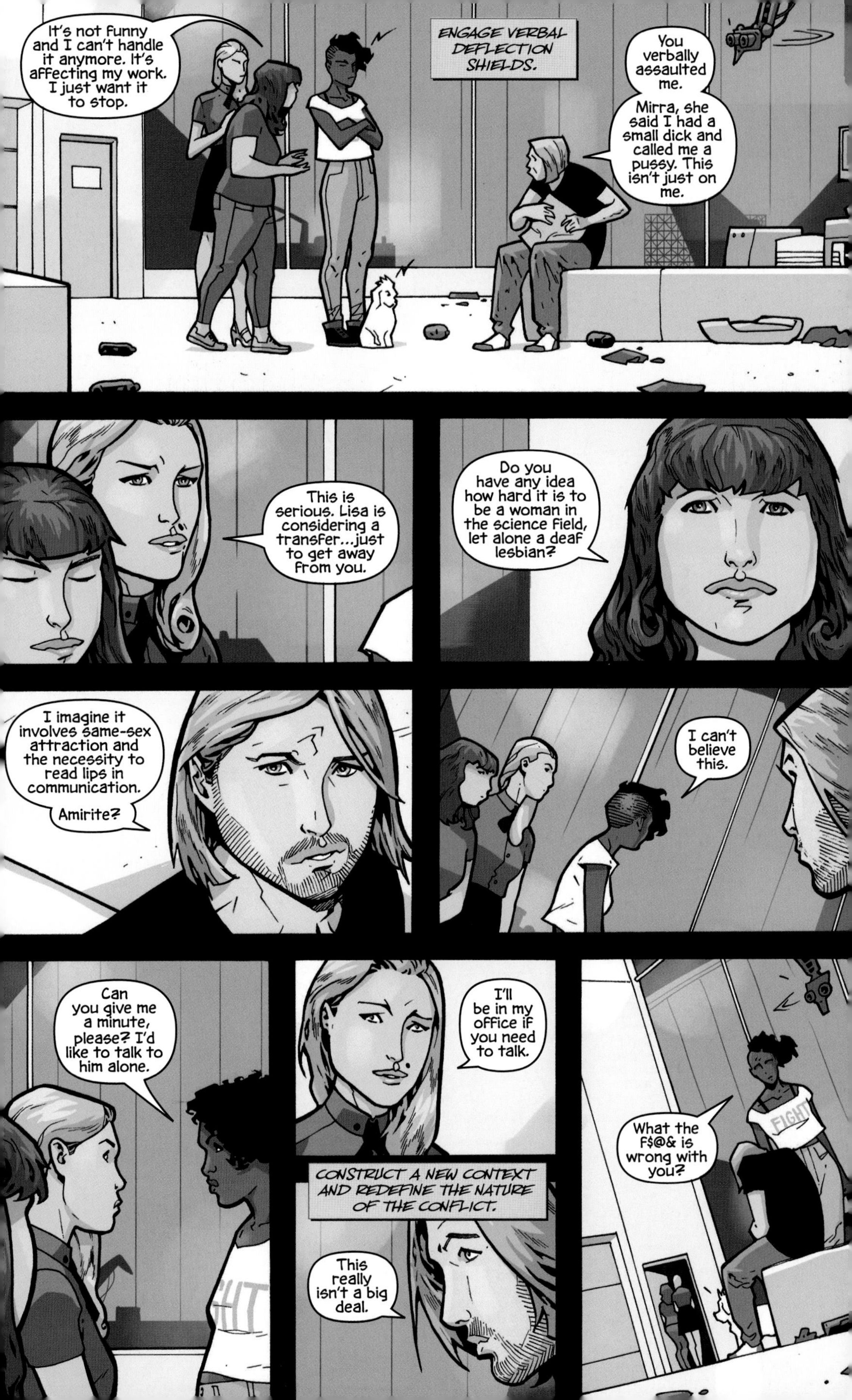
It's not funny and I can't handle it anymore. It's affecting my work. I just want it to stop.
ENGAGE VERBAL DEFLECTION SHIELDS.
You verbally assaulted me.
Mirra, she said I had a small dick and called me a pussy. This isn't just on me.
This is serious. Lisa is considering a transfer...just to get away from you.
Do you have any idea how hard it is to be a woman in the science field, let alone a deaf lesbian?
I imagine it involves same-sex attraction and the necessity to read lips in communication.
Amirite?
I can't believe this.
Can you give me a minute, please? I'd like to talk to him alone.
I'll be in my office if you need to talk.
CONSTRUCT A NEW CONTEXT AND REDEFINE THE NATURE OF THE CONFLICT.
This really isn't a big deal.
What the F$@& is wrong with you?

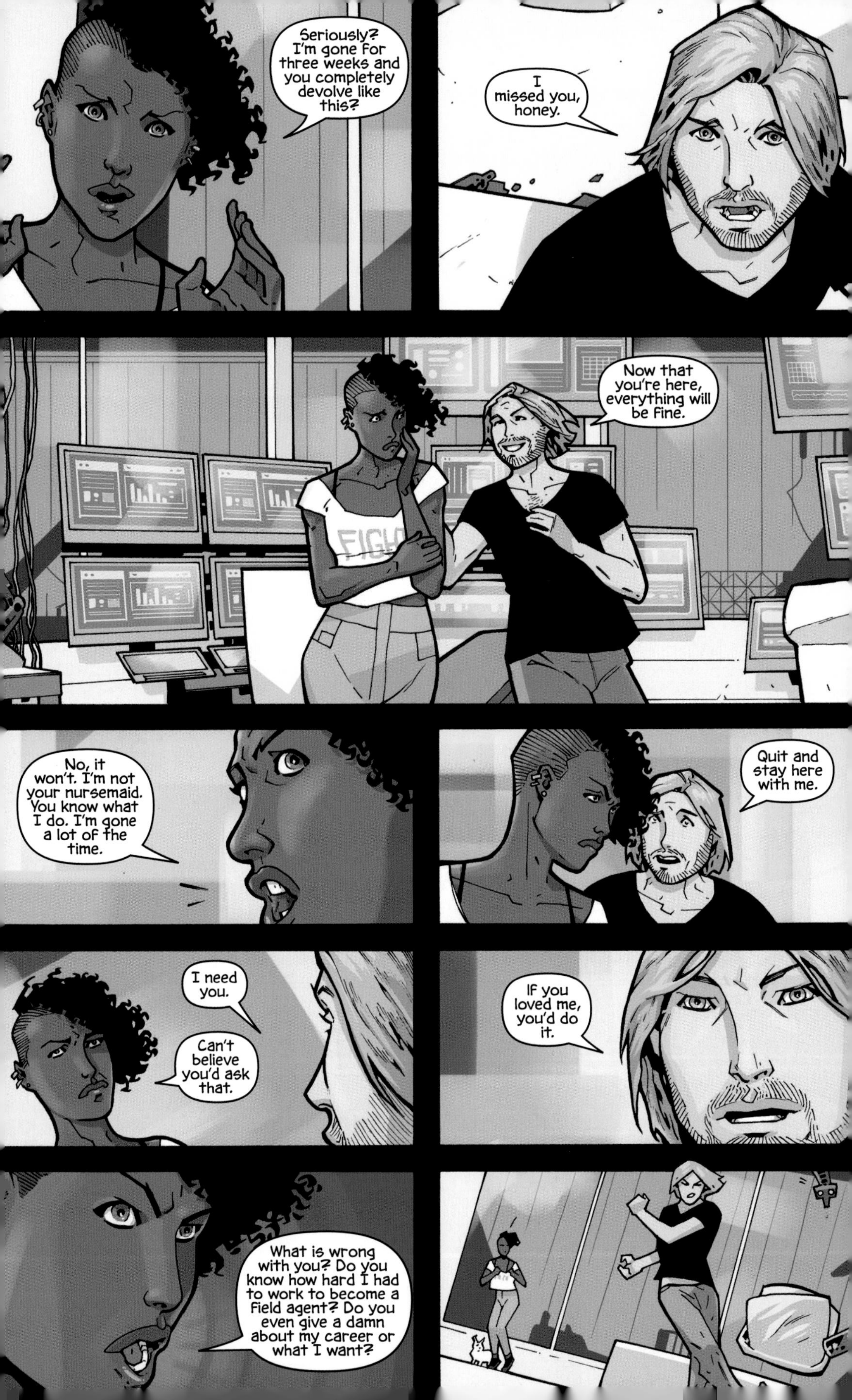
Seriously? I'm gone for three weeks and you completely devolve like this?
I missed you, honey.
Now that you're here, everything will be fine.
FIGH
No, it won't. I'm not your nursemaid. You know what I do. I'm gone a lot of the time.
Quit and stay here with me.
I need you.
Can't believe you'd ask that.
If you loved me, you'd do it.
What is wrong with you? Do you know how hard I had to work to become a field agent? Do you even give a damn about my career or what I want?

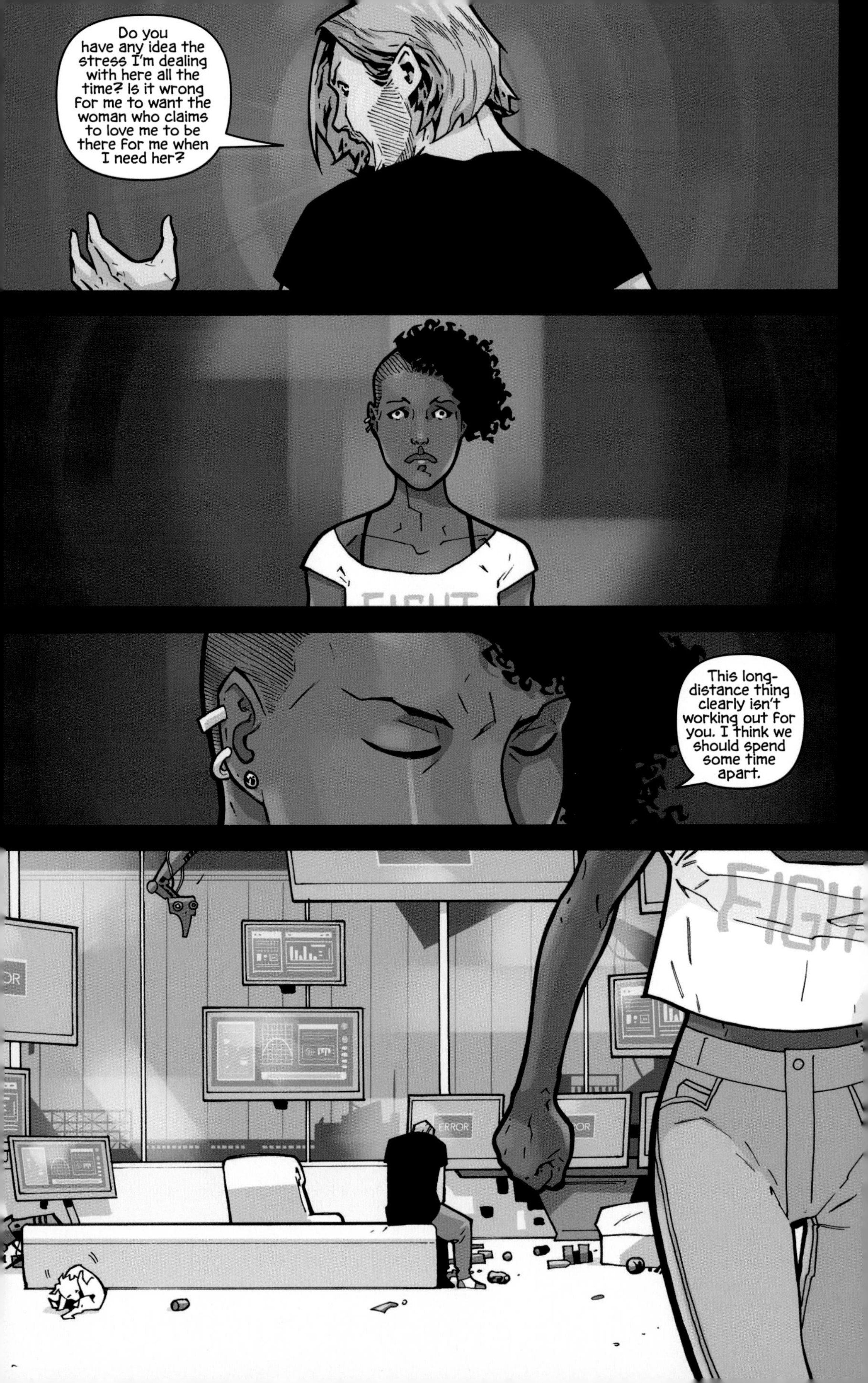
Do you have any idea the stress I'm dealing with here all the time? Is it wrong for me to want the woman who claims to love me to be there for me when I need her?
FIGHT
This long-distance thing clearly isn't working out for you. I think we should spend some time apart.
ERROR
ERROR
FIGH

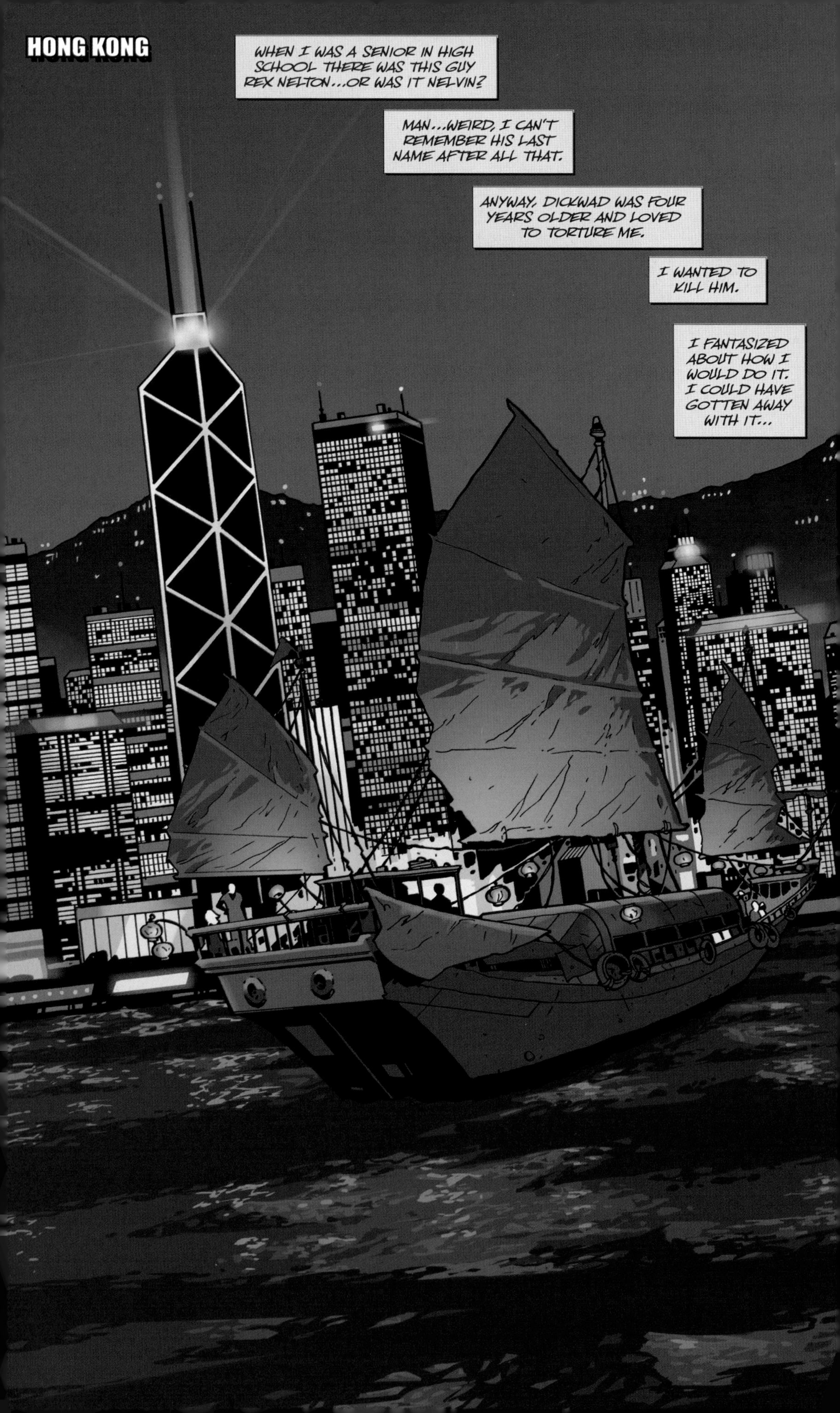
HONG KONG
WHEN I WAS A SENIOR IN HIGH SCHOOL THERE WAS THIS GUY REX NELTON...OR WAS IT NELVIN?
MAN...WEIRD, I CAN'T REMEMBER HIS LAST NAME AFTER ALL THAT.
ANYWAY, DICKWAD WAS FOUR YEARS OLDER AND LOVED TO TORTURE ME.
I WANTED TO KILL HIM.
I FANTASIZED ABOUT HOW I WOULD DO IT. I COULD HAVE GOTTEN AWAY WITH IT...

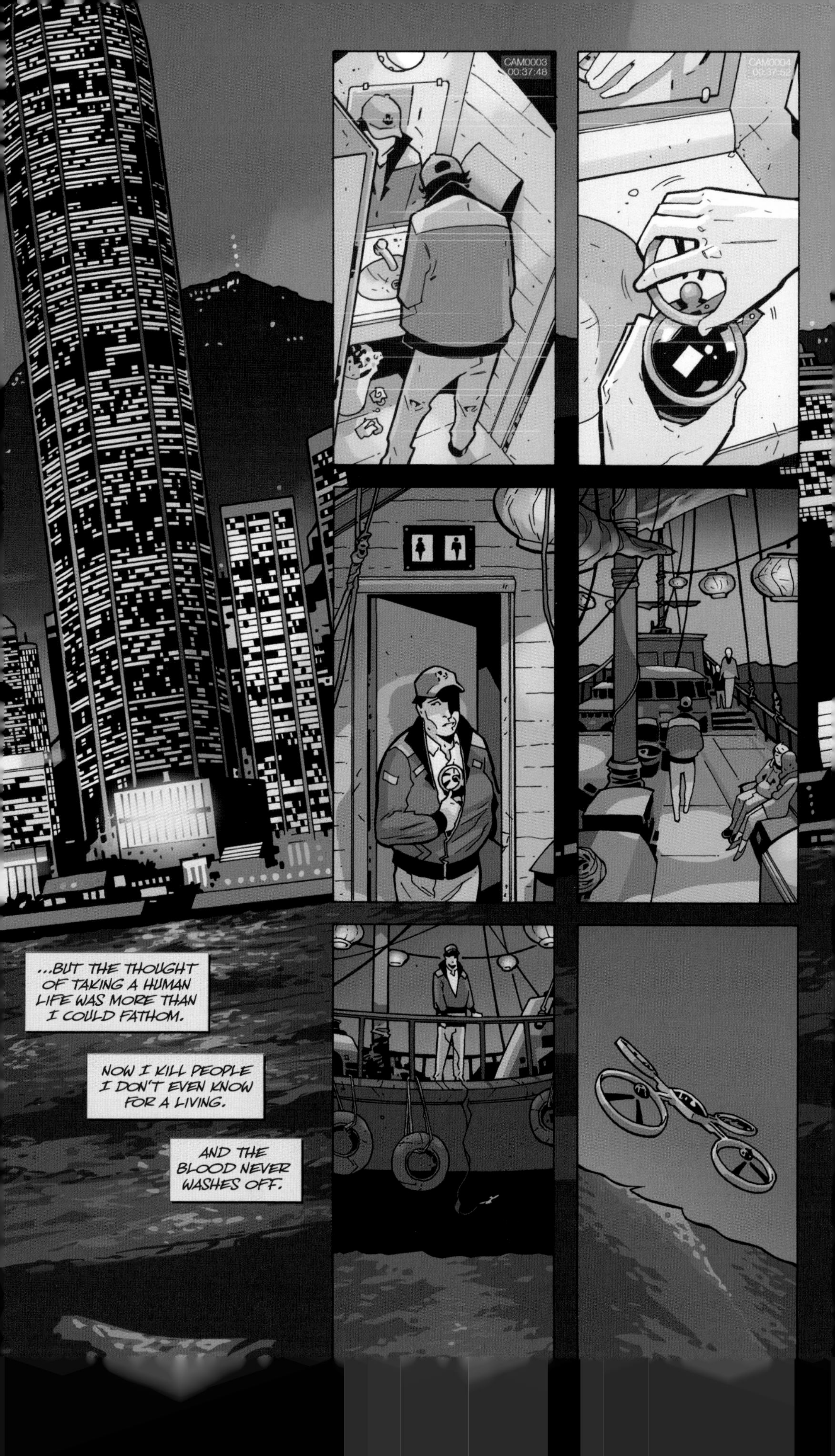
CAM0003
00:37:48
CAM0004
00:37:52
...BUT THE THOUGHT OF TAKING A HUMAN LIFE WAS MORE THAN I COULD FATHOM.
NOW I KILL PEOPLE I DON'T EVEN KNOW FOR A LIVING.
AND THE BLOOD NEVER WASHES OFF.

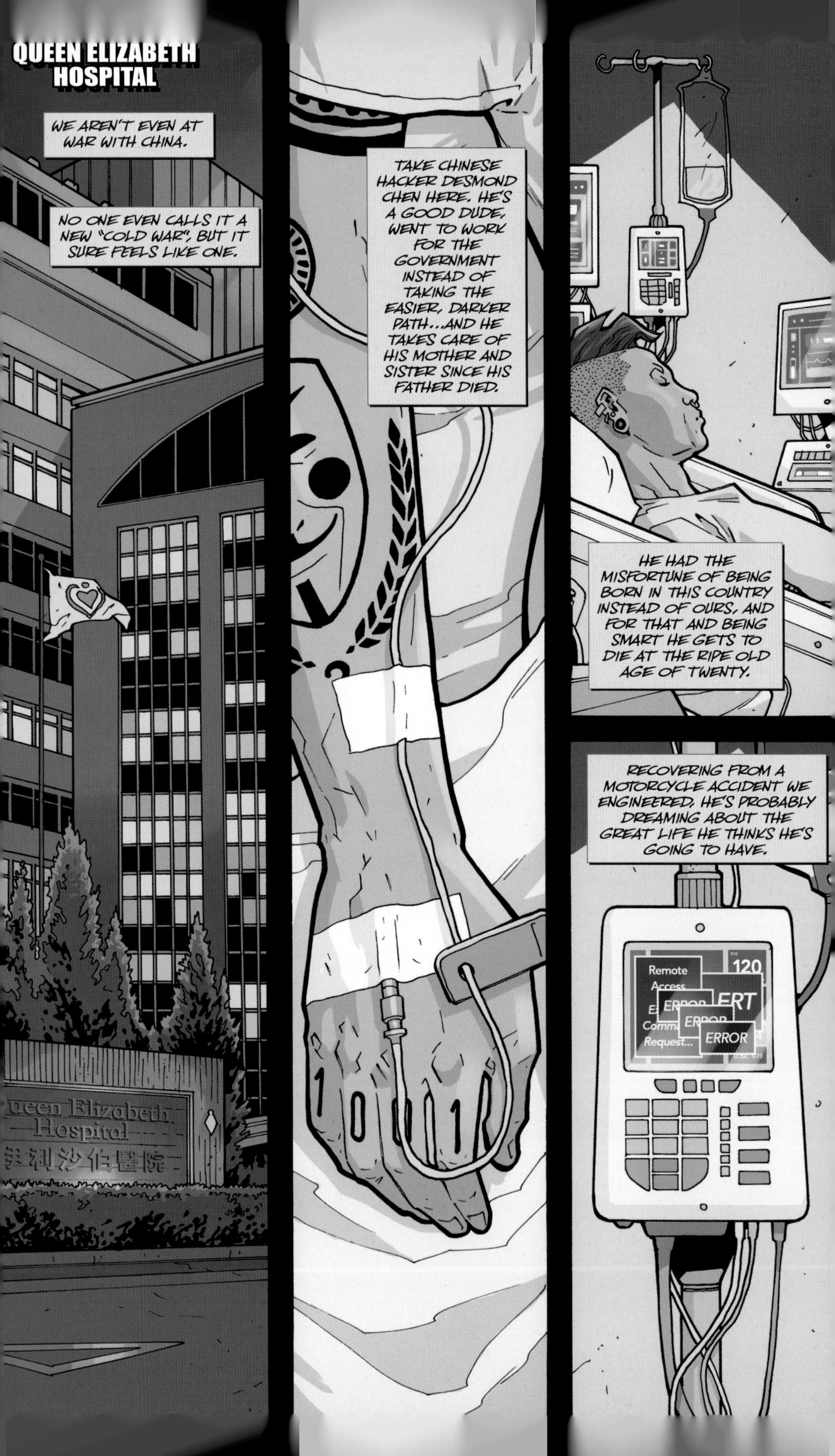
QUEEN ELIZABETH HOSPITAL
WE AREN'T EVEN AT WAR WITH CHINA.
NO ONE EVEN CALLS IT A NEW "COLD WAR", BUT IT SURE FEELS LIKE ONE.
Hospital
TAKE CHINESE HACKER DESMOND CHEN HERE. HE'S A GOOD DUDE, WENT TO WORK FOR THE GOVERNMENT INSTEAD OF TAKING THE EASIER, DARKER PATH...AND HE TAKES CARE OF HIS MOTHER AND SISTER SINCE HIS FATHER DIED.
1 0 0 1 1
HE HAD THE MISFORTUNE OF BEING BORN IN THIS COUNTRY INSTEAD OF OURS, AND FOR THAT AND BEING SMART HE GETS TO DIE AT THE RIPE OLD AGE OF TWENTY.
RECOVERING FROM A MOTORCYCLE ACCIDENT WE ENGINEERED, HE'S PROBABLY DREAMING ABOUT THE GREAT LIFE HE THINKS HE'S GOING TO HAVE.
Remote
Access
120
ERROR

LAMMA
POWER
STATION

ALL THIS TO KILL ONE KID.

WE CALL IT A **PROACTIVE MILITARY STRATEGY** TO ENSURE PEACE.

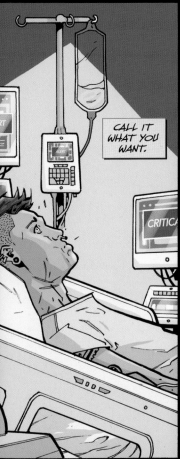

CALL IT WHAT YOU WANT.

BUT WE JUST KNOCKED OUT POWER TO MILLIONS...

...TO PREVENT AN ALARM FROM SOUNDING BEFORE THE BACKUP GENERATORS CAN KICK IN...

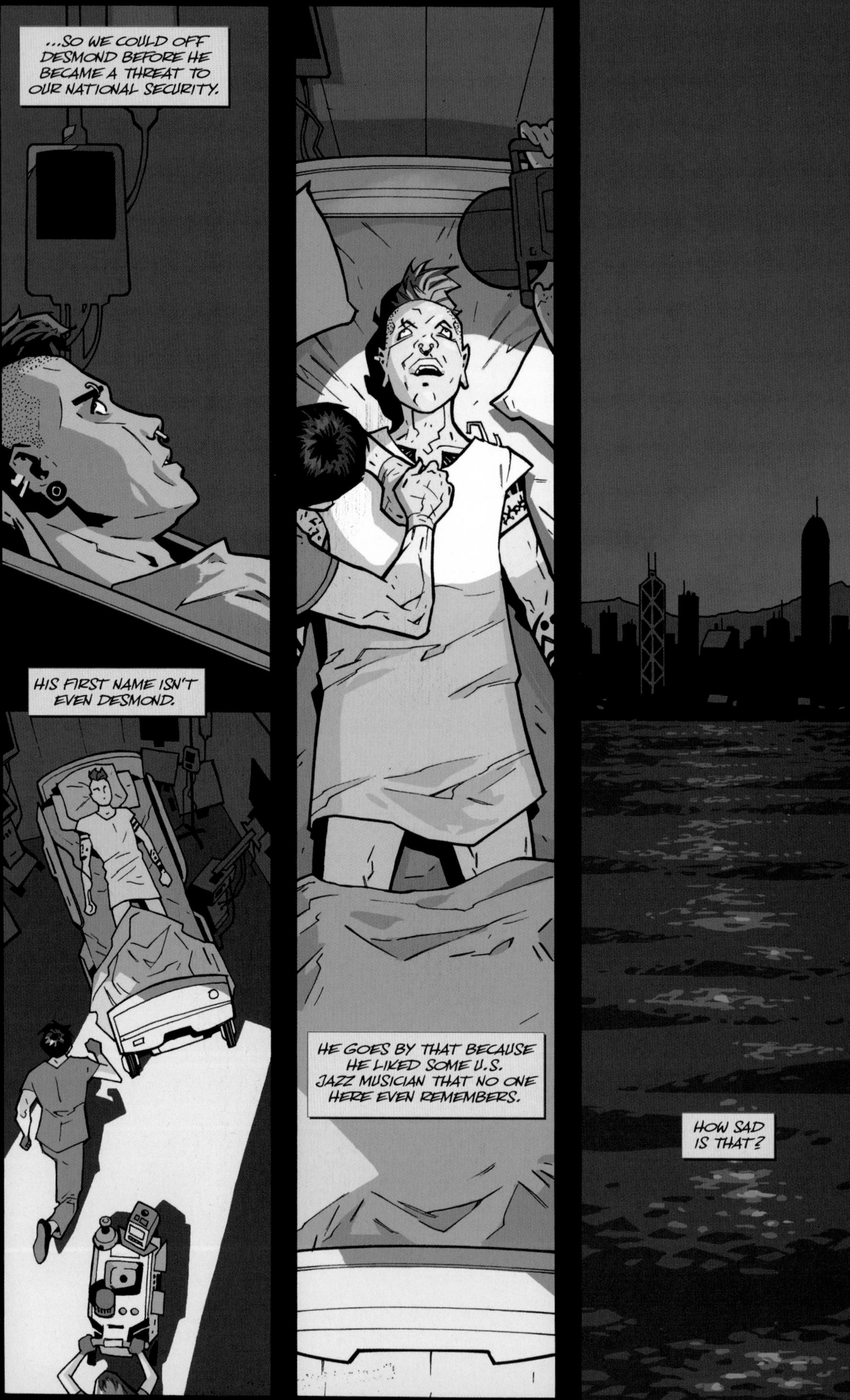
...SO WE COULD OFF DESMOND BEFORE HE BECAME A THREAT TO OUR NATIONAL SECURITY.
HIS FIRST NAME ISN'T EVEN DESMOND.
HE GOES BY THAT BECAUSE HE LIKED SOME U.S. JAZZ MUSICIAN THAT NO ONE HERE EVEN REMEMBERS.
HOW SAD IS THAT?

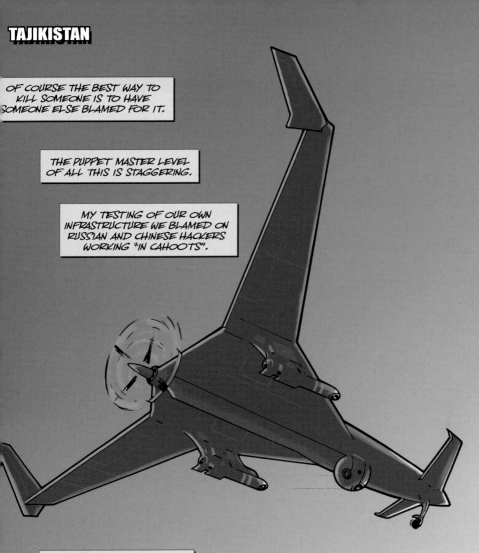

OF COURSE THE BEST WAY TO KILL SOMEONE IS TO HAVE SOMEONE ELSE BLAMED FOR IT.

THE PUPPET MASTER LEVEL OF ALL THIS IS STAGGERING.

MY TESTING OF OUR OWN INFRASTRUCTURE WE BLAMED ON RUSSIAN AND CHINESE HACKERS WORKING "IN CAHOOTS".

DESMOND'S DEATH WILL BE BLAMED ON THE RUSSIANS.

AND WE USED MY QUANTUM CRYPTO PROGRAM TO HACK THESE CHINESE DRONES AND HAVE THEM ATTACK AN OLD RUSSIAN BASE IN A FORMER SOVIET STATE.

IT'S AN OLD, INSIGNIFICANT TARGET, BUT ENOUGH TO MAKE THE POINT.

THE CHINESE LEADERSHIP CAN'T ADMIT THEY LOST CONTROL OF THEIR DRONES. THAT SHOWS WEAKNESS, AND WEAKNESS EQUALS INTERNAL REGIME CHANGE.

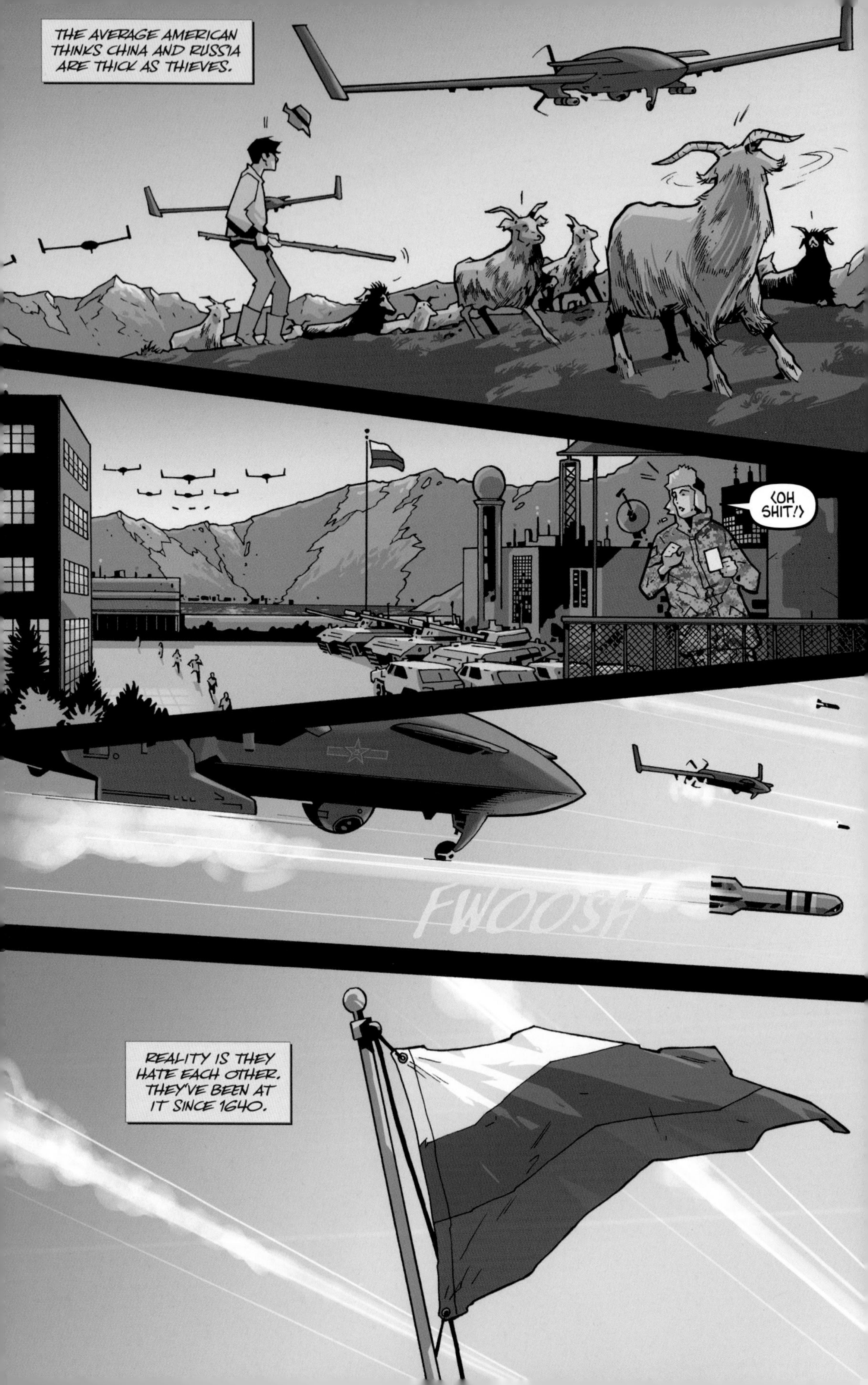
THE AVERAGE AMERICAN THINKS CHINA AND RUSSIA ARE THICK AS THIEVES.
‹OH SHIT!›
FWOOSH
REALITY IS THEY HATE EACH OTHER. THEY'VE BEEN AT IT SINCE 1640.

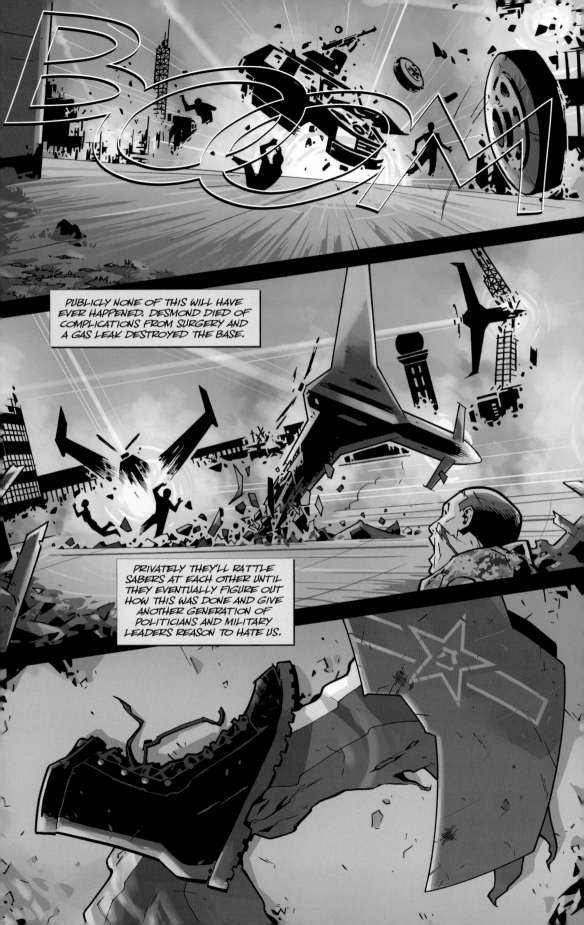

BOOM

PUBLICLY NONE OF THIS WILL HAVE EVER HAPPENED. DESMOND DIED OF COMPLICATIONS FROM SURGERY AND A GAS LEAK DESTROYED THE BASE.

PRIVATELY THEY'LL RATTLE SABERS AT EACH OTHER UNTIL THEY EVENTUALLY FIGURE OUT HOW THIS WAS DONE AND GIVE ANOTHER GENERATION OF POLITICIANS AND MILITARY LEADERS REASON TO HATE US.

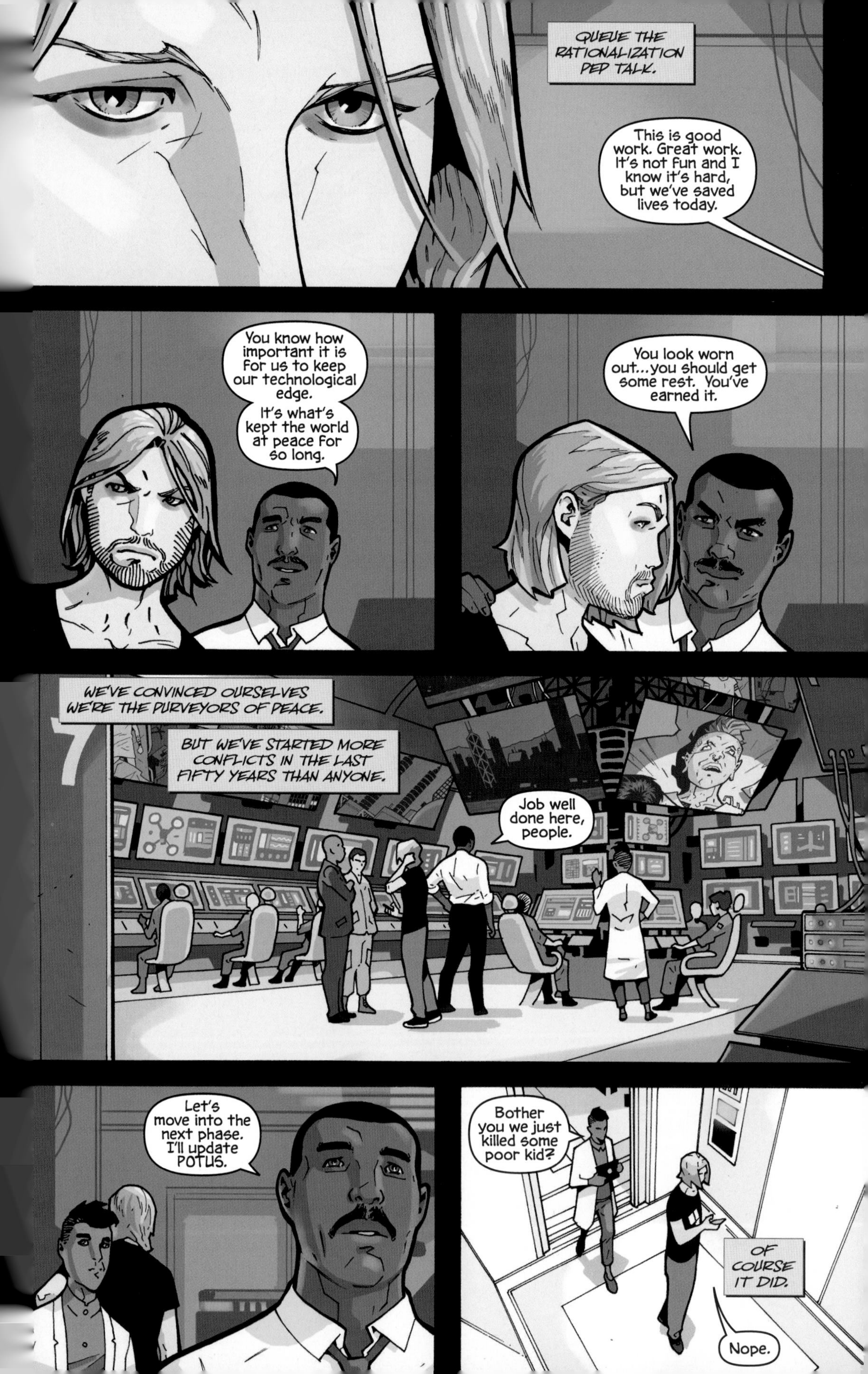
QUEUE THE RATIONALIZATION PEP TALK.
This is good work. Great work. It's not fun and I know it's hard, but we've saved lives today.
You know how important it is for us to keep our technological edge.
It's what's kept the world at peace for so long.
You look worn out...you should get some rest. You've earned it.
WE'VE CONVINCED OURSELVES WE'RE THE PURVEYORS OF PEACE.
BUT WE'VE STARTED MORE CONFLICTS IN THE LAST FIFTY YEARS THAN ANYONE.
Job well done here, people.
Let's move into the next phase. I'll update POTUS.
Bother you we just killed some poor kid?
OF COURSE IT DID.
Nope.

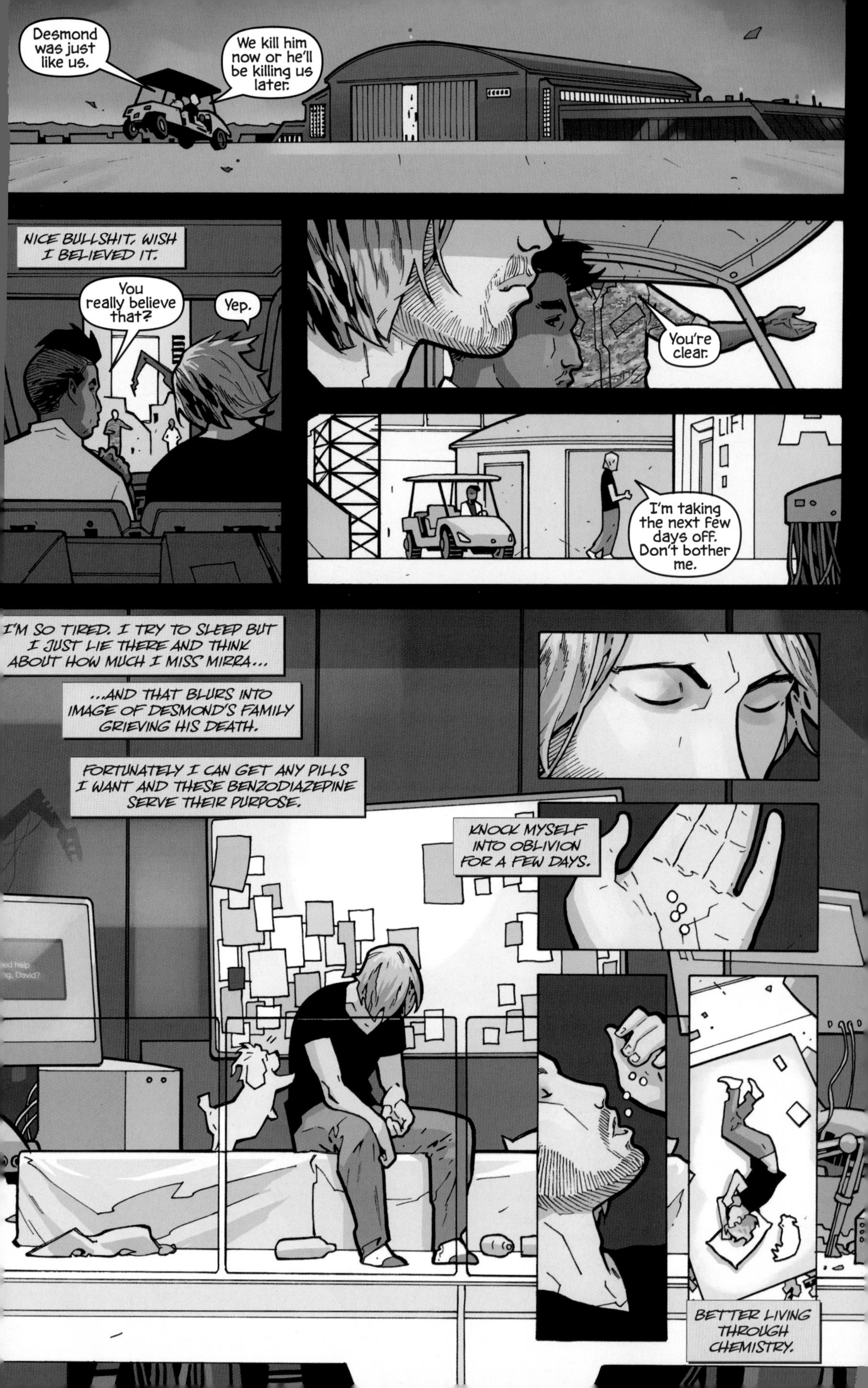
Desmond was just like us.
We kill him now or he'll be killing us later.
NICE BULLSHIT. WISH I BELIEVED IT.
You really believe that?
Yep.
You're clear.
LIFT
I'm taking the next few days off. Don't bother me.
I'M SO TIRED. I TRY TO SLEEP BUT I JUST LIE THERE AND THINK ABOUT HOW MUCH I MISS MIRRA...
...AND THAT BLURS INTO IMAGE OF DESMOND'S FAMILY GRIEVING HIS DEATH.
FORTUNATELY I CAN GET ANY PILLS I WANT AND THESE BENZODIAZEPINE SERVE THEIR PURPOSE.
KNOCK MYSELF INTO OBLIVION FOR A FEW DAYS.
BETTER LIVING THROUGH CHEMISTRY.

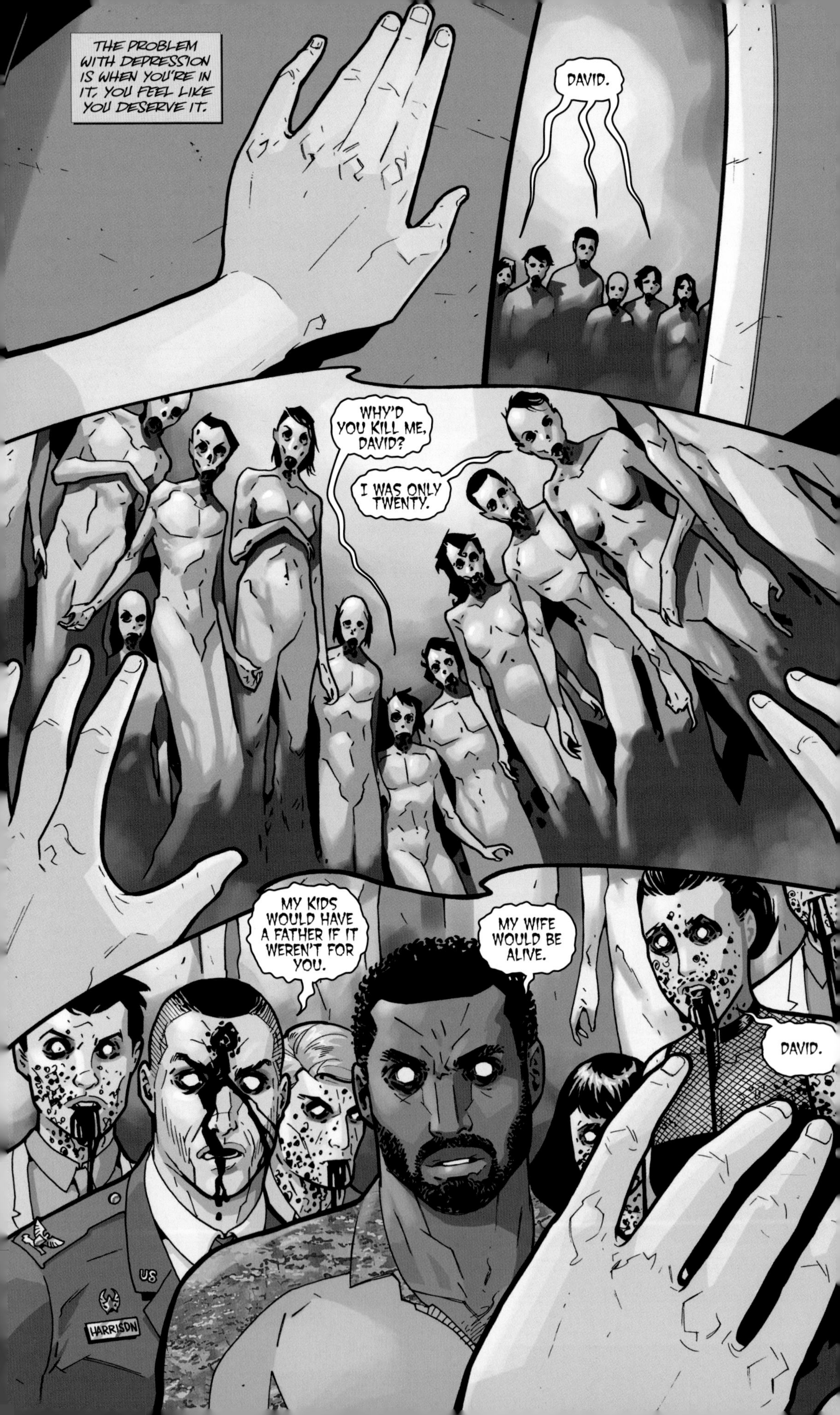
THE PROBLEM WITH DEPRESSION IS WHEN YOU'RE IN IT, YOU FEEL LIKE YOU DESERVE IT.
DAVID.
WHY'D YOU KILL ME, DAVID?
I WAS ONLY TWENTY.
MY KIDS WOULD HAVE A FATHER IF IT WEREN'T FOR YOU.
MY WIFE WOULD BE ALIVE.
DAVID.
US
HARRISON

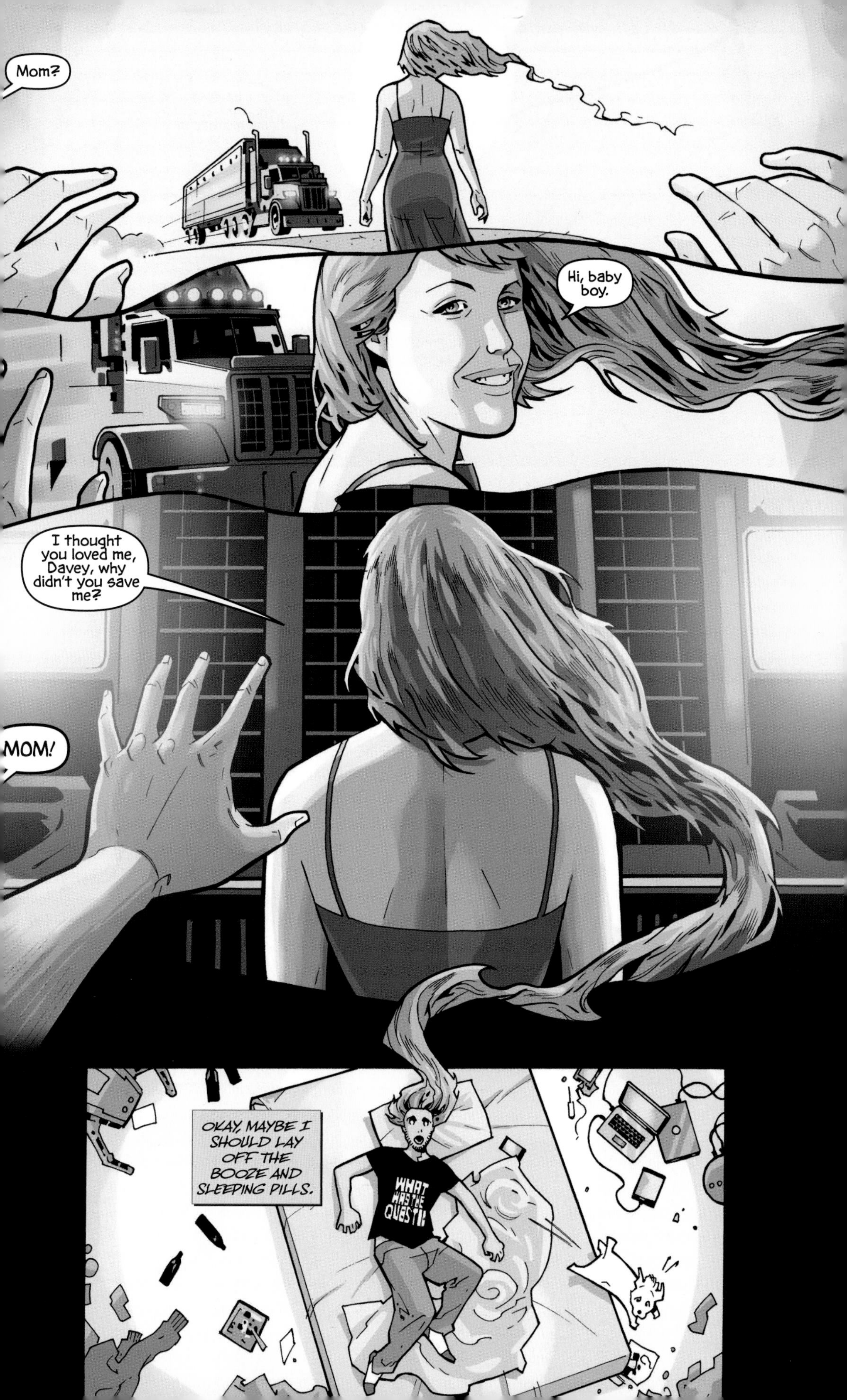

Mom?
Hi, baby boy.
I thought you loved me, Davey, why didn't you save me?
MOM!
OKAY, MAYBE I SHOULD LAY OFF THE BOOZE AND SLEEPING PILLS.

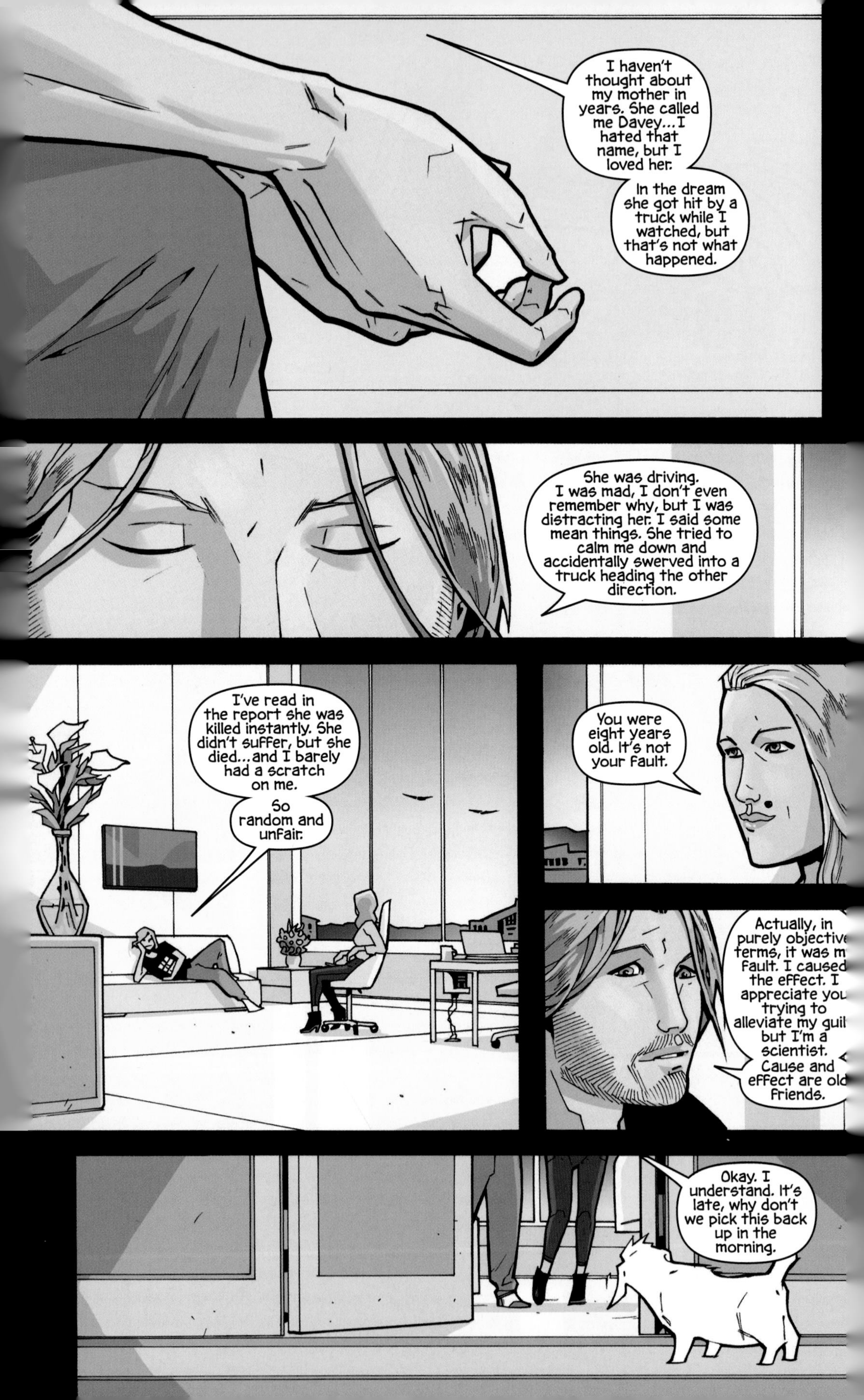
I haven't thought about my mother in years. She called me Davey... I hated that name, but I loved her.
In the dream she got hit by a truck while I watched, but that's not what happened.
She was driving. I was mad, I don't even remember why, but I was distracting her. I said some mean things. She tried to calm me down and accidentally swerved into a truck heading the other direction.
I've read in the report she was killed instantly. She didn't suffer, but she died... and I barely had a scratch on me.
So random and unfair.
You were eight years old. It's not your fault.
Actually, in purely objective terms, it was my fault. I caused the effect. I appreciate you trying to alleviate my guilt but I'm a scientist. Cause and effect are old friends.
Okay. I understand. It's late, why don't we pick this back up in the morning.

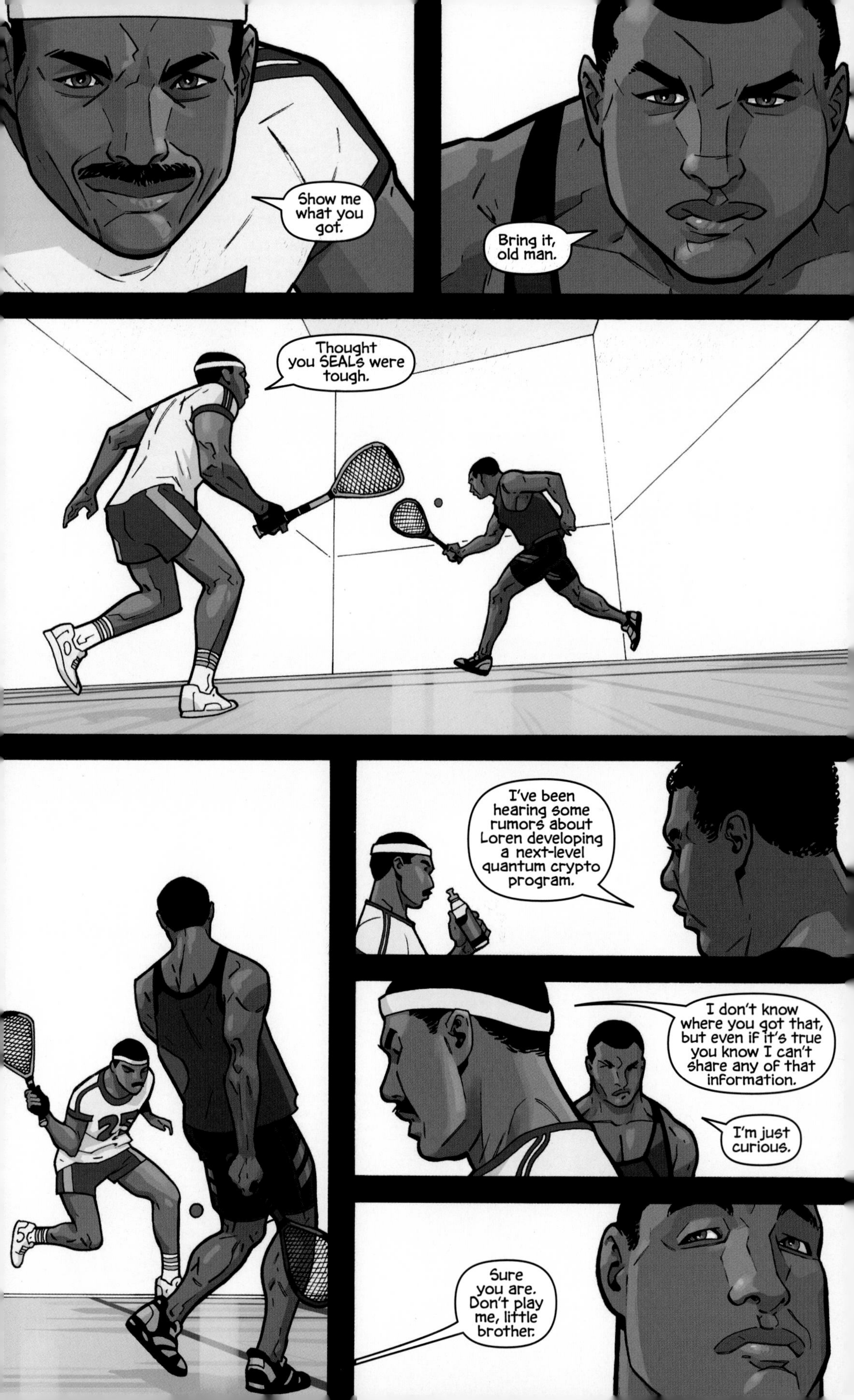
Show me what you got.
Bring it, old man.
Thought you SEALs were tough.
I've been hearing some rumors about Loren developing a next-level quantum crypto program.
I don't know where you got that, but even if it's true you know I can't share any of that information.
I'm just curious.
Sure you are. Don't play me, little brother.

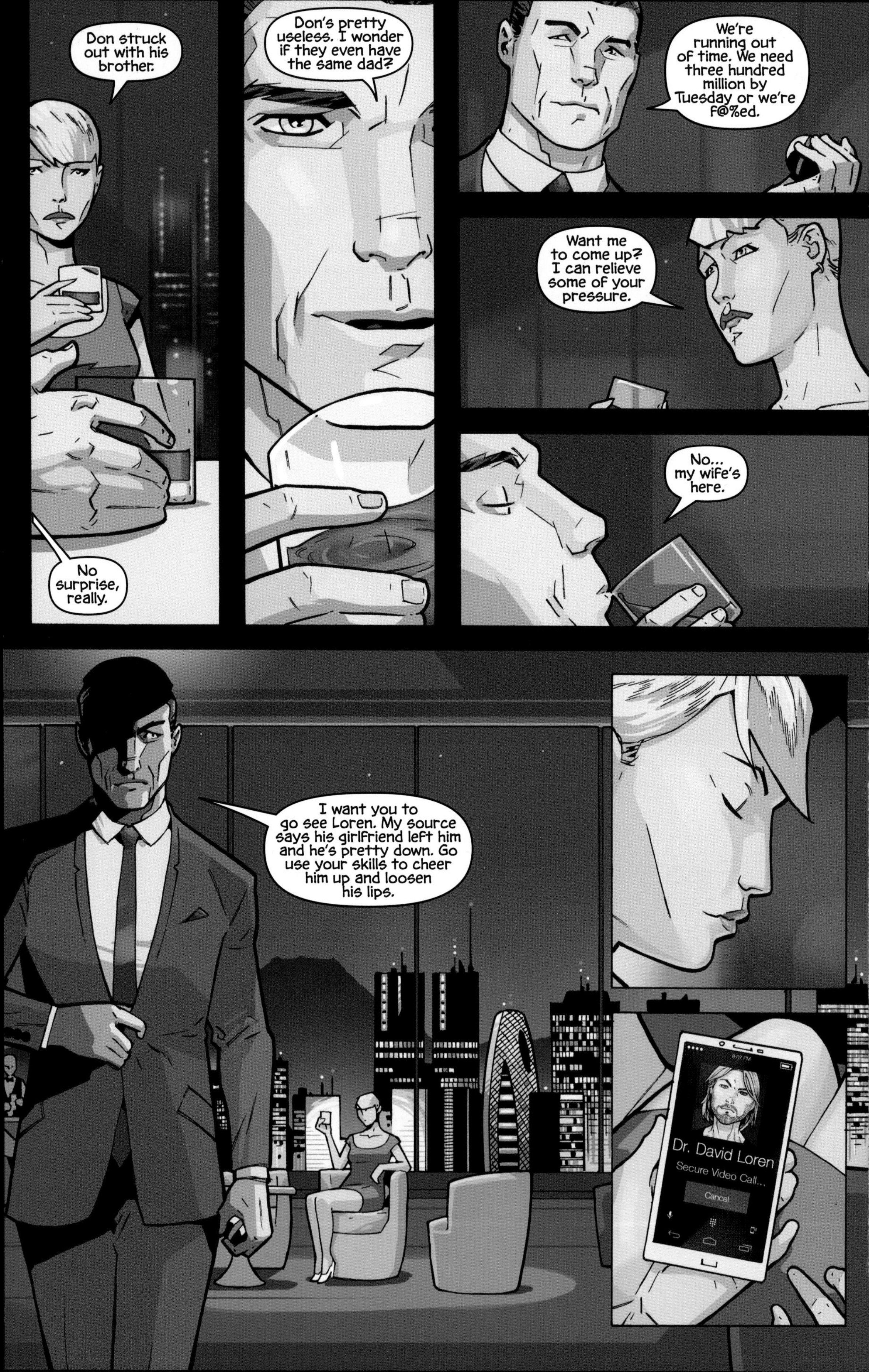
Don struck out with his brother.
No surprise, really.
Don's pretty useless. I wonder if they even have the same dad?
We're running out of time. We need three hundred million by Tuesday or we're f@%ed.
Want me to come up? I can relieve some of your pressure.
No... my wife's here.
I want you to go see Loren. My source says his girlfriend left him and he's pretty down. Go use your skills to cheer him up and loosen his lips.
8:07 PM
Dr. David Loren
Secure Video Call...
Cancel

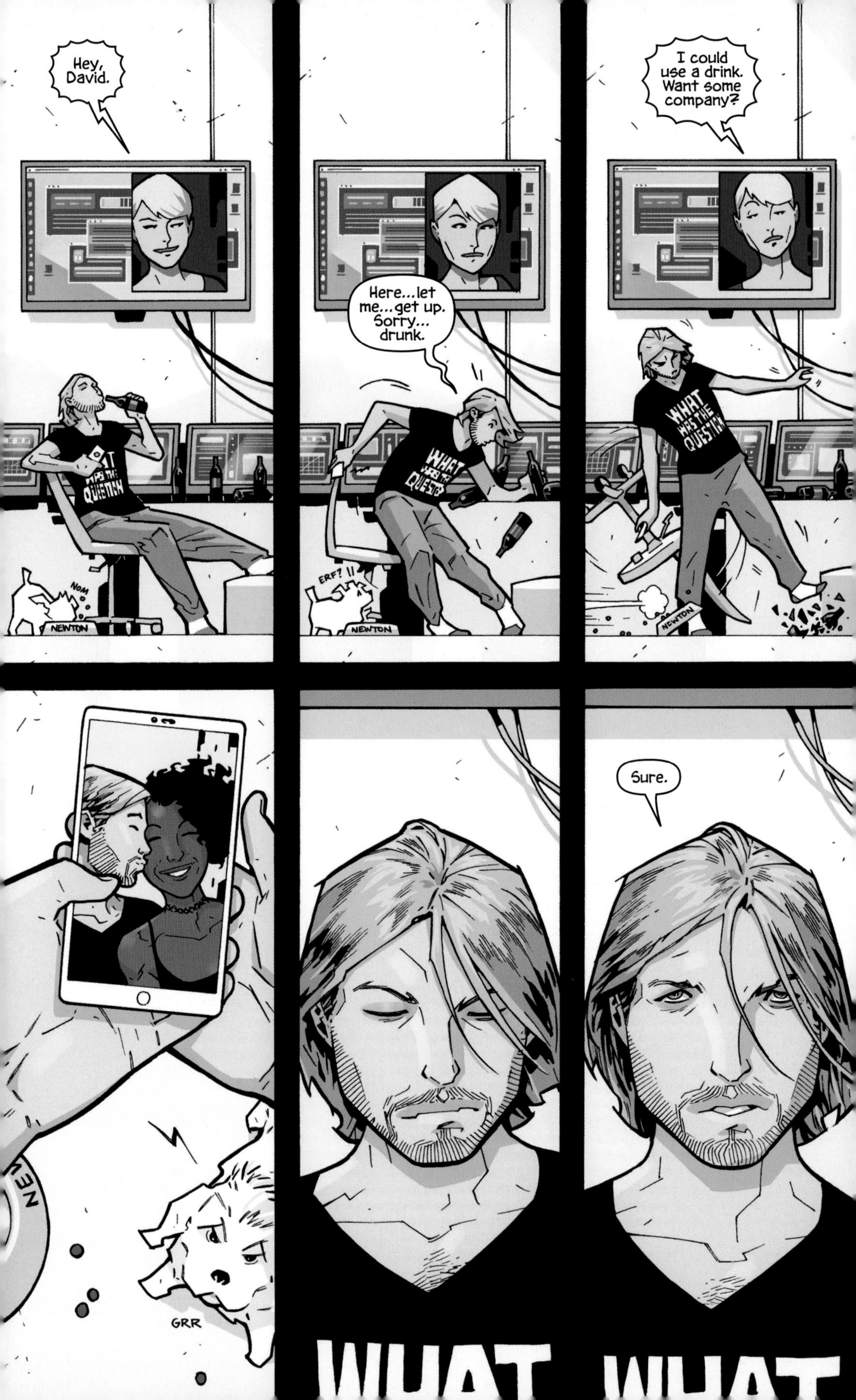
Hey, David.
Here...let me...get up. Sorry... drunk.
I could use a drink. Want some company?
NOM
NEWTON
ERF? !!
NEWTON
NEWTON
GRR
Sure.

CHAPTER FOUR

THINK TANK

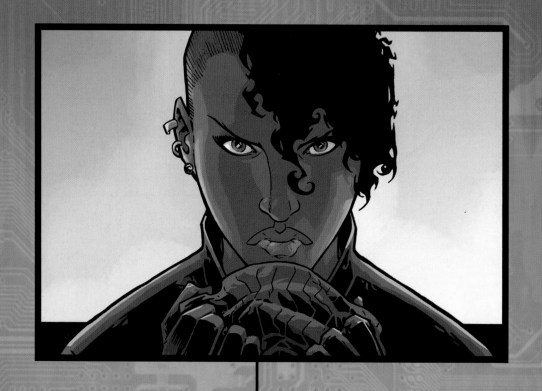

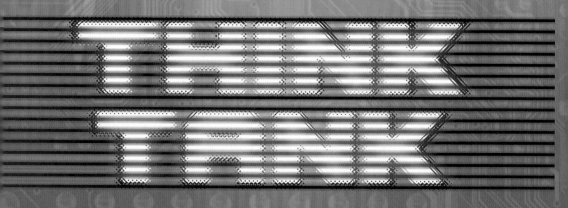

$$\oint \vec{E} \ d\vec{A} = \frac{1}{\varepsilon_o} q_{in} \qquad \oint \vec{B} \ d\vec{A} = 0 \qquad \oint \vec{E} \ d\ell = -\frac{d}{dt} \int \vec{B} \ dA$$

$$\oint \vec{B} \ d\vec{\ell} = \mu_o I_{in} \qquad \vec{F} = q(\vec{v} \times \vec{B} + \vec{E}) \qquad i = \frac{dq}{dt}$$

nt charge $\quad E = \frac{1}{4\pi \varepsilon_o} \frac{q}{r^2} \qquad V = \frac{1}{4\pi \varepsilon_o} \frac{q}{r} \qquad \qquad p = qd$

Depression is the inability to construct a future.

$V_f - V_i = -\int_i^f \vec{E}$ $\qquad \qquad \vec{\tau} = \vec{p} \times \vec{E}$

Rollo May

$C = \frac{Q}{V} \qquad U_E = \frac{1}{2} QV = \frac{1}{2} CV^2 = \frac{1}{2} \frac{Q^2}{C} \qquad C = \varepsilon_o \frac{A}{d}$

$R = \frac{V}{i} \qquad P = Vi \qquad P = i^2 R = \frac{V^2}{R} \qquad R = \rho \frac{L}{A}$

$R_{eq} = R_1 + R_2 + \cdots \qquad \qquad C_{eq} = C_1 + C_2 + \cdots$

$\frac{1}{R_{eq}} = \frac{1}{R_1} + \frac{1}{R_2} + \cdots \qquad \frac{1}{C_{eq}} = \frac{1}{C_1} + \frac{1}{C_2} + \cdots$

$d\vec{B} = \frac{\mu_o}{4\pi} \frac{i d\vec{s} \times \hat{r}}{r^2} \qquad B = \frac{\mu_o}{2\pi} \frac{i}{r} \qquad B = \mu_o n i \qquad \vec{\tau} = \vec{\mu} \times \vec{B}$

$\phi = -\frac{d\Phi}{dt} \qquad \mathcal{E} = -N \frac{d\Phi}{dt} \qquad L = \frac{|\mathcal{E}|}{|\frac{di}{dt}|} = \frac{N\Phi}{i}$

$u_E = \frac{1}{2} \varepsilon_o E^2 \qquad u_B = \frac{1}{2} \frac{B^2}{\mu_o} \qquad U_B = \frac{1}{2} L i^2$

$q_o e^{-t/\tau_c} \qquad q = C\mathcal{E}(1 - e^{-t/\tau_c}) \qquad i = i_o e^{-t/\tau_L} \qquad i = \frac{\mathcal{E}}{R}(1 - e^{-t/\tau_L})$

$\frac{L}{R} \qquad \tau_c = RC \qquad \mu = N i A \qquad \frac{1}{4\pi \varepsilon_o} = 9 \times 10^9 \qquad \frac{\mu_o}{4\pi} = 10^{-7}$

means $10^6 \qquad \mu$ means 10^{-6}

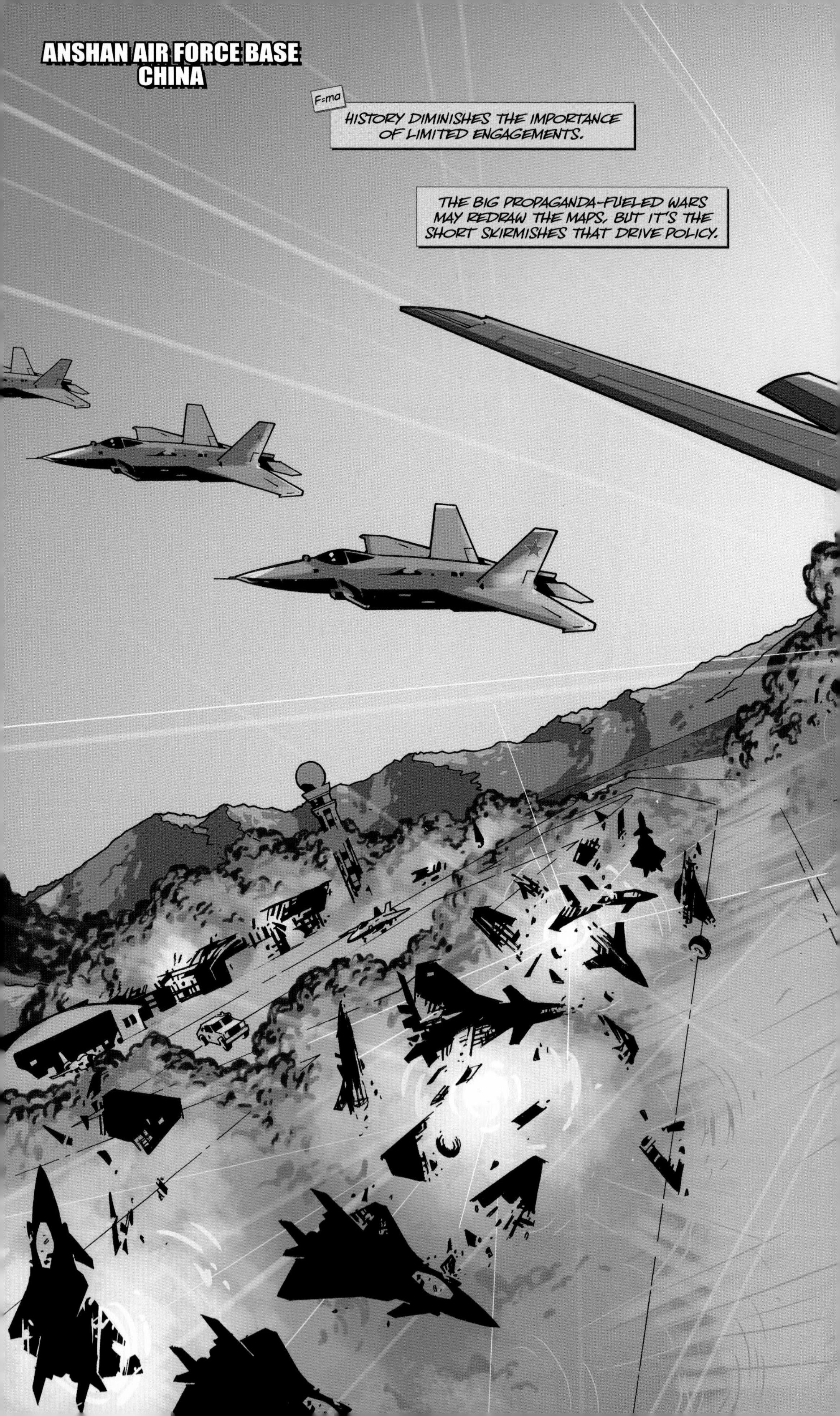
ANSHAN AIR FORCE BASE
CHINA
F=ma
HISTORY DIMINISHES THE IMPORTANCE OF LIMITED ENGAGEMENTS.
THE BIG PROPAGANDA-FUELED WARS MAY REDRAW THE MAPS, BUT IT'S THE SHORT SKIRMISHES THAT DRIVE POLICY.

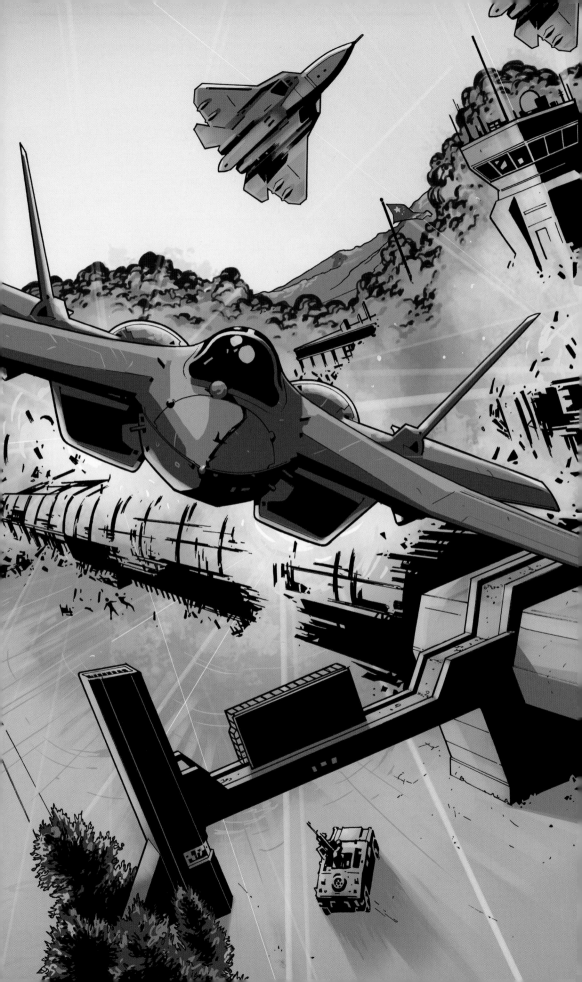

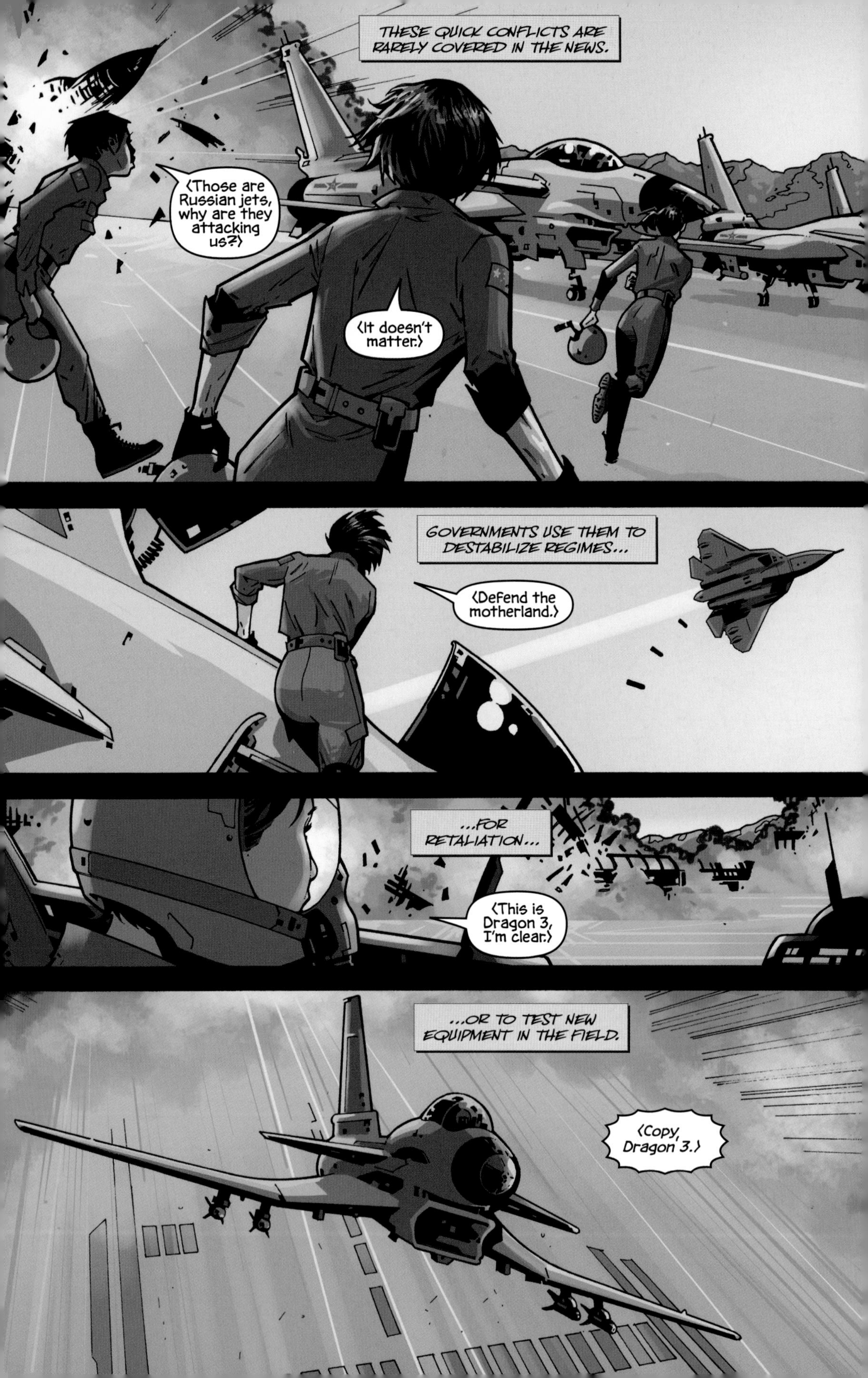
THESE QUICK CONFLICTS ARE RARELY COVERED IN THE NEWS.
⟨Those are Russian jets, why are they attacking us?⟩
⟨It doesn't matter.⟩
GOVERNMENTS USE THEM TO DESTABILIZE REGIMES...
⟨Defend the motherland.⟩
...FOR RETALIATION...
⟨This is Dragon 3, I'm clear.⟩
...OR TO TEST NEW EQUIPMENT IN THE FIELD.
⟨Copy, Dragon 3.⟩

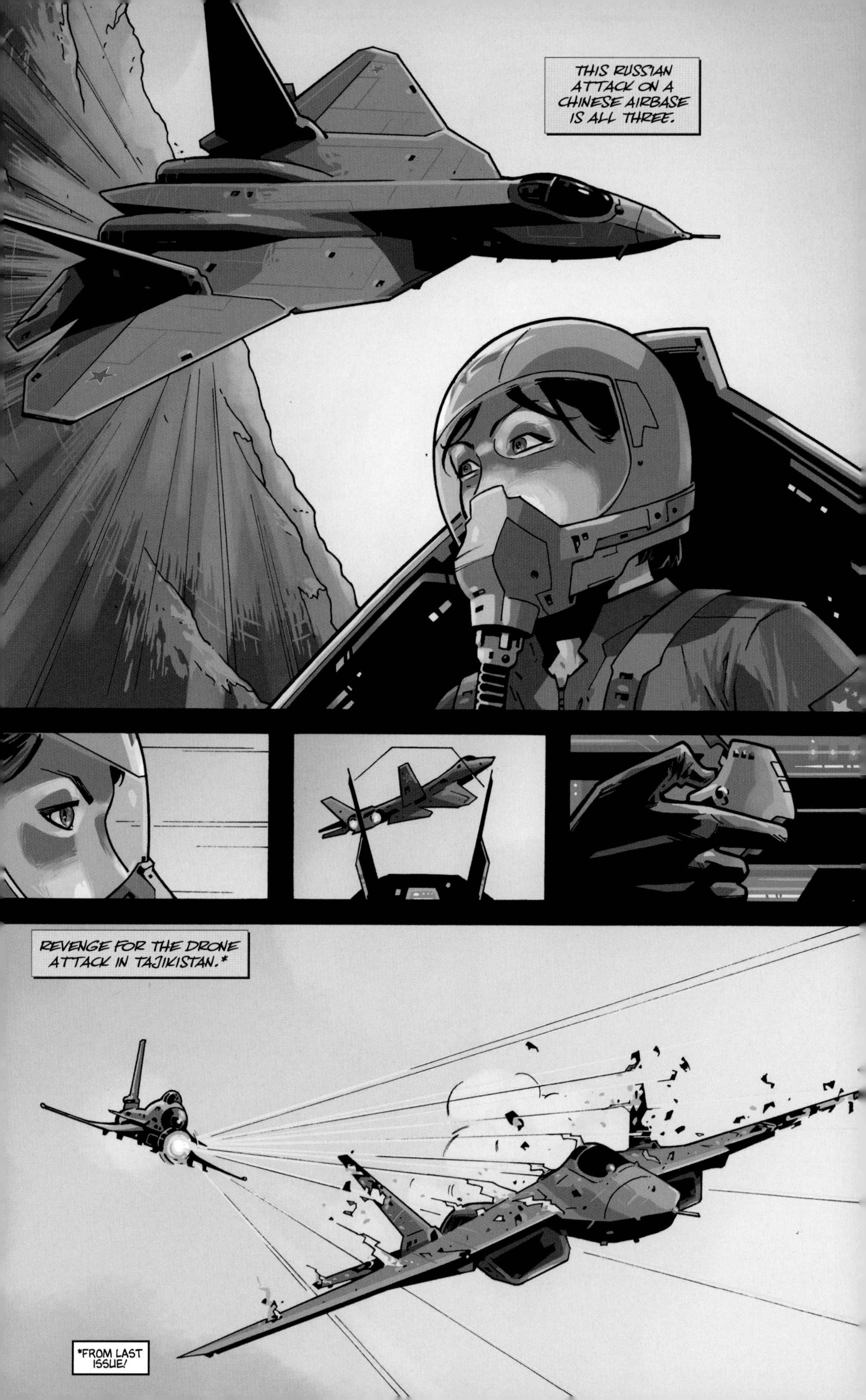
THIS RUSSIAN ATTACK ON A CHINESE AIRBASE IS ALL THREE.
REVENGE FOR THE DRONE ATTACK IN TAJIKISTAN.*
*FROM LAST ISSUE!

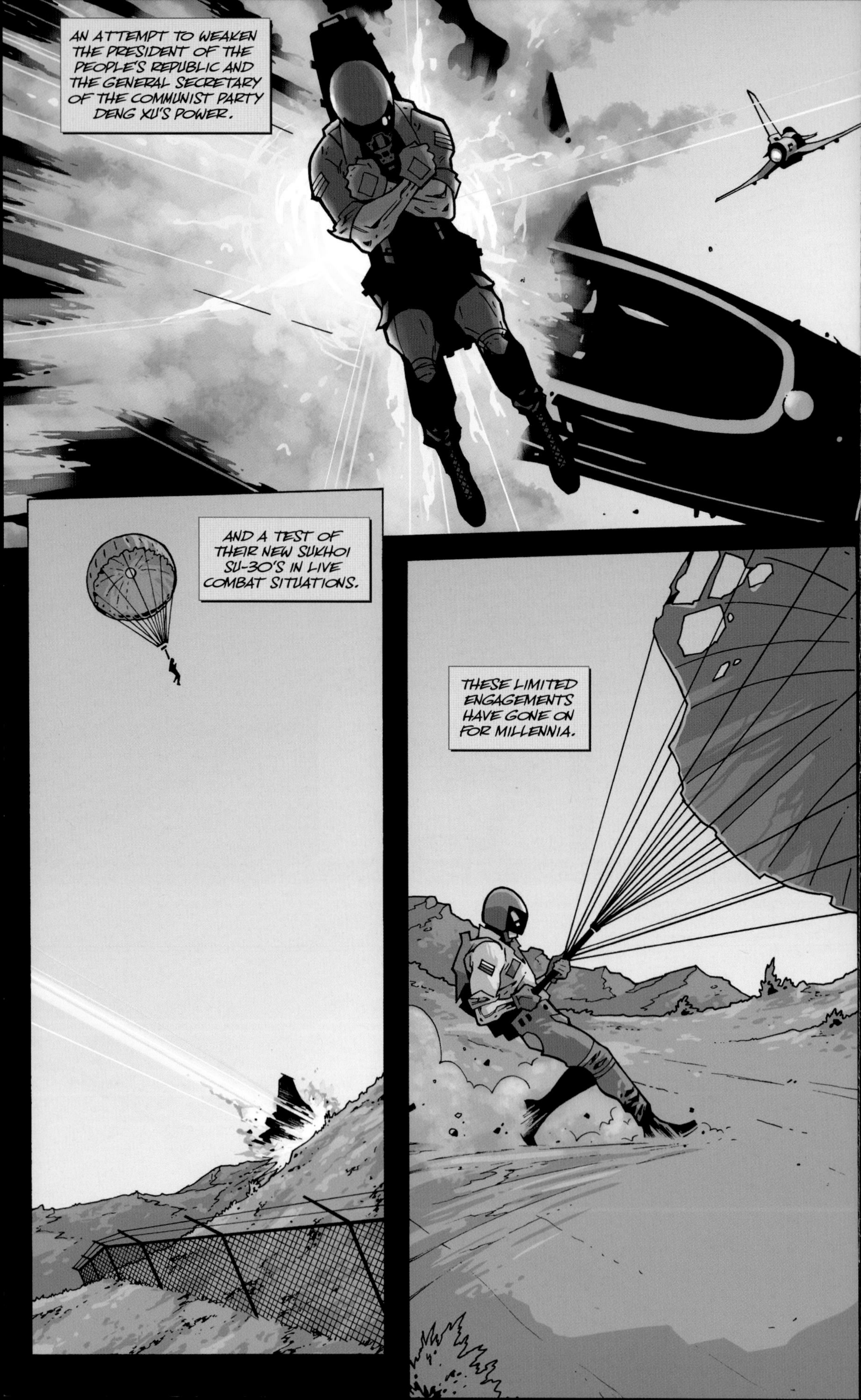
AN ATTEMPT TO WEAKEN THE PRESIDENT OF THE PEOPLE'S REPUBLIC AND THE GENERAL SECRETARY OF THE COMMUNIST PARTY DENG XU'S POWER.
AND A TEST OF THEIR NEW SUKHOI SU-30'S IN LIVE COMBAT SITUATIONS.
THESE LIMITED ENGAGEMENTS HAVE GONE ON FOR MILLENNIA.

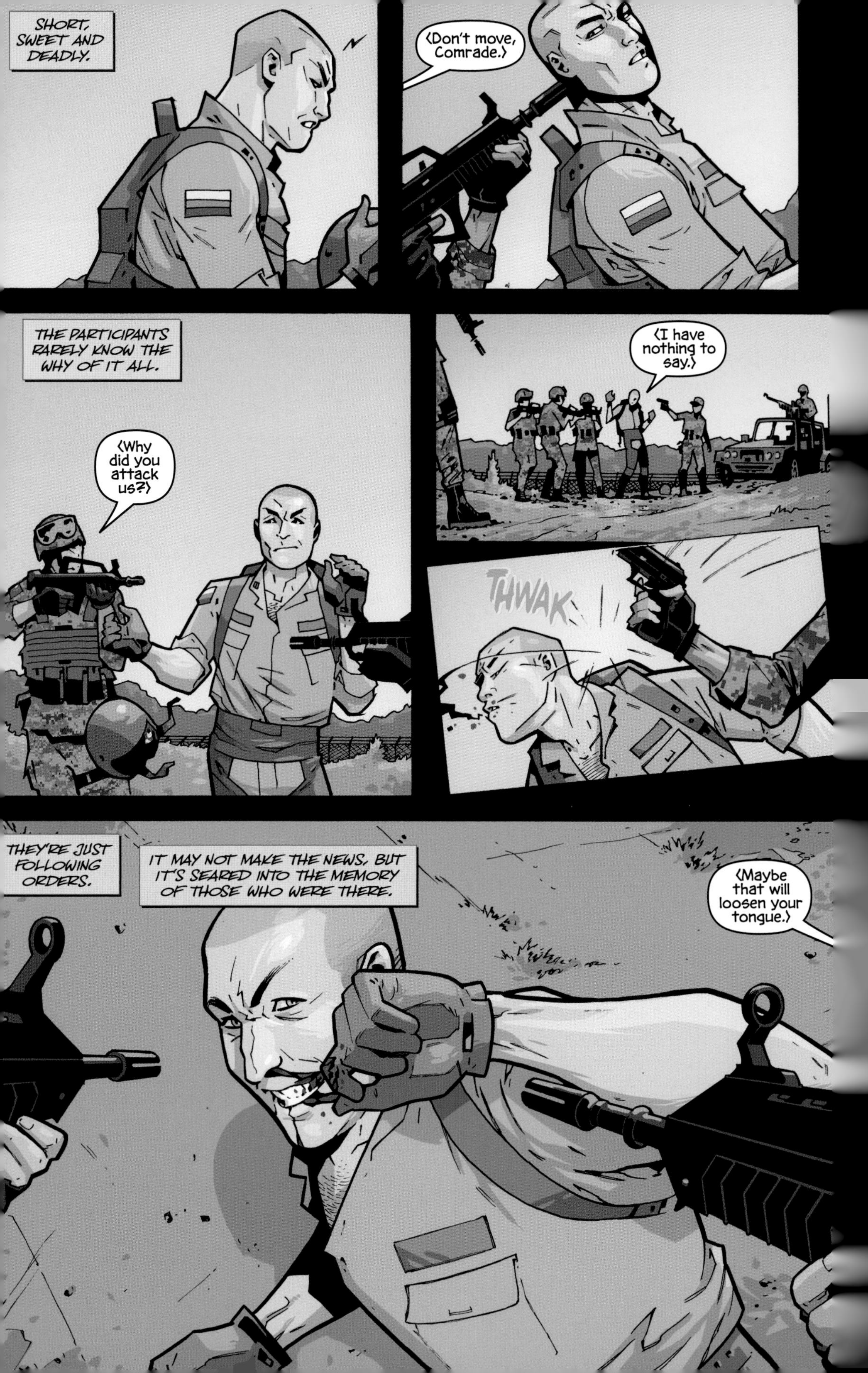
SHORT, SWEET AND DEADLY.
‹Don't move, Comrade.›
THE PARTICIPANTS RARELY KNOW THE WHY OF IT ALL.
‹Why did you attack us?›
‹I have nothing to say.›
THWAK
THEY'RE JUST FOLLOWING ORDERS.
IT MAY NOT MAKE THE NEWS, BUT IT'S SEARED INTO THE MEMORY OF THOSE WHO WERE THERE.
‹Maybe that will loosen your tongue.›

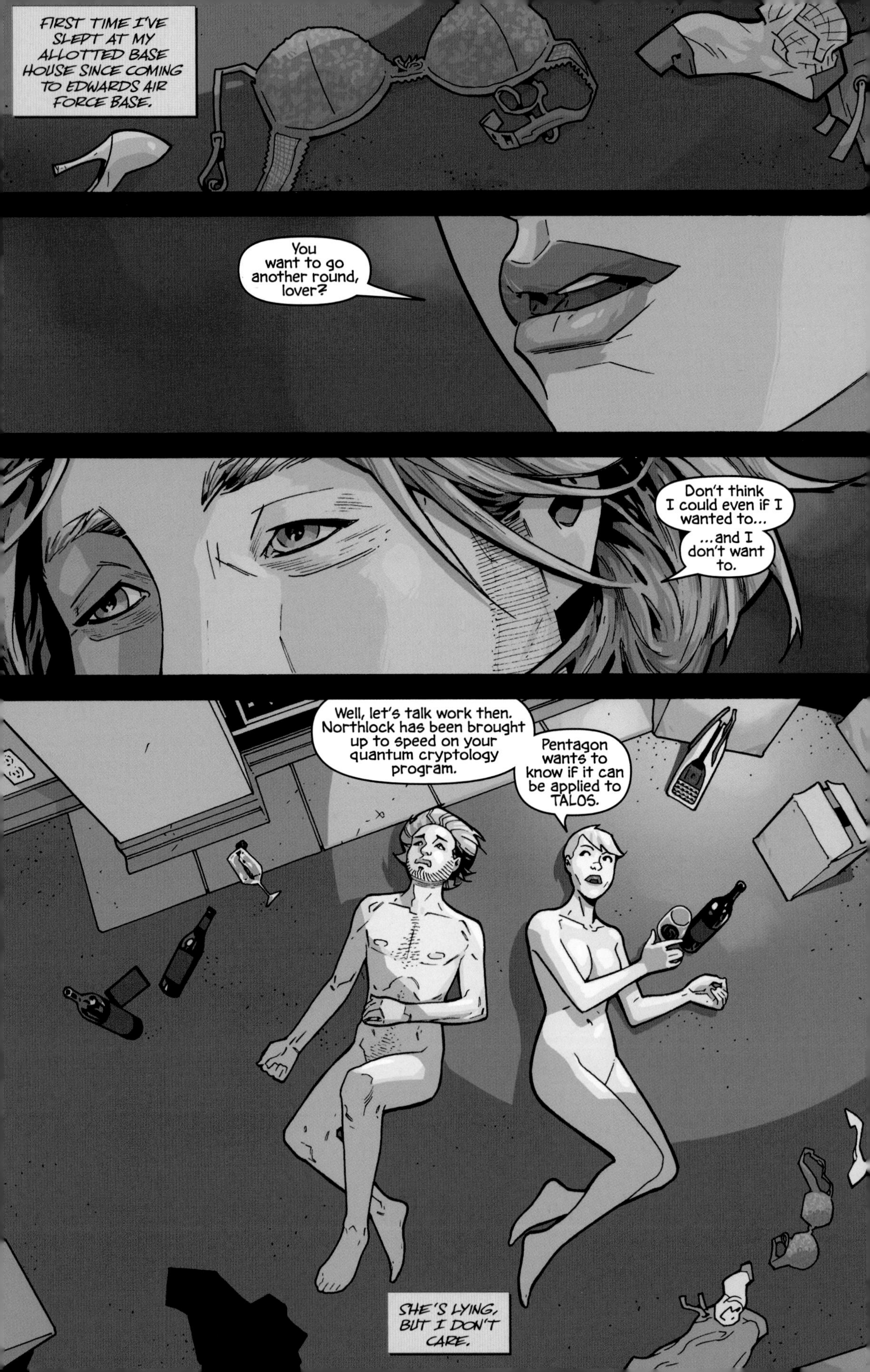
FIRST TIME I'VE SLEPT AT MY ALLOTTED BASE HOUSE SINCE COMING TO EDWARDS AIR FORCE BASE.
You want to go another round, lover?
Don't think I could even if I wanted to...
...and I don't want to.
Well, let's talk work then. Northlock has been brought up to speed on your quantum cryptology program.
Pentagon wants to know if it can be applied to TALOS.
SHE'S LYING, BUT I DON'T CARE.

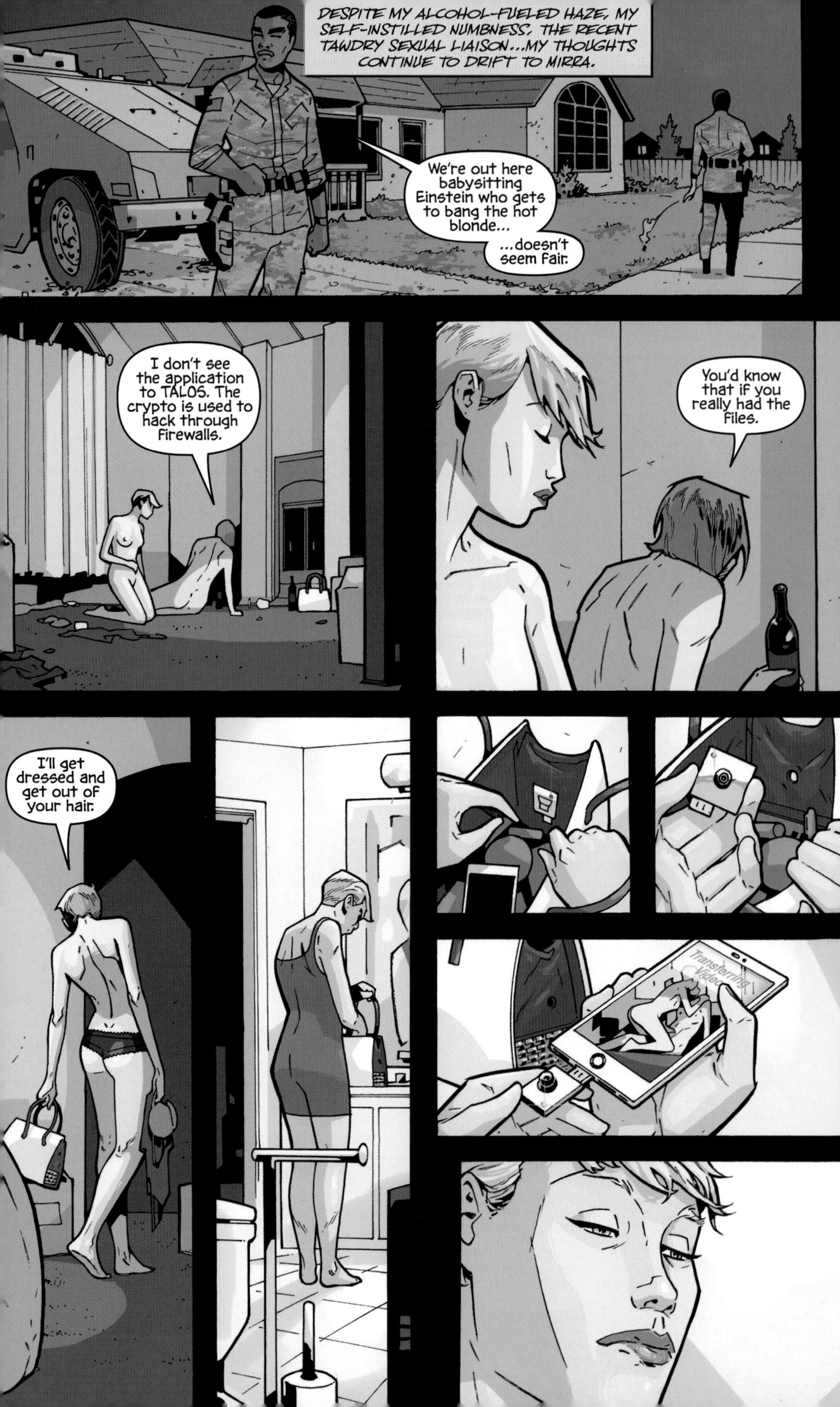
DESPITE MY ALCOHOL-FUELED HAZE, MY SELF-INSTILLED NUMBNESS, THE RECENT TAWDRY SEXUAL LIAISON...MY THOUGHTS CONTINUE TO DRIFT TO MIRRA.
We're out here babysitting Einstein who gets to bang the hot blonde...
...doesn't seem fair.
I don't see the application to TALOS. The crypto is used to hack through firewalls.
You'd know that if you really had the Files.
I'll get dressed and get out of your hair.
Transferring Video

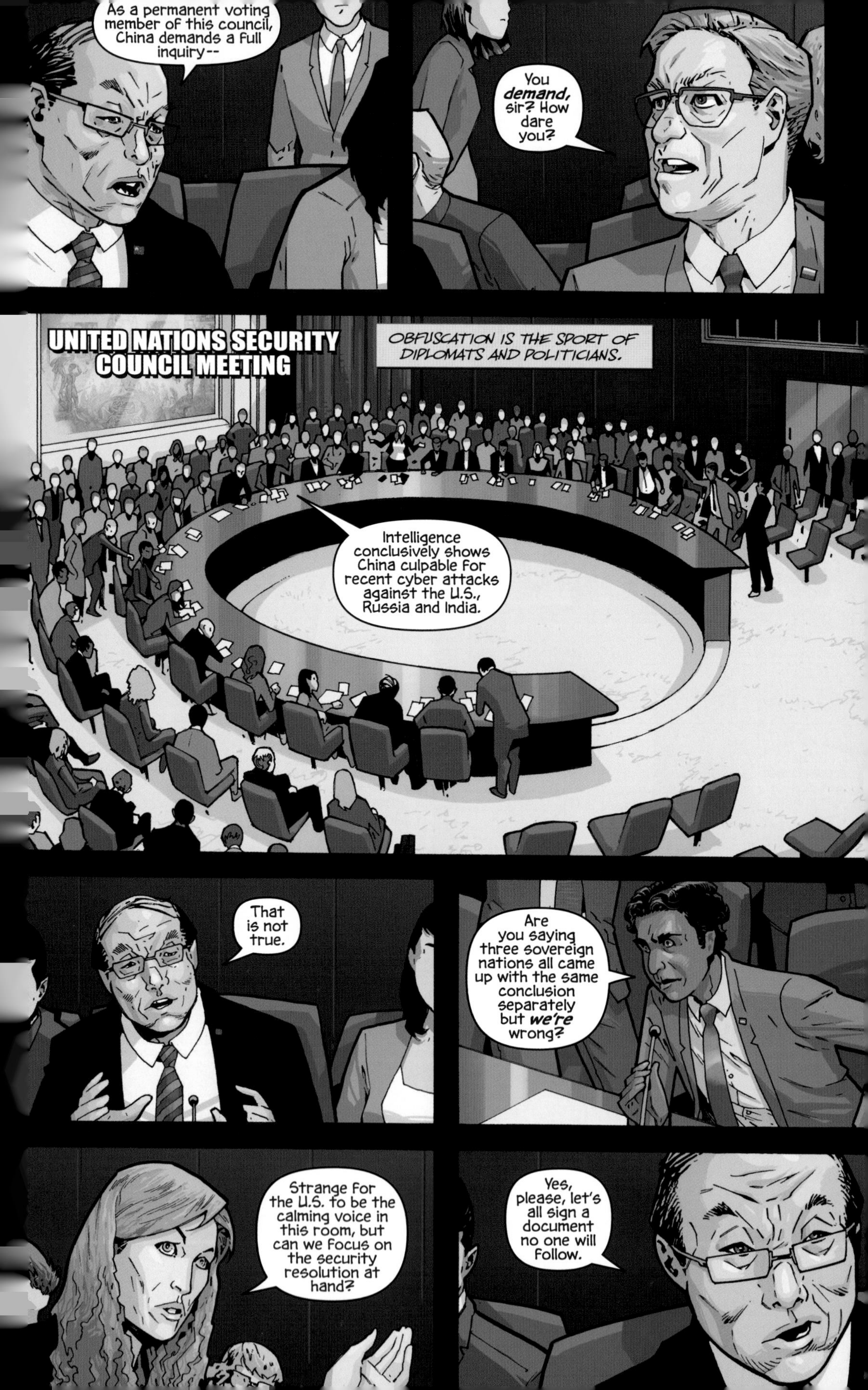
As a permanent voting member of this council, China demands a full inquiry--
You demand, sir? How dare you?
UNITED NATIONS SECURITY COUNCIL MEETING
OBFUSCATION IS THE SPORT OF DIPLOMATS AND POLITICIANS.
Intelligence conclusively shows China culpable for recent cyber attacks against the U.S., Russia and India.
That is not true.
Are you saying three sovereign nations all came up with the same conclusion separately but we're wrong?
Strange for the U.S. to be the calming voice in this room, but can we focus on the security resolution at hand?
Yes, please, let's all sign a document no one will follow.

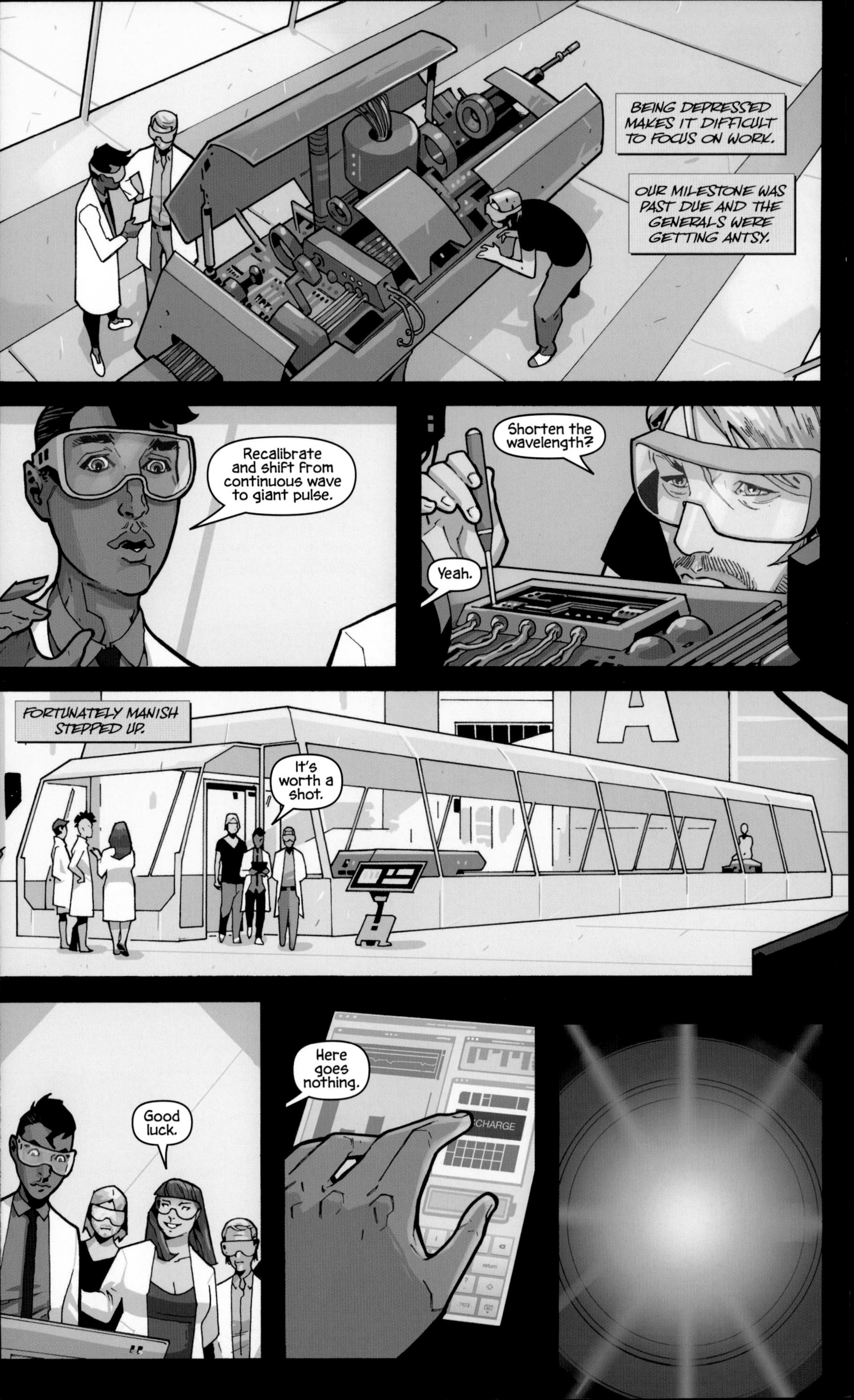
BEING DEPRESSED MAKES IT DIFFICULT TO FOCUS ON WORK.
OUR MILESTONE WAS PAST DUE AND THE GENERALS WERE GETTING ANTSY.
Recalibrate and shift from continuous wave to giant pulse.
Shorten the wavelength?
Yeah.
FORTUNATELY MANISH STEPPED UP.
It's worth a shot.
Good luck.
Here goes nothing.

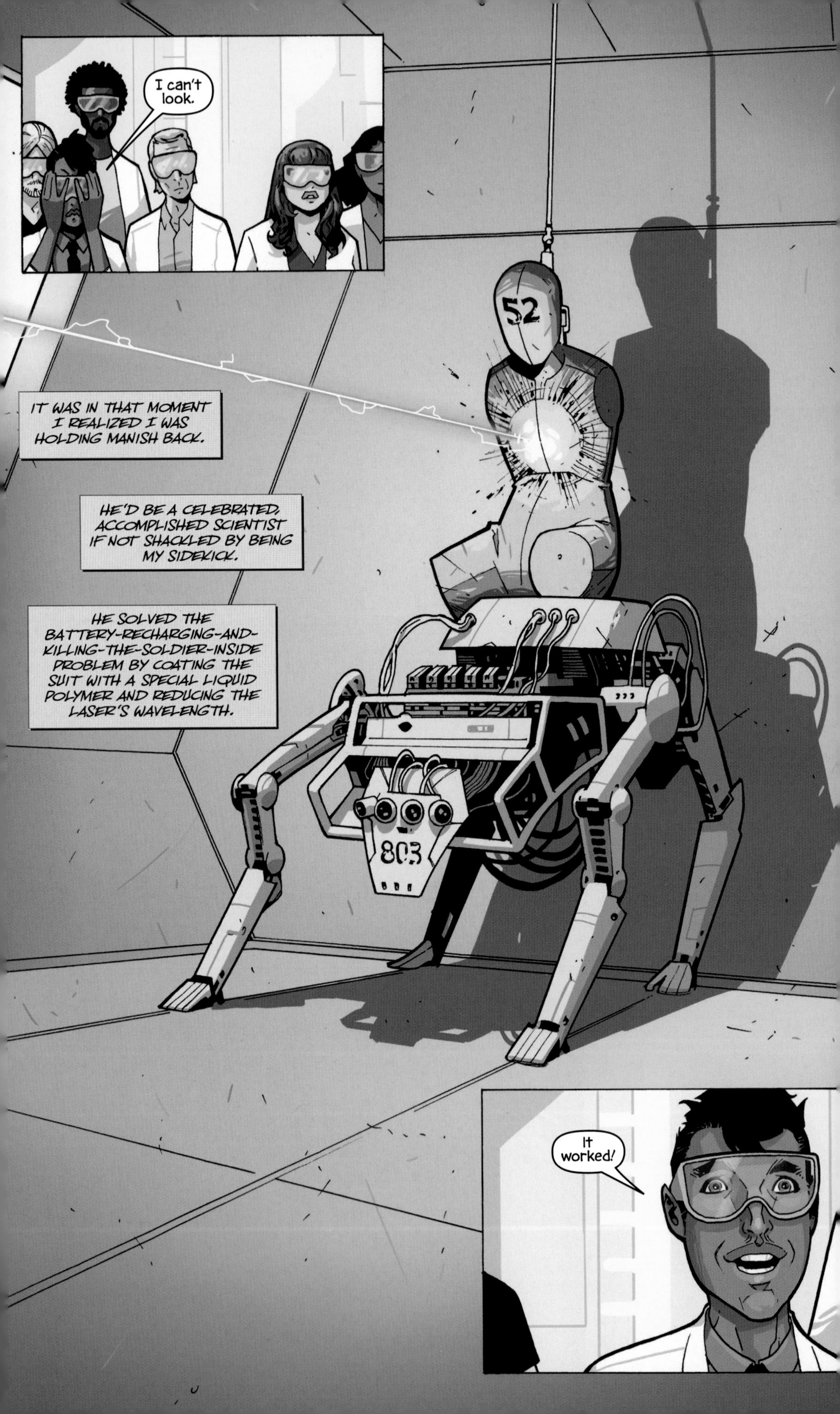
I can't look.
IT WAS IN THAT MOMENT I REALIZED I WAS HOLDING MANISH BACK.
52
HE'D BE A CELEBRATED, ACCOMPLISHED SCIENTIST IF NOT SHACKLED BY BEING MY SIDEKICK.
HE SOLVED THE BATTERY-RECHARGING-AND-KILLING-THE-SOLDIER-INSIDE PROBLEM BY COATING THE SUIT WITH A SPECIAL LIQUID POLYMER AND REDUCING THE LASER'S WAVELENGTH.
803
It worked!

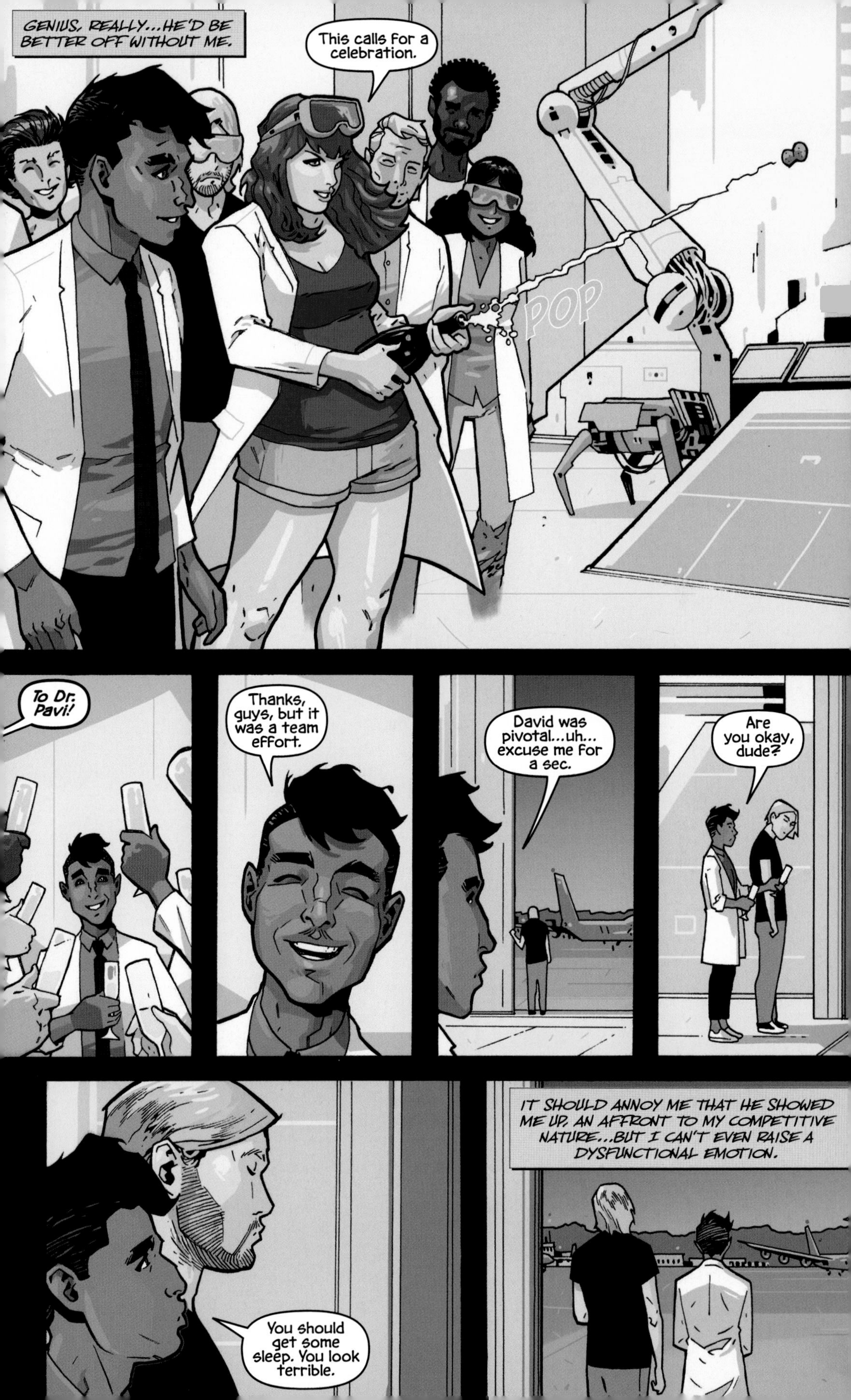
GENIUS, REALLY...HE'D BE BETTER OFF WITHOUT ME.
This calls for a celebration.
POP
To Dr. Pavi!
Thanks, guys, but it was a team effort.
David was pivotal...uh... excuse me for a sec.
Are you okay, dude?
You should get some sleep. You look terrible.
IT SHOULD ANNOY ME THAT HE SHOWED ME UP, AN AFFRONT TO MY COMPETITIVE NATURE...BUT I CAN'T EVEN RAISE A DYSFUNCTIONAL EMOTION.

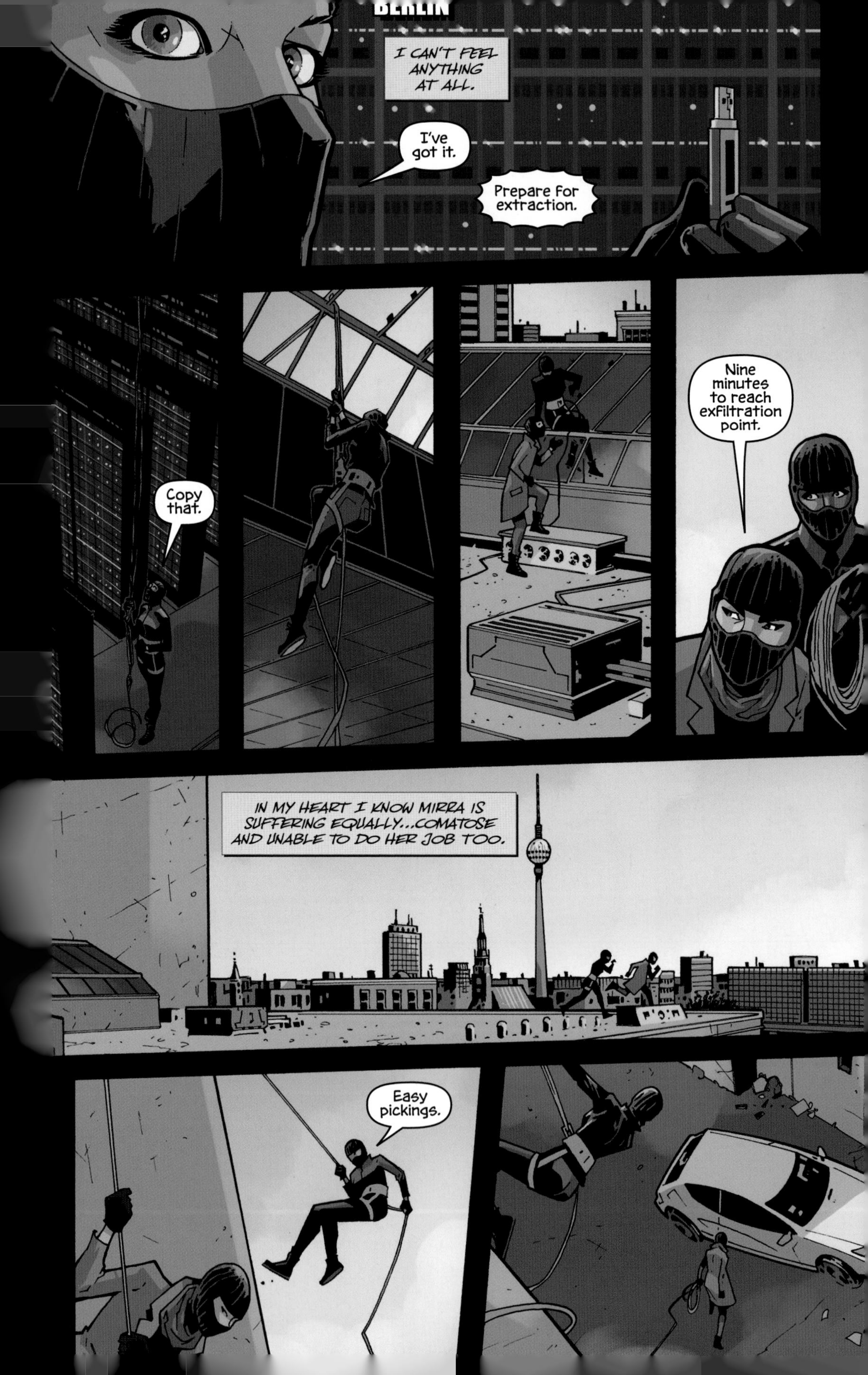
BERLIN
I CAN'T FEEL ANYTHING AT ALL.
I've got it.
Prepare for extraction.
Copy that.
Nine minutes to reach exfiltration point.
IN MY HEART I KNOW MIRRA IS SUFFERING EQUALLY...COMATOSE AND UNABLE TO DO HER JOB TOO.
Easy pickings.

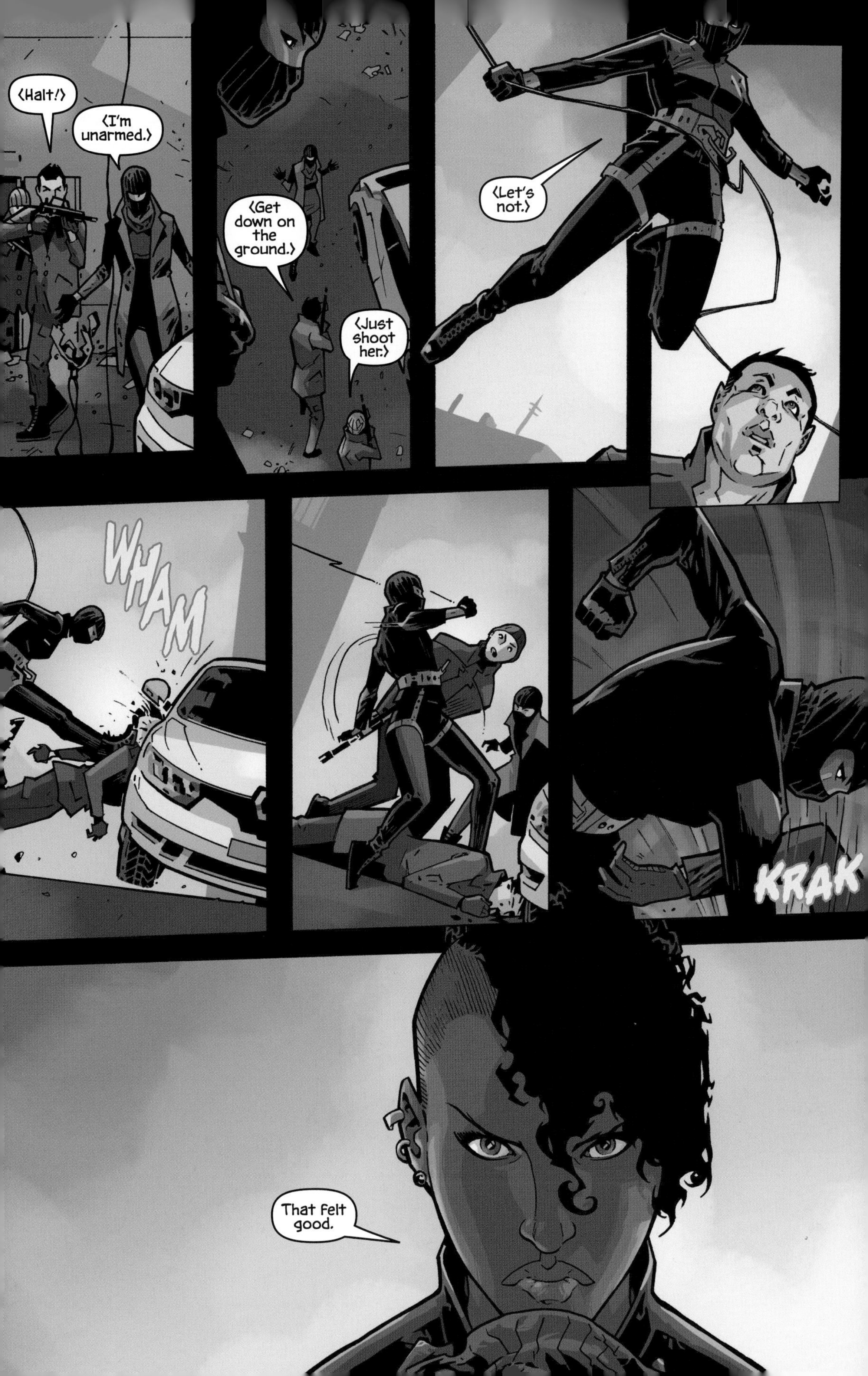
‹Halt!›
‹I'm unarmed.›
‹Get down on the ground.›
‹Just shoot her.›
‹Let's not.›
WHAM
KRAK
That felt good.

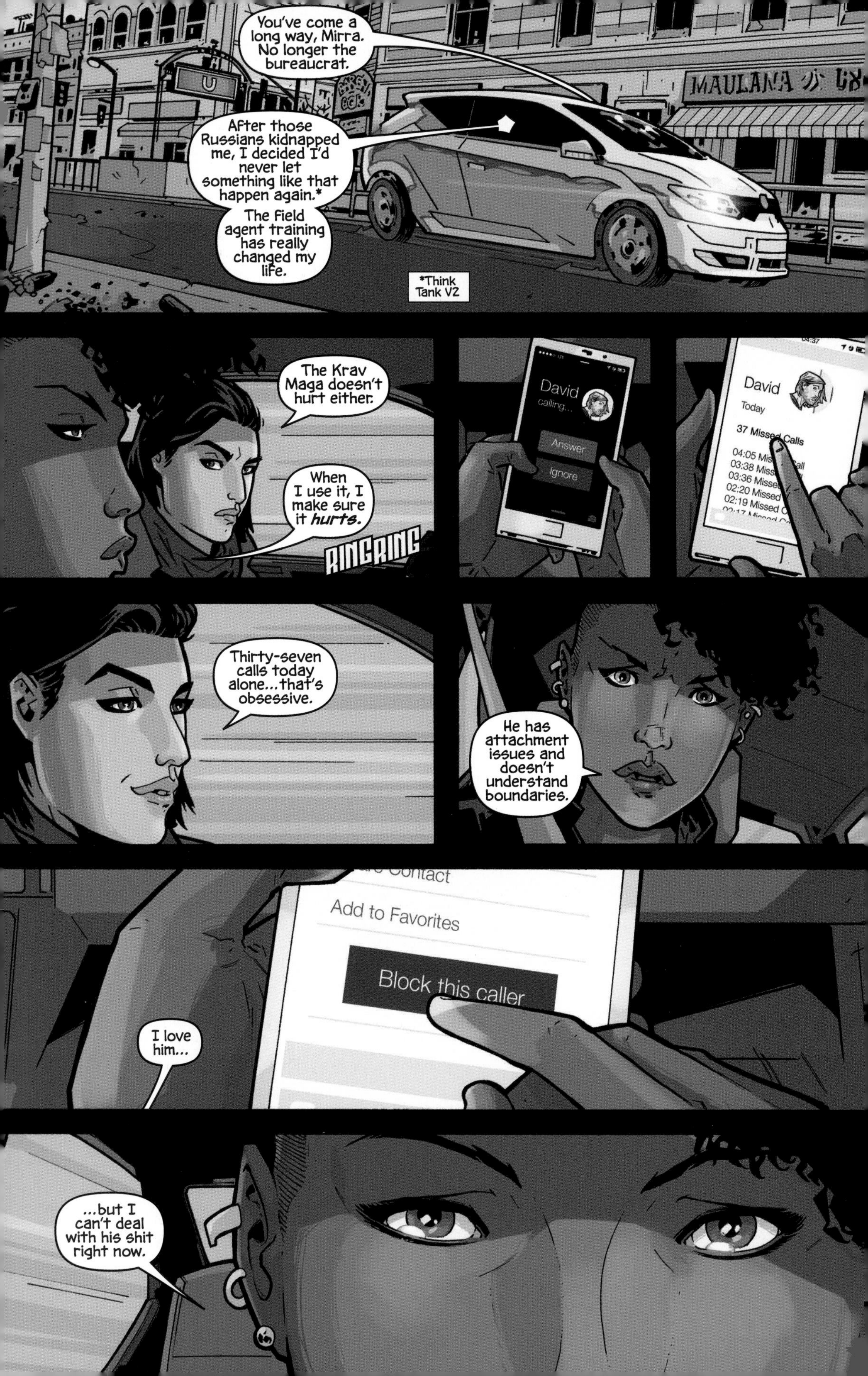
You've come a long way, Mirra. No longer the bureaucrat.
After those Russians kidnapped me, I decided I'd never let something like that happen again.*
The field agent training has really changed my life.
*Think Tank V2
The Krav Maga doesn't hurt either.
When I use it, I make sure it *hurts*.
RINGRING
David calling...
Answer
Ignore
David
Today
37 Missed Calls
Thirty-seven calls today alone...that's obsessive.
He has attachment issues and doesn't understand boundaries.
Add to Favorites
Block this caller
I love him...
...but I can't deal with his shit right now.

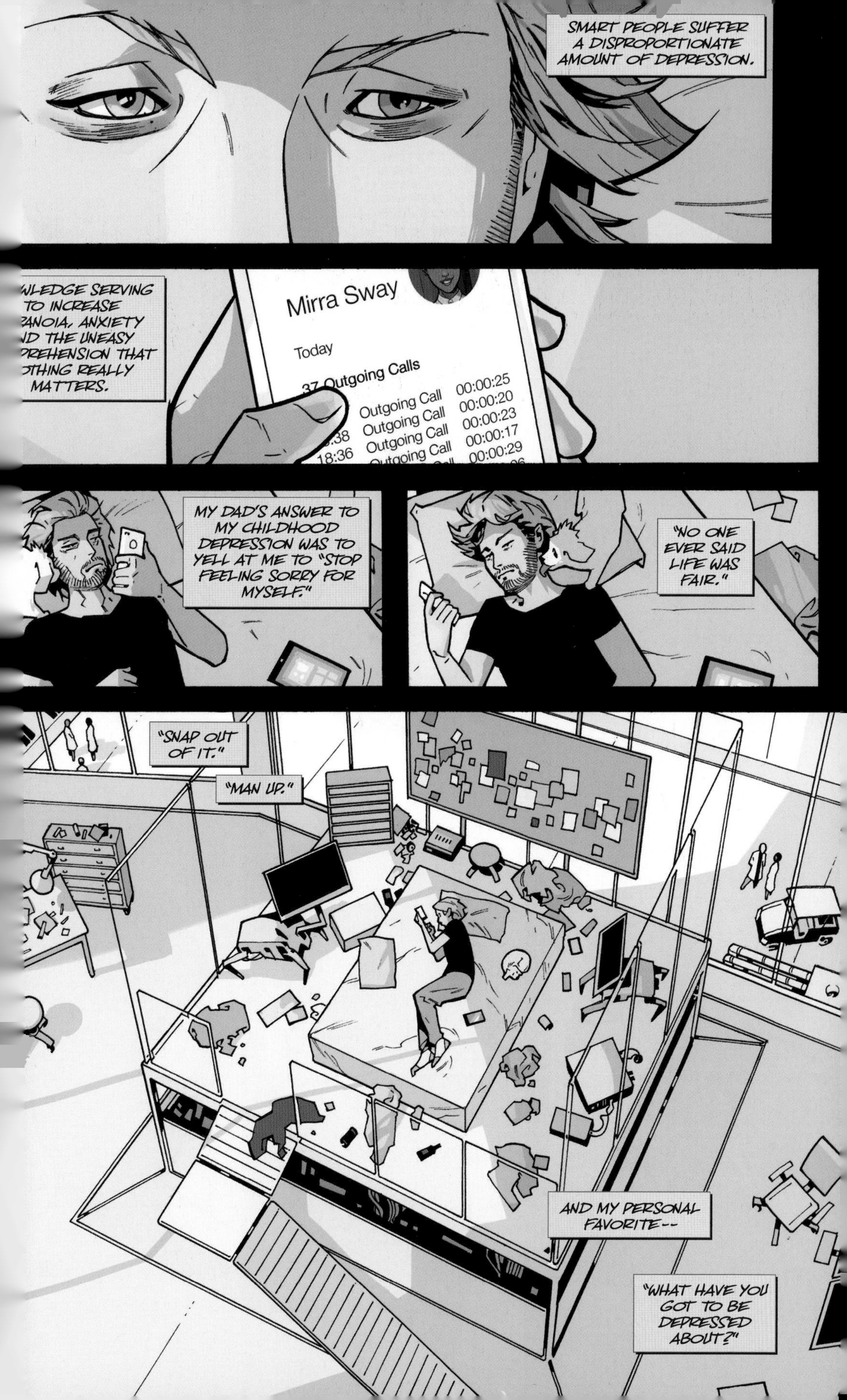

SMART PEOPLE SUFFER A DISPROPORTIONATE AMOUNT OF DEPRESSION.
WLEDGE SERVING TO INCREASE RANOIA, ANXIETY ND THE UNEASY PREHENSION THAT OTHING REALLY MATTERS.
Mirra Sway
Today
37 Outgoing Calls
Outgoing Call 00:00:25
Outgoing Call 00:00:20
Outgoing Call 00:00:23
38 Outgoing Call 00:00:17
18:36 Outgoing Call 00:00:29
MY DAD'S ANSWER TO MY CHILDHOOD DEPRESSION WAS TO YELL AT ME TO "STOP FEELING SORRY FOR MYSELF."
"NO ONE EVER SAID LIFE WAS FAIR."
"SNAP OUT OF IT."
"MAN UP."
AND MY PERSONAL FAVORITE--
"WHAT HAVE YOU GOT TO BE DEPRESSED ABOUT?"

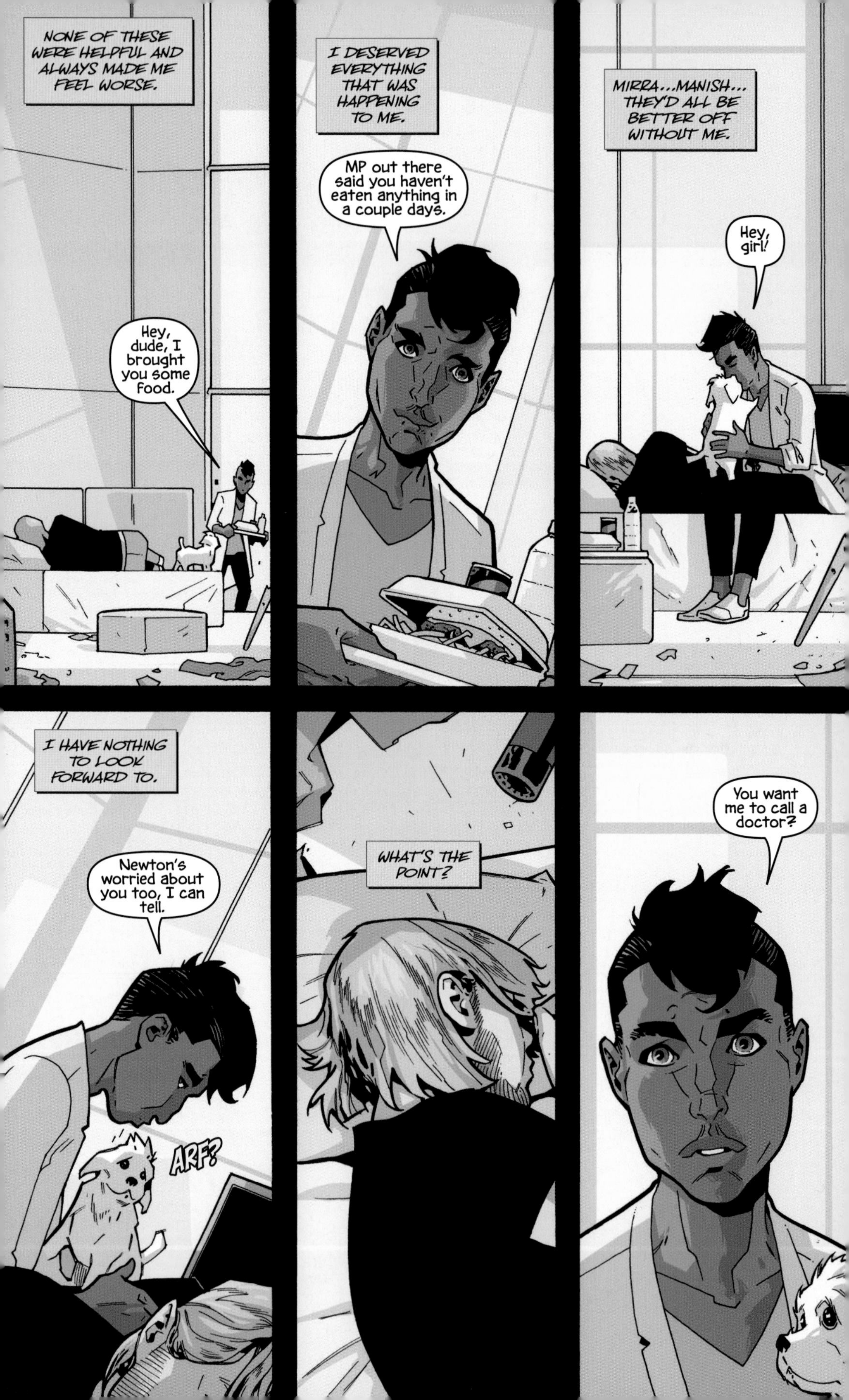
NONE OF THESE WERE HELPFUL AND ALWAYS MADE ME FEEL WORSE.
Hey, dude, I brought you some food.
I DESERVED EVERYTHING THAT WAS HAPPENING TO ME.
MP out there said you haven't eaten anything in a couple days.
MIRRA...MANISH... THEY'D ALL BE BETTER OFF WITHOUT ME.
Hey, girl!
I HAVE NOTHING TO LOOK FORWARD TO.
Newton's worried about you too, I can tell.
ARF?
WHAT'S THE POINT?
You want me to call a doctor?

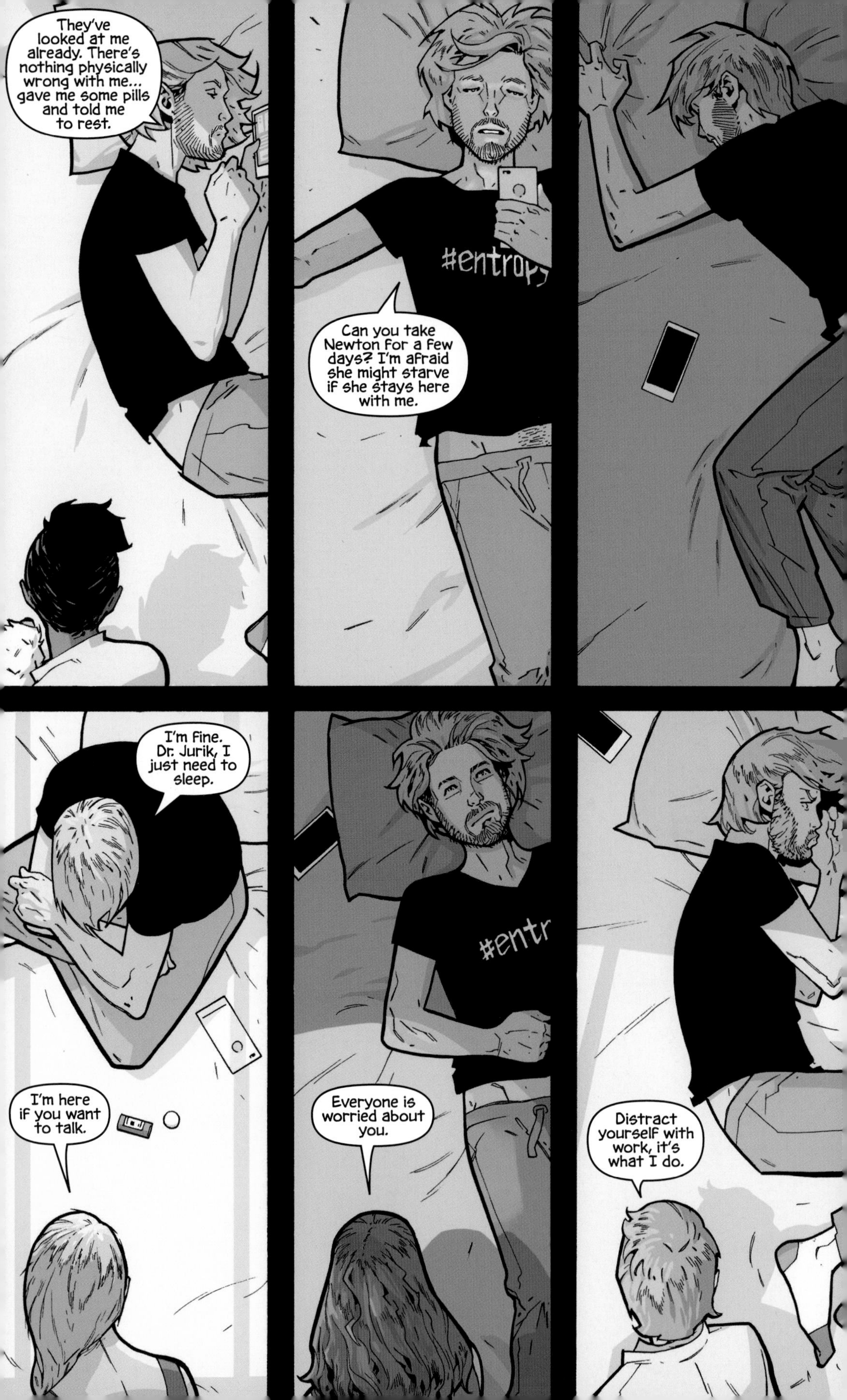
They've looked at me already. There's nothing physically wrong with me... gave me some pills and told me to rest.
Can you take Newton for a few days? I'm afraid she might starve if she stays here with me.
#entropy
I'm fine. Dr. Jurik, I just need to sleep.
I'm here if you want to talk.
#entr
Everyone is worried about you.
Distract yourself with work, it's what I do.

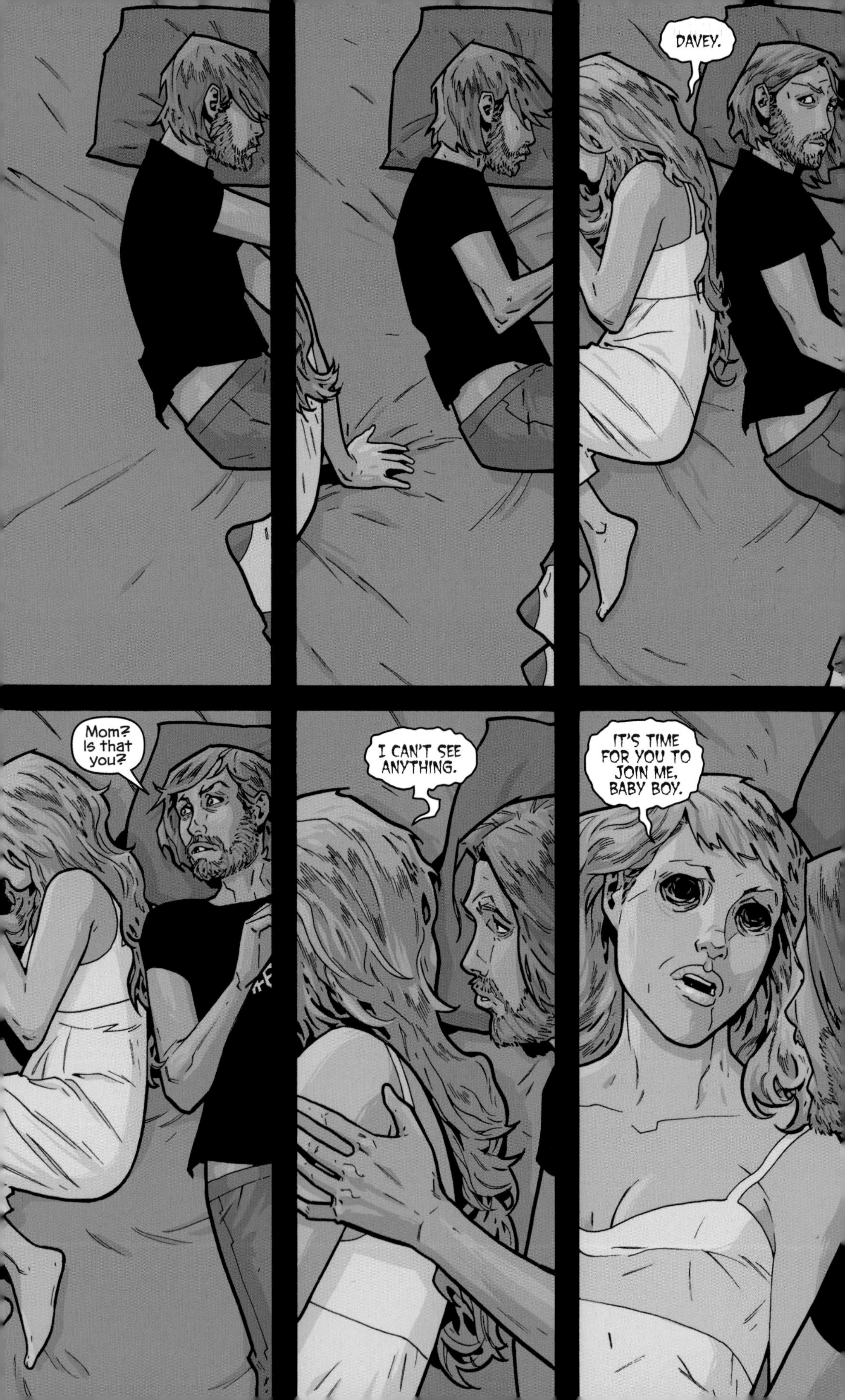
DAVEY.
Mom? Is that you?
I CAN'T SEE ANYTHING.
IT'S TIME FOR YOU TO JOIN ME, BABY BOY.

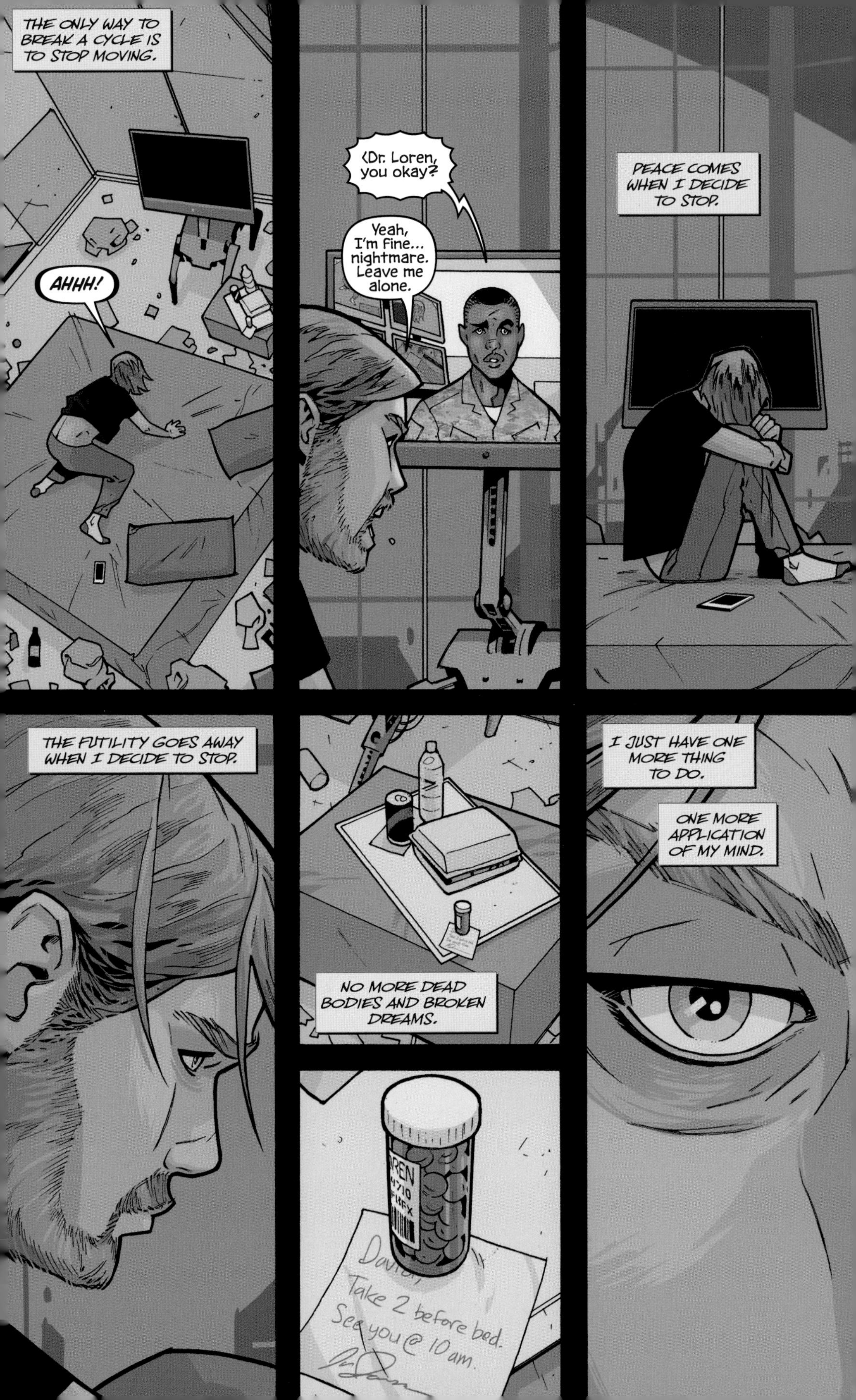
THE ONLY WAY TO BREAK A CYCLE IS TO STOP MOVING.
AHHH!
<Dr. Loren, you okay?>
Yeah, I'm fine... nightmare. Leave me alone.
PEACE COMES WHEN I DECIDE TO STOP.
THE FUTILITY GOES AWAY WHEN I DECIDE TO STOP.
NO MORE DEAD BODIES AND BROKEN DREAMS.
David,
Take 2 before bed.
See you @ 10 am.
I JUST HAVE ONE MORE THING TO DO.
ONE MORE APPLICATION OF MY MIND.

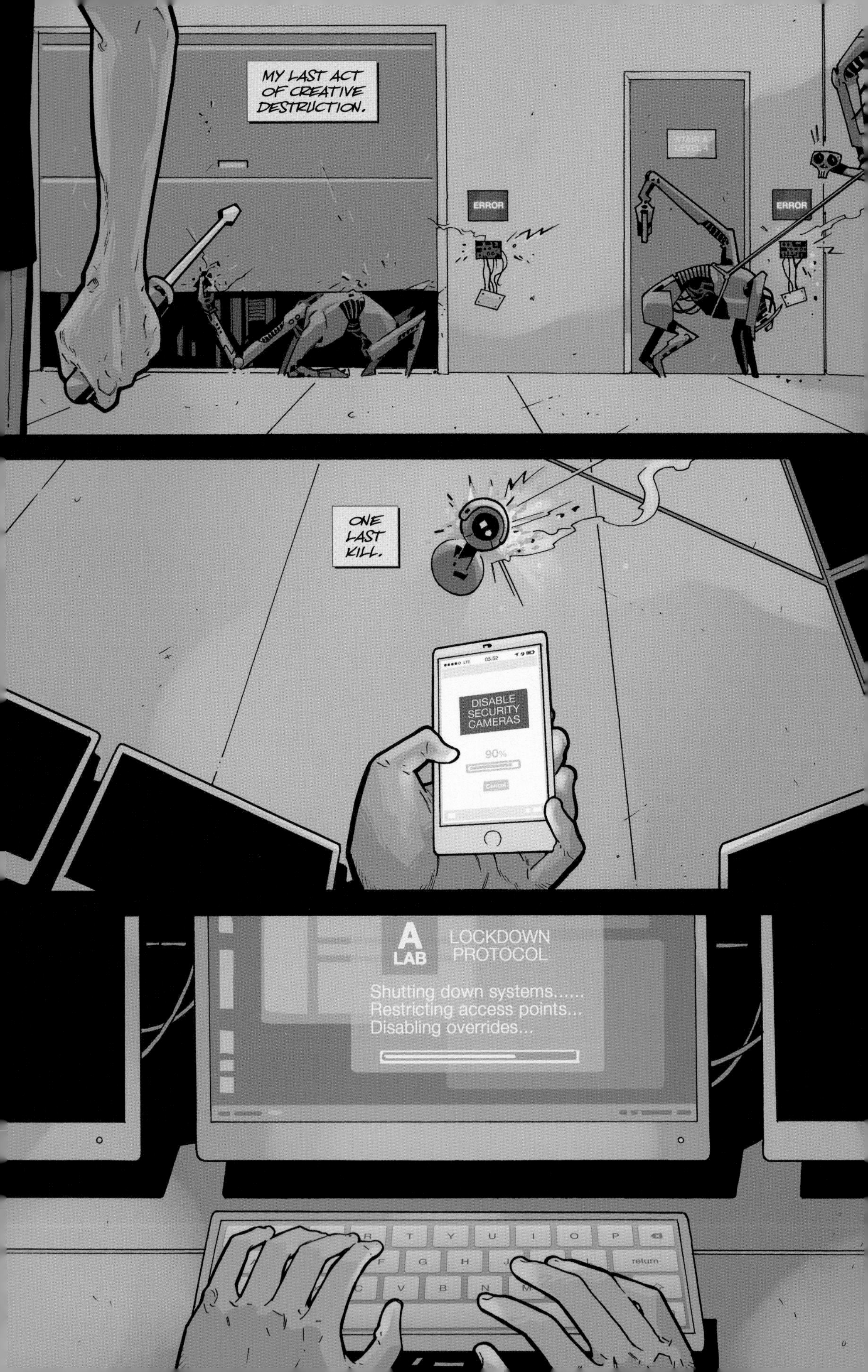
MY LAST ACT OF CREATIVE DESTRUCTION.
ERROR
STAIR A LEVEL 4
ERROR
ONE LAST KILL.
DISABLE SECURITY CAMERAS
90%
Cancel
LOCKDOWN PROTOCOL
A LAB
Shutting down systems......
Restricting access points...
Disabling overrides...

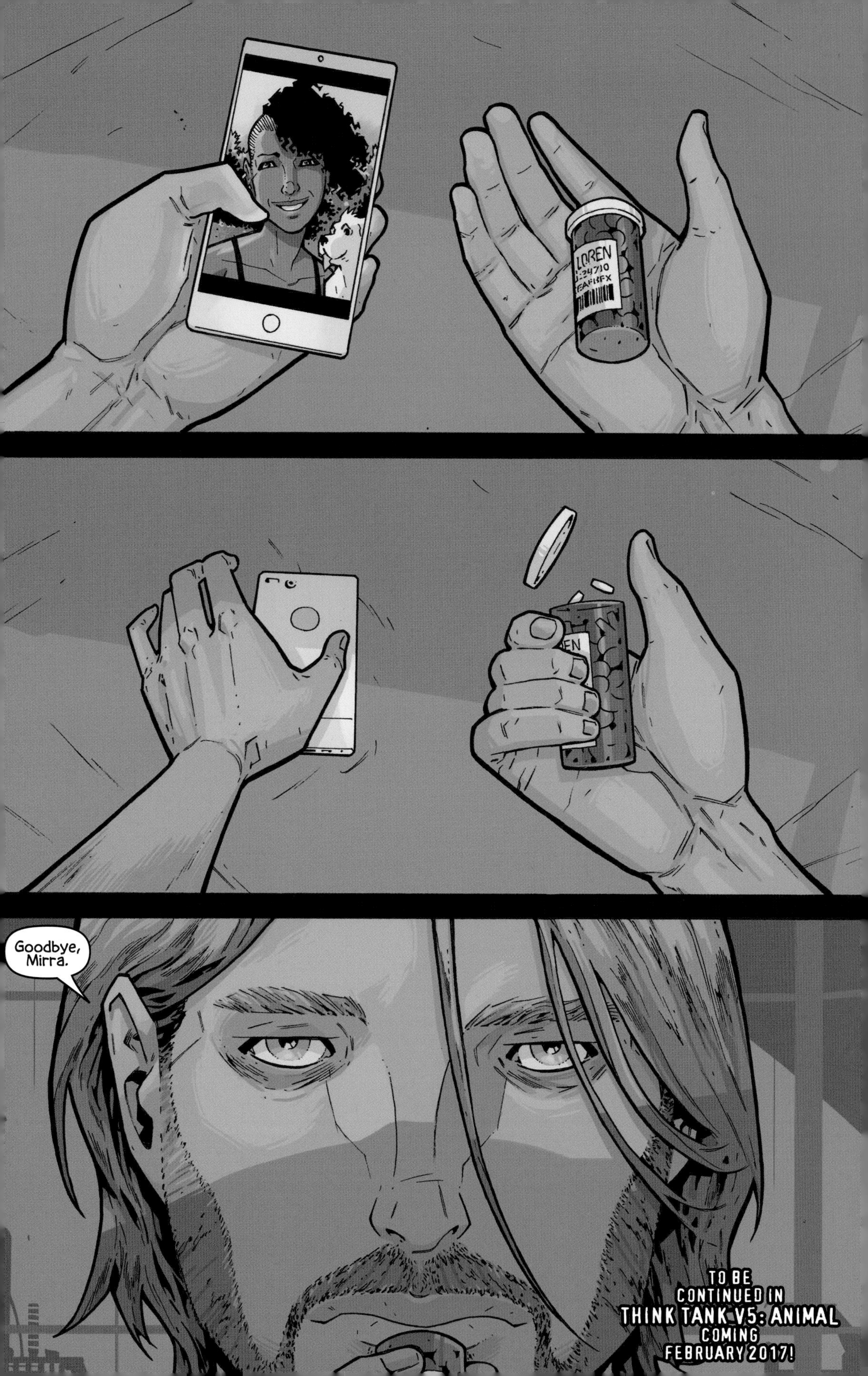
LOREN
Goodbye, Mirra.
TO BE CONTINUED IN THINK TANK V5: ANIMAL COMING FEBRUARY 2017!

COVER GALLERY

TANK TANK

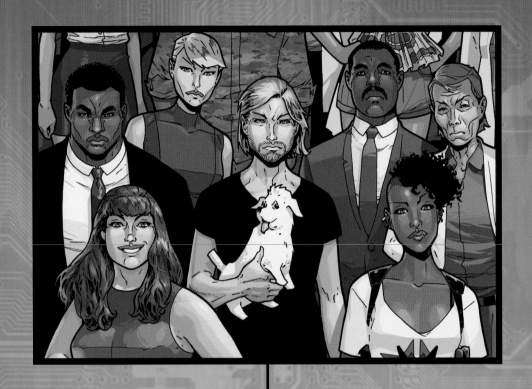

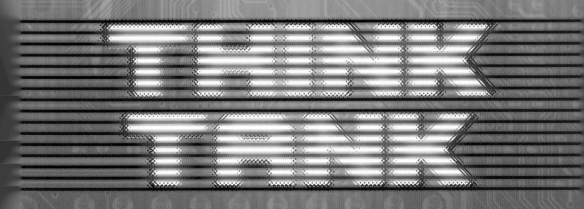

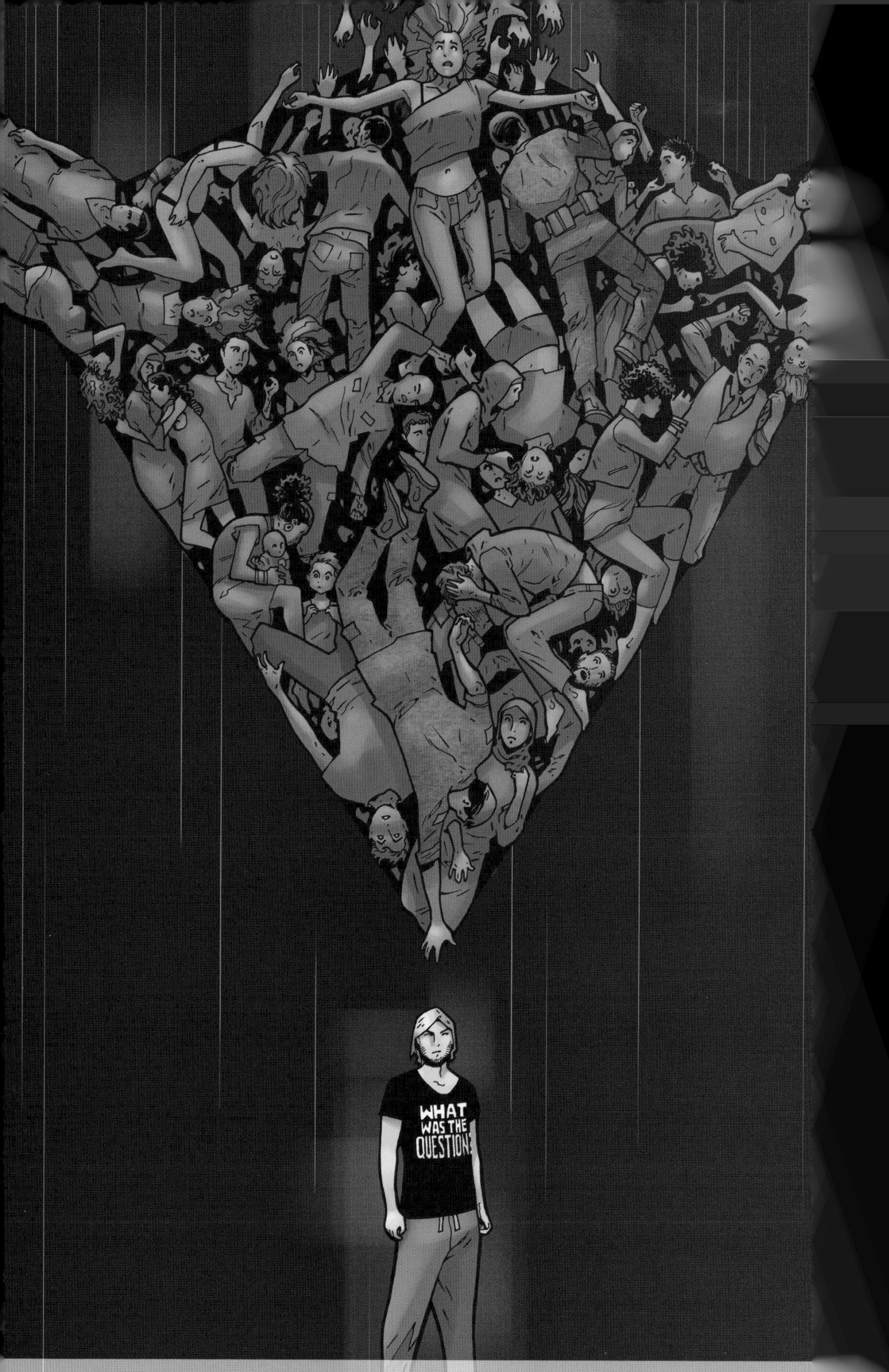
WHAT
WAS THE
QUESTION?

Think Tank: Creative Destruction #1 cover A art by **Rahsan Ekedal**

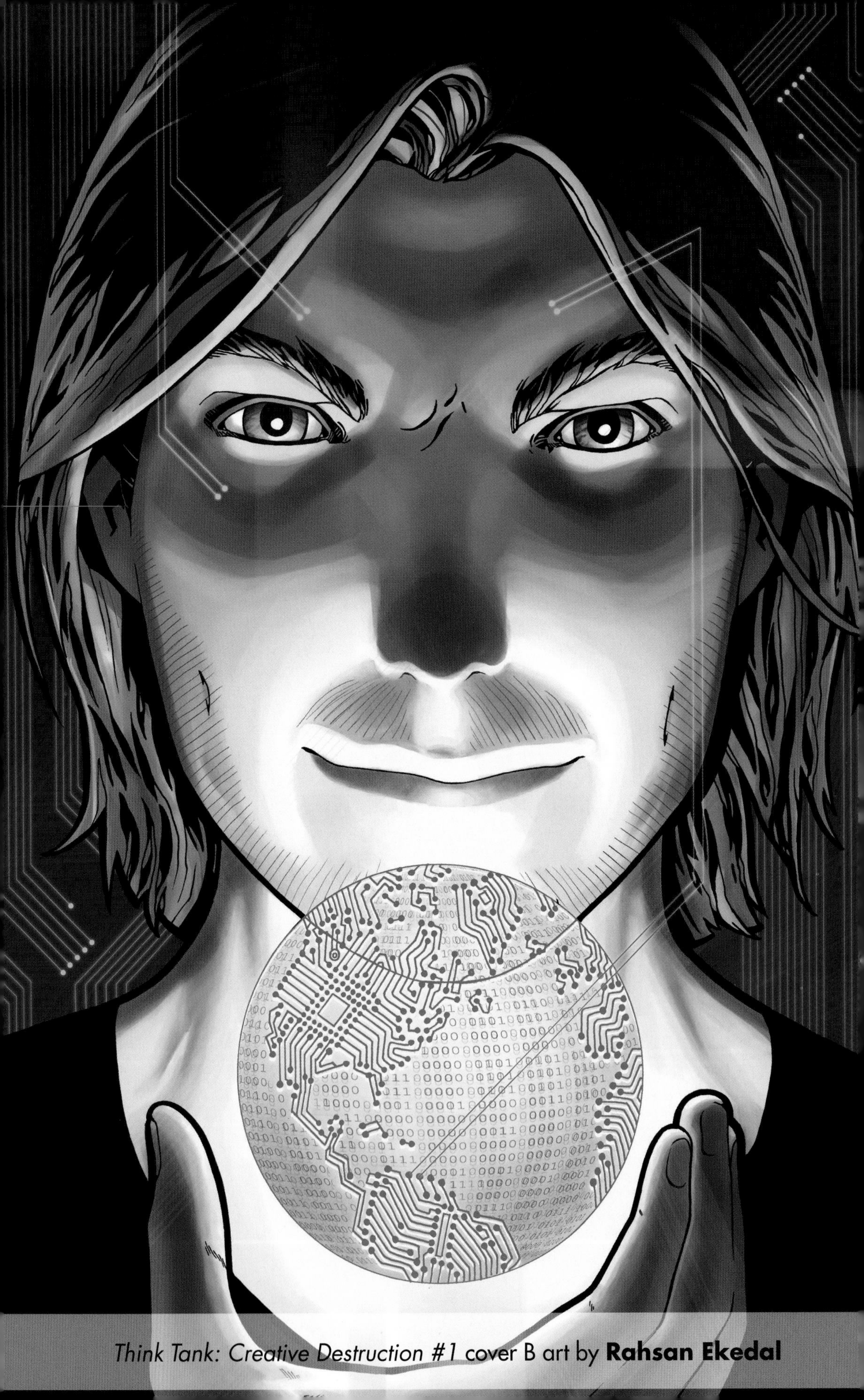

Think Tank: Creative Destruction #1 cover B art by **Rahsan Ekedal**

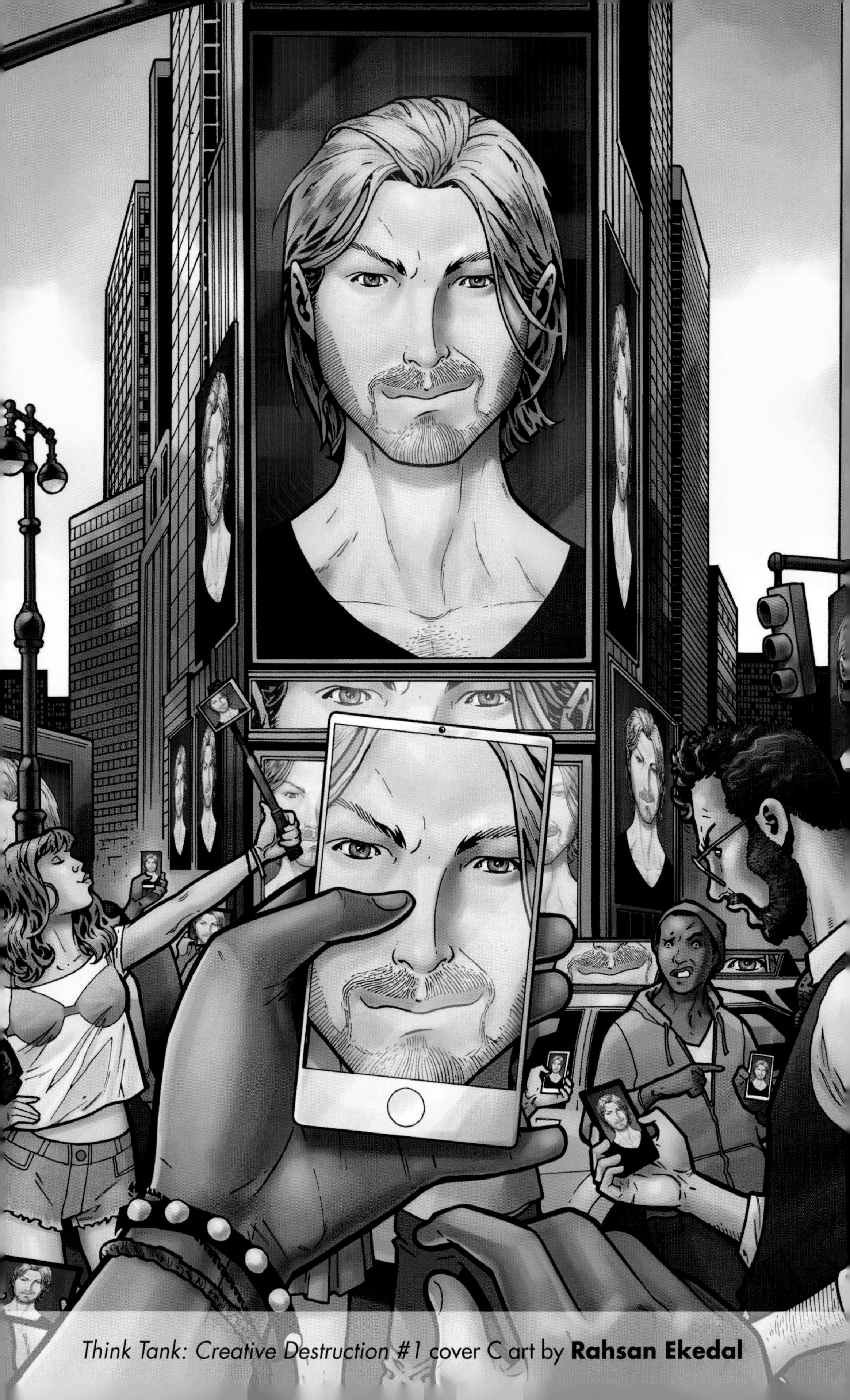

Think Tank: Creative Destruction #1 cover C art by **Rahsan Ekedal**

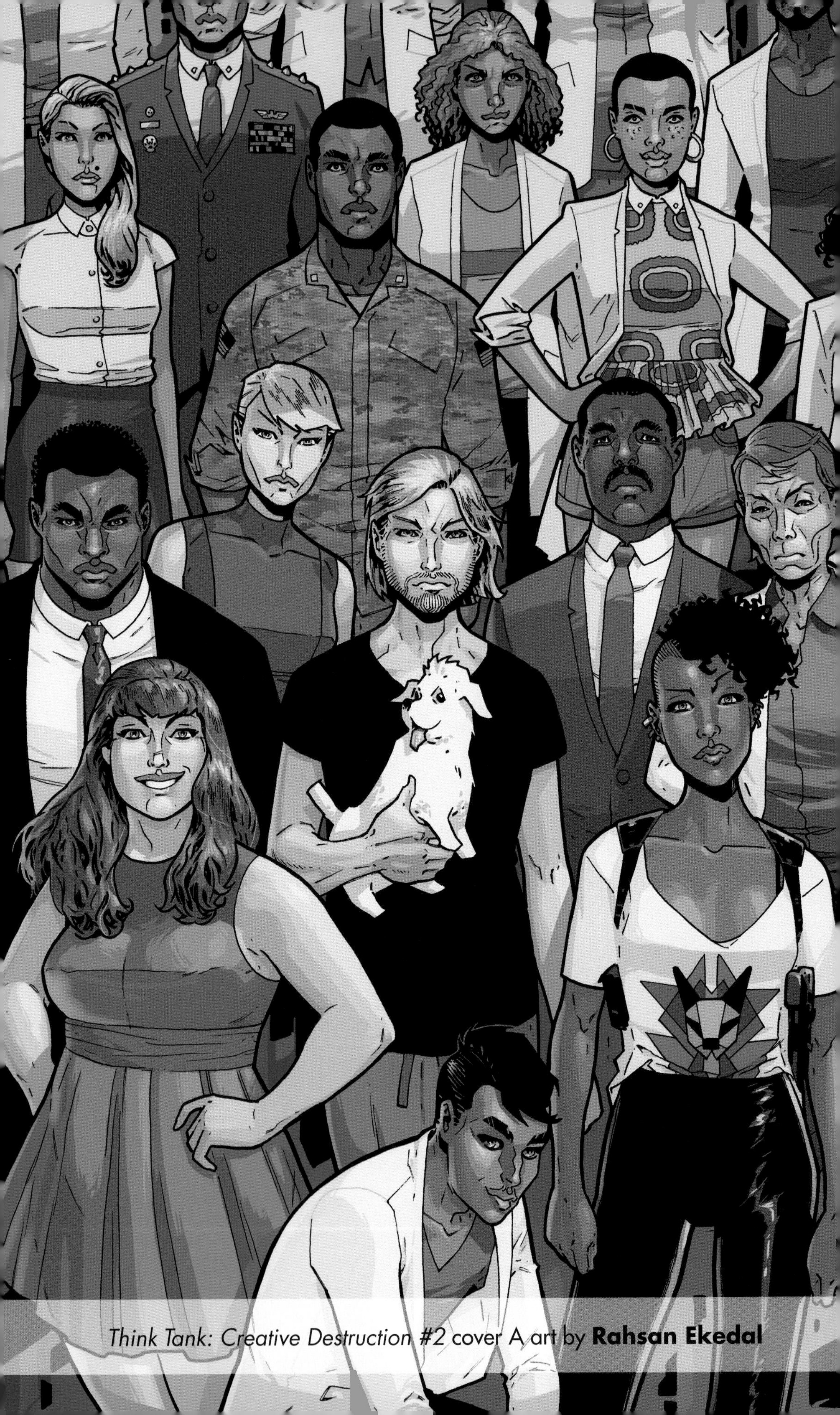

Think Tank: Creative Destruction #2 cover A art by **Rahsan Ekedal**

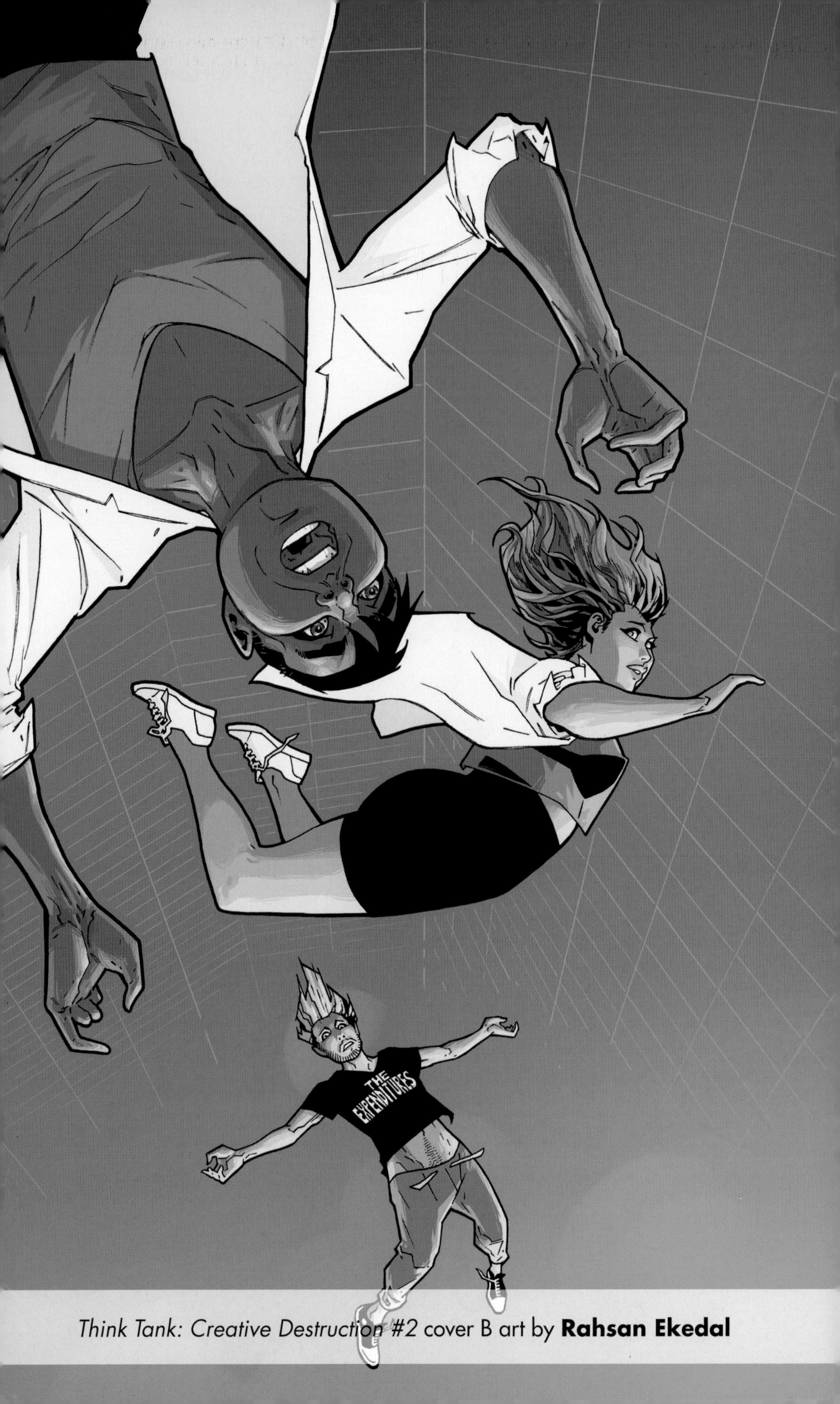
THE
EXPENDITURES
Think Tank: Creative Destruction #2 cover B art by **Rahsan Ekedal**

Think Tank: Creative Destruction #3 cover A art by **Rahsan Ekedal**

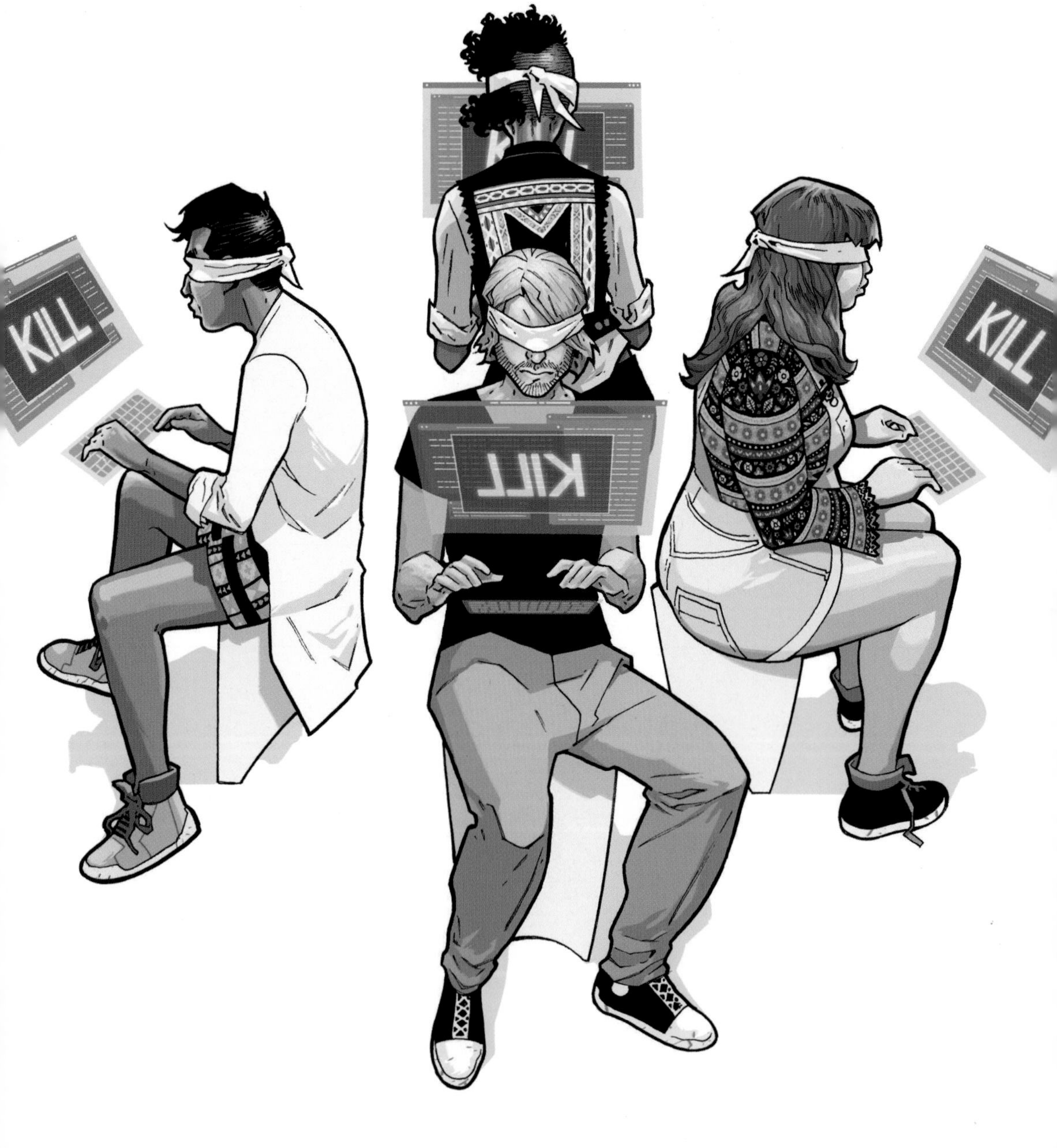
KILL
KILL
KILL
KILL

Think Tank: Creative Destruction #3 cover B art by **Rahsan Ekedal**

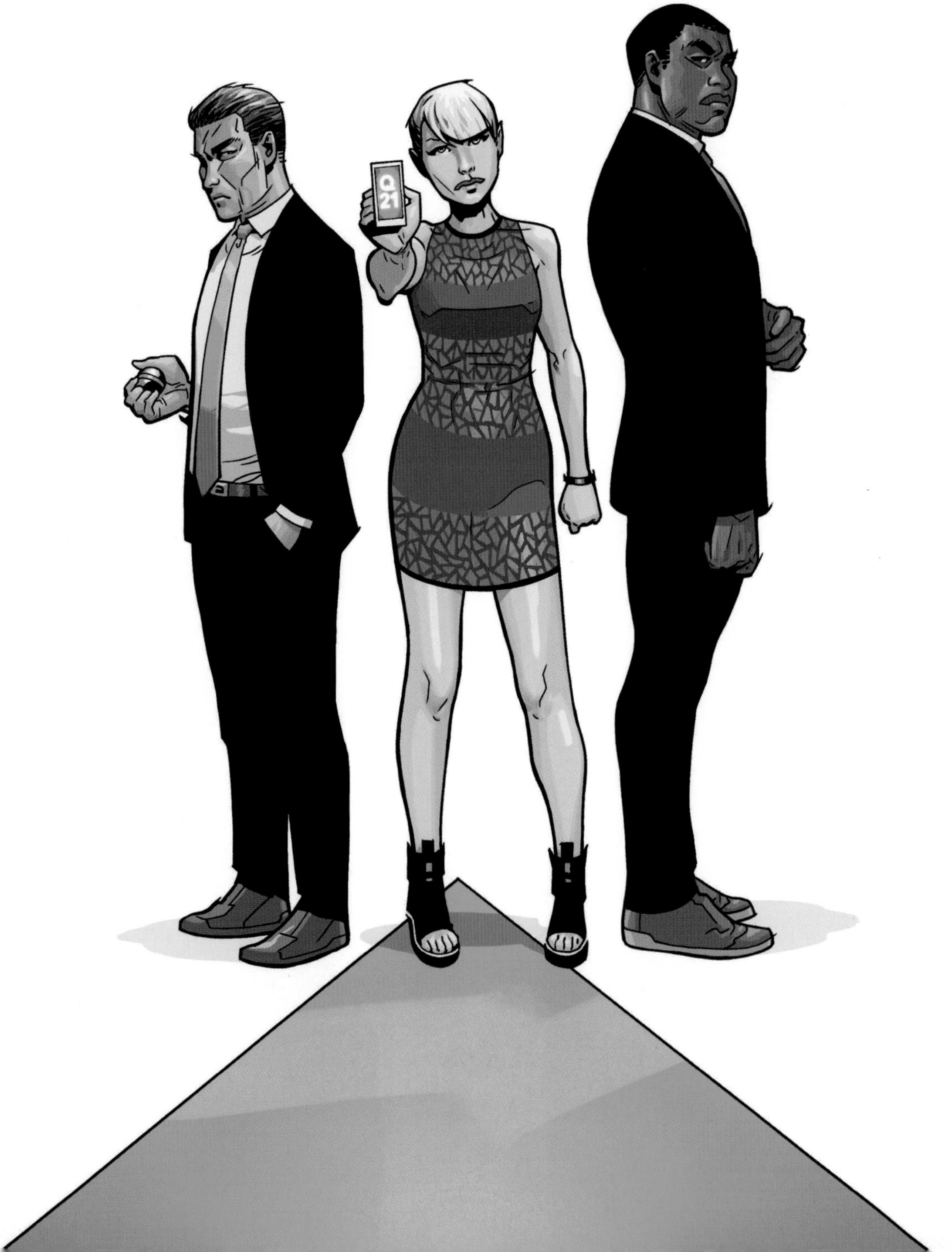
Q
21

Think Tank: Creative Destruction #4 cover A art by **Rahsan Ekedal**

Think Tank: Creative Destruction #4 cover B art by **Rahsan Ekedal**

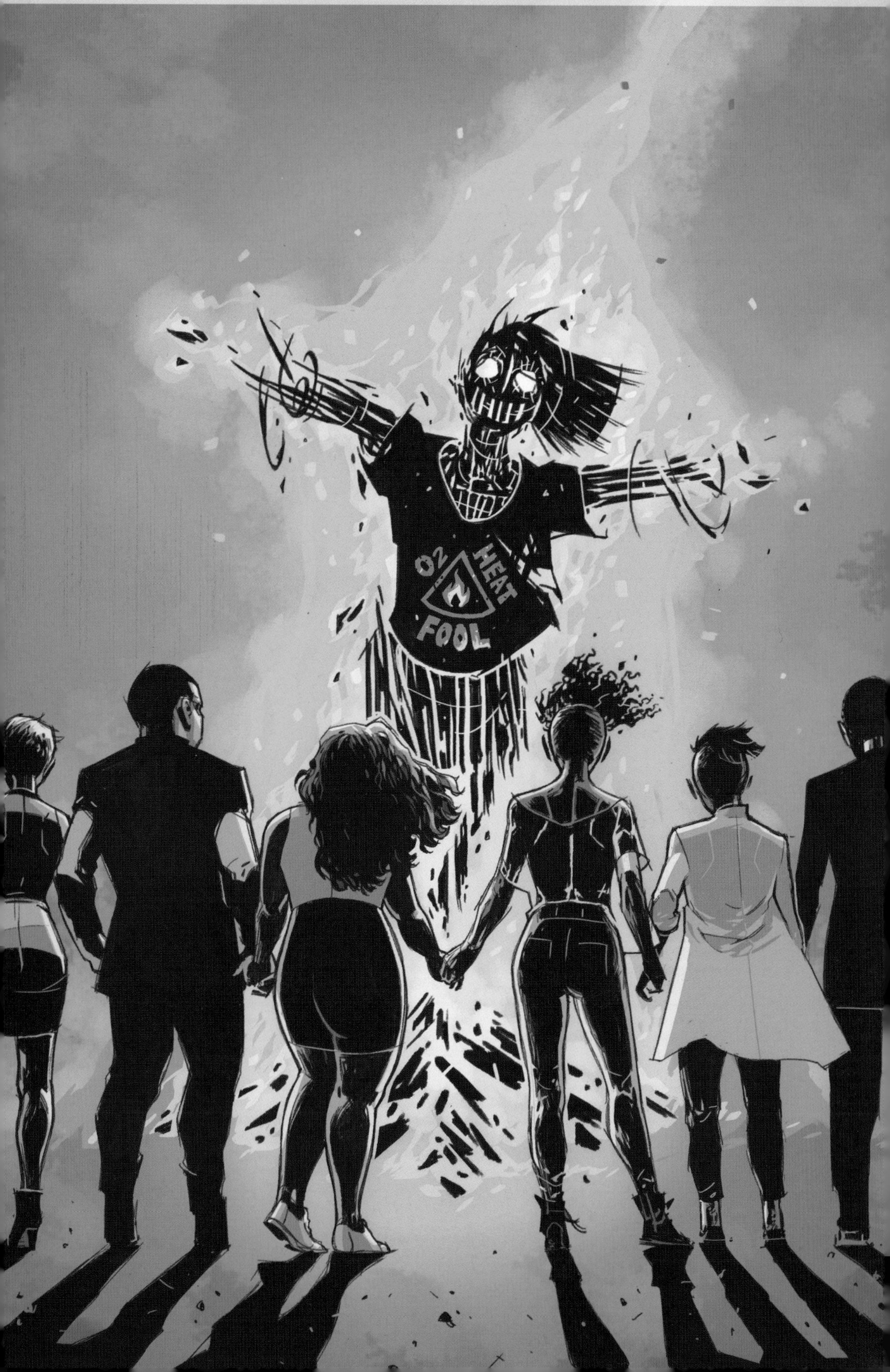

O2
HEAT
FOOL

/QUANTUM21

SCIENCE CLASS

THINK TANK

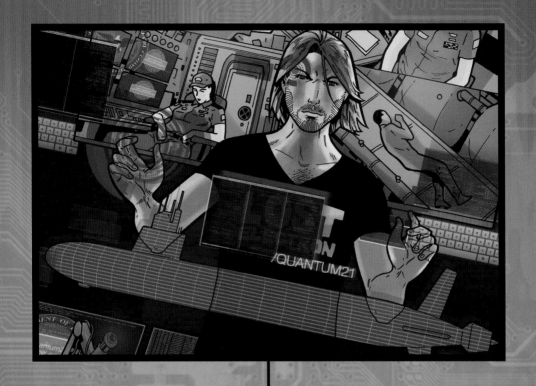

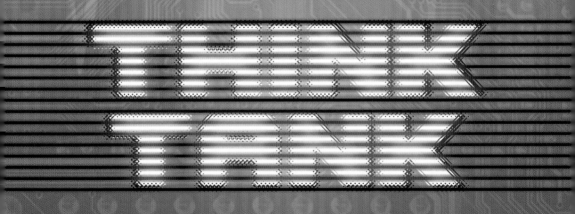

SCIENCE CLASS

Howdy! So it's been two years since the last volume of Think Tank came out. If this is your first experience with Think Tank, welcome! There are three previous volumes and a one-shot called *Think Tank: Fun with PTSD.* These are available in print in comic shops, bookstores and Amazon now. As always, I'd ask if you like this book to please recommend it to a friend.

THINK
TANK

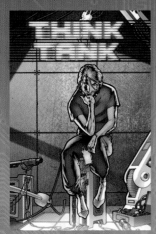

Think Tank vol. 1

ISBN: 978-160706-660-6

DANGER | READING THIS BOOK WILL MAKE YOU SMARTER
THINK
TANK
VOLUME 2
MY MILITARY INDUSTRIAL COMPLEX IS BIGGER THAN YOURS

Think Tank vol. 2

ISBN: 978-160706-745-0

THINK
TANK
SEAL TEAM SEXY

Think Tank vol. 3

ISBN: 978-160706-851-8

INFRASTRUCTURE WEAKNESS

NEW YORK TIMES BESTSELLING AUTHOR OF ONE SECOND AFTER
WILLIAM R.
FORSTCHEN
ONE YEAR
AFTER
"Forstchen is the prophet of a new Dark Age. The wise will listen."
—STEPHEN COONTS, New York Times bestselling author of Saucer: Savage Planet
A NOVEL

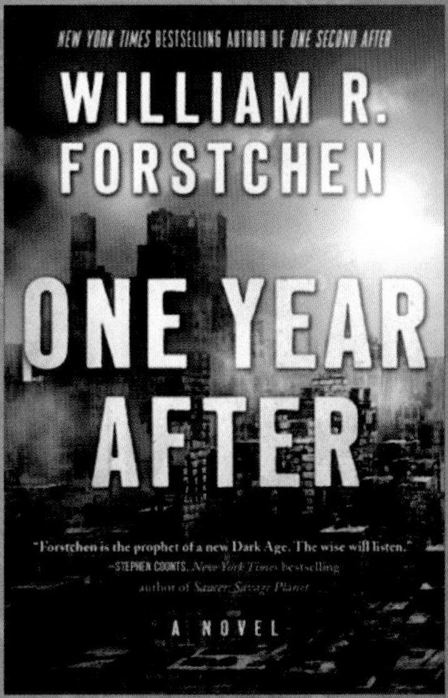

This is for real. I'll get into this more in a couple pages, but if you want to read a book (very realistic) that will scare the shit out of you about this, read *One Year After* by William R. Forstchen.

The electrical grid is insanely out of date and it's all connected. This has worked well to keep continuous power available as needed, but makes us very vulnerable. Check these links if you wish to be further frightened.

http://blog.nema.org/2015/05/12/u-s-electric-infrastructure-by-the-numbers/
https://en.wikipedia.org/wiki/Northeast_blackout_of_2003
http://insider.foxnews.com/2014/02/23/our-death-toll-would-be-staggering-judge-jeanine-explains-threats-power-grid

ATSAC

Is real and handles traffic in Los Angeles. I didn't realize they intentionally lengthen red light times on certain streets to help with congestion.

https://www.youtube.com/watch?v=ZfY5rEetk7s
https://www.youtube.com/watch?v=1TZ0PISonSw
http://trafficinfo.lacity.org/about-atsac.php

TALOS

The Army's Tactical Assault Light Operator Suit is very real. I'm going to get into this in detail in the next issue, but here are a couple videos.

https://www.youtube.com/watch?v=CgiGU7y-CvQM

https://www.youtube.com/watch?v=rBcM8161i-hE

EXISTING GEAR
HELMET
Basic helmets provide modest protection from bullets, shrapnel and explosions. Troops often attach night-vision goggles for better visibility on missions.
BODY ARMOR
U.S. troops wear limited amounts of body armor designed to protect vital organs and allow them to move with speed and agility.
LOWER BODY
Current uniforms provide limited lower-body protection.
GEAR
U.S. forces can carry more than 125 pounds of gear, including grenades, knives, radios, ammunition magazines and flashlights.
FUTURE IRON MAN SUIT
HELMET
Future helmets may include visors, sensors and Google Glass-type interfaces to help U.S. forces spot hidden threats.
COOLING SYSTEM
Suits could include a cooling system to help regulate the body temperatures of U.S. troops encased in the the body armor.
MOTORIZED EXOSKELETON
The suit would likely include a motorized exoskeleton to help carry the hundreds of pounds of added weight from the body armor and high-tech components.
POWER
Future suits might be powered by a small engine.
BODY ARMOR
The full-body suit would provide dramatically increased body-

SOME OTHER COOL THINGS TO CHECK OUT

ART OF RAHSAN EKEDAL

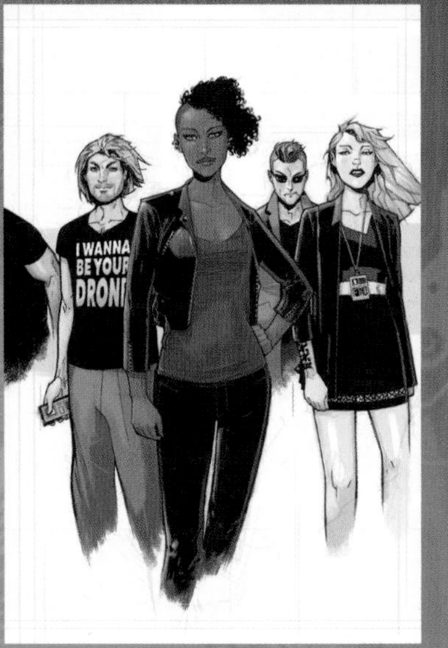
I WANNA BE YOUR DRONE

Diamond code: DEC150632
ISBN: 163215661X

I want to start by plugging Rahsan's *Art of* Hardcover book that is coming out soon.

It has a ton of behind-the-scene sketches and development along with some of Rahsan's best covers and illustrations over the years.

If you're a fan of *Think Tank*, *The Tithe*, *Echoes*, or Rahsan's work in general, this limited edition hardcover is a nice book to have.

The next project we are working on together brings many of our past characters together in a story called *Eden's Fall*, but more on that in a couple pages.

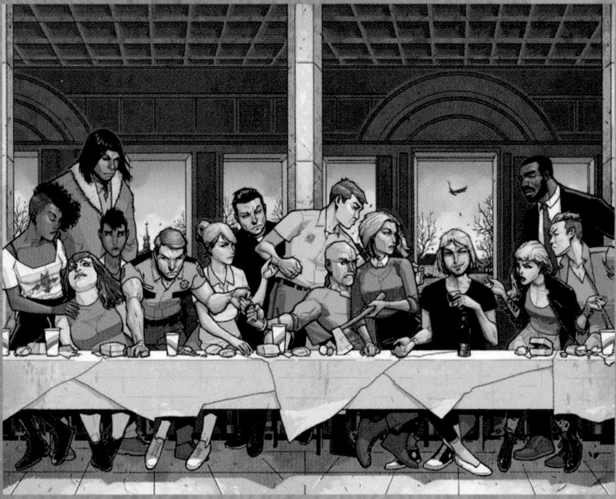

INFRASTRUCTURE VULNERABILITY

So how screwed are we?

In 2013, a military-style raid tried to take out a transformer substation. No one was apprehended. Less than a week later someone on a boat opened fire on a nuclear power plant in Tennessee and engaged police, then fled. That blackout in 2003 from a tree falling in Ohio is real.

WAYS TO CRIPPLE THE U.S.A.

1) EMP – two EMP bursts strategically detonated above the U.S. would knock out our power for years. This scenario is game over. Studies suggest 8 out of 10 people would die. If it makes you feel any better, our subs could still nuke back…if we know who fired them.

http://www.thefederalistpapers.org/us/emp-attack-on-us-power-grid-could-kill-9-in-10-americans
http://science.howstuffworks.com/7102-electromagnetic-pulse-bomb-video.htm)

2) PORTS – one port takes the majority of goods in and out of this country, that's the Port of Los Angeles in Long Beach. You take that out and the economic fallout alone would have a dramatic long-term effect.

http://www.ncbi.nlm.nih.gov/pubmed/17640206

WAYS TO CRIPPLE THE U.S.A. (cont.)

3)　　　CHLORINE CLOUD – we store chlorine all over the place and there are tankers driving on the roads with it as you read this. A single RPG hitting one of these trucks driving near a large city would kill millions of people as the chlorine cloud spreads.

http://www.scientificamerican.com/article/chlorine-accidents-take-big-human-toll/

4)　　　ROADS – most of our food is distributed via the trucking system. Take out some key roads, bridges, tunnels, and you can stop distribution in its tracks. Most food is not grown "locally" so think about that for a second.

https://info.publicintelligence.net/TSAhighwaysthreat.pdf

5)　　　WATER – our water system is already rickety. You could take out the supply, people would die within three days of not having water. You can contaminate the water with some sort of bio-viral threat. So many ways this could go bad.

http://www.mrws.org/Terror/Counterterrorism.htm

 A guy pissed in an aqueduct and ruined 38 million gallons, and he was just an asshole.

http://www.usatoday.com/story/news/nation/2014/04/17/water-reservoir-urination/7814581/

6)　　　HACKING SYSTEMS/CHANGING THRESHOLDS – so how concerned are authorities on this? Insanely concerned. Some Iranians recently hacked into a New York dam. They didn't cause any real damage, but they could have. So many ways to destroy things.

http://www.popularmechanics.com/military/a4096/4307521/

These are just a few examples. I could write (and people have) entire books on just one of these. Should you be scared? Yeah, I think you should. I am. I'm not trying to promote hysteria, but something needs to be done. Our infrastructure is more important than a lot of other things this country wastes money on.

http://www.nytimes.com/2003/08/15/nyregion/blackout-2003-overview-power-surge-blacks-northeast-hitting-cities-8-states.html?pagewanted=all
http://www.wired.com/2015/01/time-fix-americas-infrastructure-heres-start/
http://nationalinterest.org/feature/the-days-after-cyberattack-strikes-the-us-power-grid-15028

MILITARY INDUSTRIAL COMPLEX

I could go on and on about this, but our system is flawed. It's better than most, but listen to President Eisenhower's speech as he left office. And he was PART of the creation of the modern military.

Text here:
http://coursesa.matrix.msu.edu/~hst306/documents/indust.html

Video here:
https://www.youtube.com/watch?v=8y06NSBBRtY

CRACKERS

When I stumbled across this I laughed for a while. I've been called a "cracker" a few times in my life and every time it makes me giggle a bit inside. I know that's probably not the intended effect.

http://www.security-faqs.com/what-are-the-main-differences-between-hackers-and-crackers.html

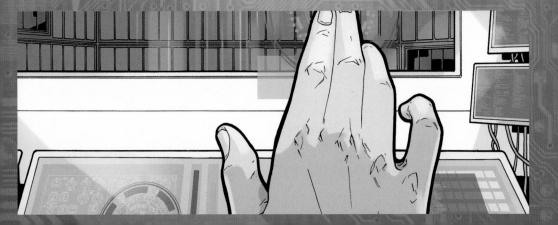

NARRATION

For you long-time *Think Tank* readers, you'll be well aware that I use a lot of first person David Loren narrative to convey an additional level of the story. One of the things I love about comics is narration. This is rare in TV and film and even when used feels kind of forced. In comics and novels, we can explore the space between what a person actually says and what they're thinking. I'm endlessly fascinated with human behavior, and Loren is an interesting case study in psychology.

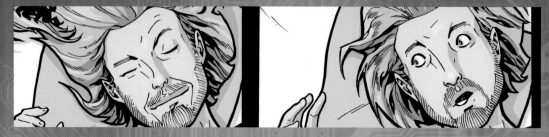

PROACTIVE MILITARY STRATEGY

Or "Is this plot remotely plausible?" Do proactive military strategies happen and would someone kill a twenty-year-old hacker as a proactive move? Well DARPA's primary goal is to prevent technological surprise by staying ahead of foreign powers, ally or not. There's also a Proactive Preemptive Operations Group at the Pentagon whose purpose is to evaluate strategies to prevent future problems. Google "proactive military strategy" and you get 13.6 million hits. Political figures, scientists die all the time under some mysterious circumstances. Every government has black ops groups of some kind. The CIA's budget is between 30-40 billion dollar. Maybe I'm paranoid, maybe I exaggerate for fictional purposes…but I can look you in the eye and tell you that I believe this is 100% plausible. And I think it happens all the time. How scary is that?

Mysterious scientist deaths
http://www.stevequayle.com/?s=146

Proactive strategies:

ISIS/U.S.A.
http://nation.com.pk/blogs/17-Nov-2015/proactive-not-reactive-military-action-is-needed-against-isis

China/U.S.A. South China Sea
http://www.ibtimes.com/china-military-strategy-white-paper-pledges-active-defense-more-proactive-navy-amid-1937401

India/Pakistan
http://southasianvoices.org/proactive-operations-and-massive-retaliation-whither-deterrence-stability/

U.S. FOREIGN POLICY

For 50 years we've maintained ourselves as the police of the world. One theme you'll see running throughout my story is that I think this is no longer viable and we're dealing with the shockwaves of trying to maintain that status quo despite it not working and the problems it causes. We give billions in aid, have military all over the world to "help" people, but they generally all despise us. We've also made countless errors and blunders. I'm not advocating an isolationist policy, BUT why are we spending trillions on other countries that don't seem to want our help when our own infrastructure is falling apart? I believe it's time for a serious look at how we spend money internationally and question why we do it. Time for a line-by-line audit!

http://www.foreignpolicyjournal.com/2014/09/08/the-failures-of-us-foreignmilitary-policy/
http://nationalinterest.org/feature/mistakes-were-made-americas-five-biggest-foreign-policy-11160

HACKING DRONES

Is this possible? Yes, and it has been done many times already.
You don't hear about it because most of it gets covered up.

http://security.blogs.cnn.com/2012/07/19/aerial-drones-vulnerable-to-being-hacked-congress-told/
http://www.ibtimes.co.uk/wondering-how-hack-military-drone-its-all-google-1500326
http://www.wired.co.uk/news/archive/2015-08/19/drone-hack-defcon

REMOTE KILLING FROM HACKING HOSPITALS

Hospitals are a new target for hackers. For the most part they are being held hostage to pay a fee to have their systems left alone. It's kind of like modern-day protection racket. And hospitals are paying. So, if hospitals are vulnerable and they use equipment that's networked…then it's vulnerable too. It's happening. Read that last link.

http://www.forbes.com/sites/kalevleetaru/2016/03/29/hacking-hospitals-and-holding-hostages-cy-bersecurity-in-2016/#500d804d3e2e
http://bigstory.ap.org/article/86401c5c2f7e43b79d7decb04a0022b4/hackers-broke-hospitals-de-spite-software-flaw-warnings

http://investmentwatchblog.com/hospitals-found-to-be-easily-hacked-patient-identities-sto-len-and-medication-schedules-altered/
PTSD AND TOLL ON OPERATORS

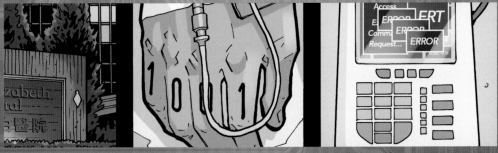

I wrote extensively on PTSD in the book *Think Tank: Fun with PTSD* one shot. If you go to topcow.com and scroll down to the bottom right, that and 50 other books are there-for free if you want to read them. The point on the "toll on operators" is that scientists like Loren here are people too. They deal with the same kind of pressures and realizations of their hand in the killing. This takes a dramatic toll on their emotional stability. David is in a bit of a negative spiral now. How he reacts and what will happen going forward is going to be very interesting. Depression is a real thing obviously and once you're in that spiral it's hard to get out.

EDEN'S FALL

You may know that in a couple different places it says Volume 5 will come out in February 2017. I intended to relaunch this as an ongoing series and have three-month gaps between arcs as Rahsan caught up. Sales on the trade paperbacks are pretty good, digital is solid, but the 32-page monthly book sales aren't great. So…given that and financial realities and my passion to continue this book no matter what…we're going to do a volume a year for the next couple years and hope to build the readership up enough to warrant more. So please! If you like this book, recommend it to a friend.

Up next, *Eden's Fall*! This special three-issue story arc combines characters from *Think Tank*, *The Tithe*, and *Postal* and the first issue was released last month (August 2016)!

Here's some preview art:

DEPRESSION

So I suffer from depression. I started recently taking Lexapro. I never knew there was such a stigma for coming out and saying that, but I do. So if you do, we're in it together =)

SUICIDE

In 2011 I did consider suicide because of personal issues. So this issue I wrote with some experience. I had convinced myself that my children and family would be better off without me. I had people telling me I was crazy, I had such a great life. "What do you have to be depressed about?" This is the worst thing you can tell someone that's depressed. That or buck up, or get over it. People in a depressed state feel like they deserve to be that way. Words like that do NOT help. Educate yourself a bit because words can unintentionally cause more harm than good despite your good intentions.

Things to say and not to say to a depressed person:

http://www.health.com/health/gallery/0,,20393228,00.html
http://psychcentral.com/lib/worst-things-to-say-to-someone-whos-depressed/

Article about my flirtation with suicide here:

http://robot6.comicbookresources.com/2012/11/matt-hawkins-celebrates-life-by-sharing-his-own-struggle-with-suicide/

ARE YOU STRUGGLING WITH SUICIDAL THOUGHTS?

If so, there is help out there for you. There's a national suicide prevention hotline where you can talk anonymously to someone who will listen and want to help you. I've been in dark places. It always gets better. And if you think no one cares, I do. I care. If you want someone to talk to you can IM me on Facebook, but since I may not be online, if you need to please call the Suicide Prevention Hotline. 1-800-273-8255

UNITED NATIONS SECURITY COUNCIL

"Under the U.N. Charter, the Security Council has primary responsibility for the maintenance of international peace and security. It has 15 Members, and each Member has one vote. Under the Charter, all Member States are obligated to comply with Council decisions."

"The permanent members of the United Nations Security Council, also known as the Permanent Five, Big Five, or P5, include the following five governments: China, France, Russia, the United Kingdom, and the United States."

http://www.un.org/en/sc/
http://worldpress.org/specials/iraq/unsc.htm

LASERS

I play with some serious laser power in this story. If you're curious about lasers and how they work this is a good document to read:

http://www.pro-lite.co.uk/File/laser_safety_laser_basics.php

COST-PLUS BUDGETING

From Wikipedia the definition is "A cost-plus contract, also termed a cost reimbursement contract, is a contract where a contractor is paid for all of its allowed expenses to a set limit plus additional payment to allow for a profit."

Think about that for a second. What they're saying is you don't need to know what your costs are in advance. In *Think Tank* we set the story up that they underbid it to secure the deal and were planning on using the cost plus to then charge more. This is so common it's ridiculous. Anyone who's ever had to bid on a job knows how stupid this is.

Fraud examples:
http://www.motherjones.com/politics/2013/05/contractors-385-billion-military-bases

Thank you for sticking with us for this new series. Look for *Eden's Fall*, out now and a new *Think Tank* volume starting February 2017.

Carpe Diem!

Matt Hawkins
Twitter: @topcowmatt | http://www.facebook.com/selfloathingnarcissist

OTHER BOOKS WRITTEN BY ME AND RAHSAN EKEDAL

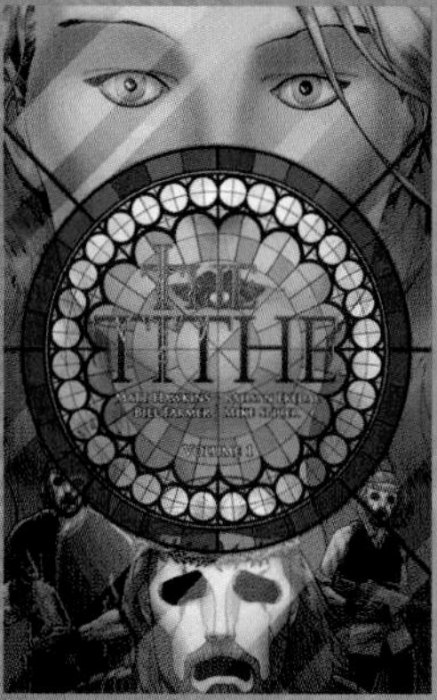
TITHE

The Tithe, Vol. 1
ISBN: 978-1632153241
Written by Matt Hawkins
Art by Rahsan Ekedal
A heist story like no other, with fraudalent mega-churches pitted against Robin Hood hackers.

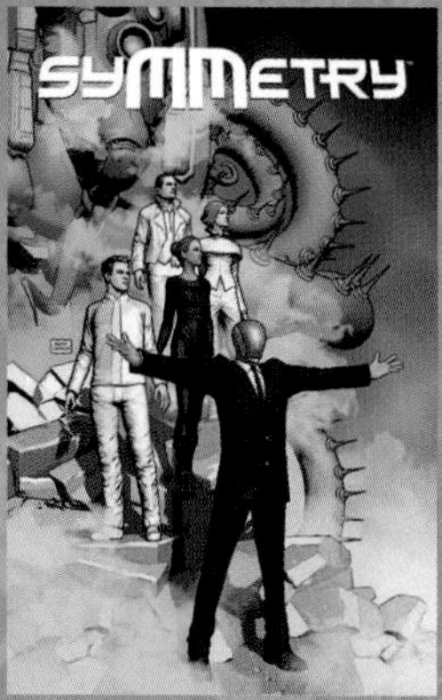
SYMMETRY

Symmetry, Vol. 1
ISBN: 978-1632156990
Written by Matt Hawkins
Art by Raffaele Ienco
Unlikely love sparks a dangerous revolution in a Utopian future!

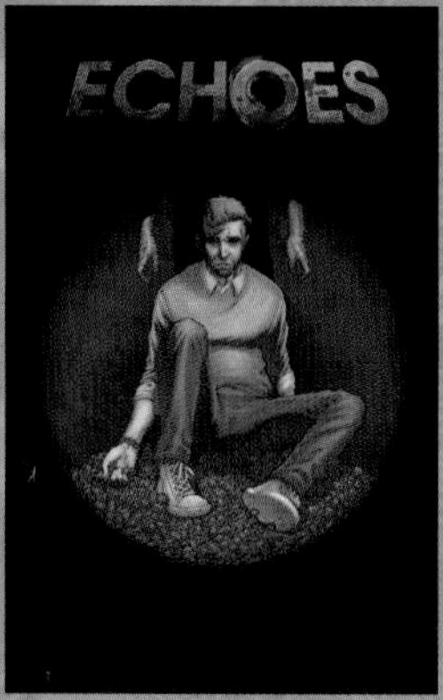
ECHOES

Echoes, Vol. 1
ISBN: 978-1632156600
Written by Joshua Fialkov
Art by Rahsan Ekedal
A young man stricken with schizophrenia discovers his abusive father's horrifying legacy.

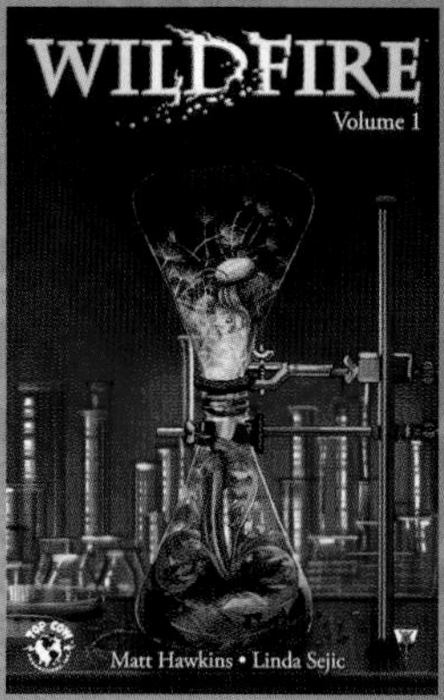
WILDFIRE
Volume 1
Matt Hawkins • Linda Sejic

Wildfire, Vol. 1
ISBN: 978-1632150240
Written by Matt Hawkins
Art by Linda Sejic
In this GMO conspiracy thriller, a plant-growth formula leads to the destruction of Los Angeles.

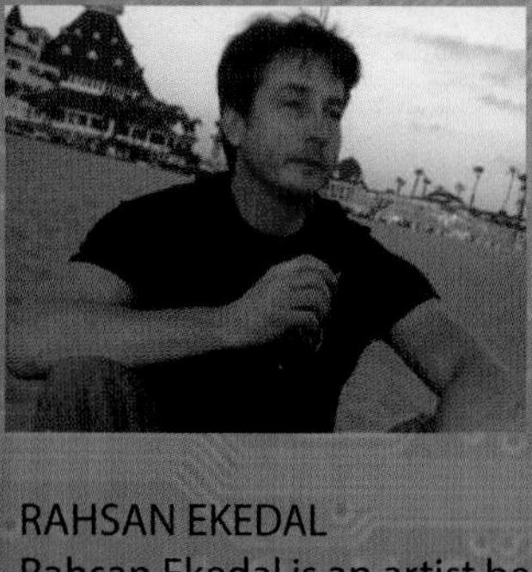

MATT HAWKINS
A veteran of the initial Image Comics launch, Matt started his career in comic book publishing in 1993 and has been working with Image as a creator, writer and executive for over twenty years. President/COO of Top Cow since 1998, Matt has created and written over thirty new franchises for Top Cow and Image including *Think Tank*, *The Tithe*, *Necromancer*, *VICE*, *Lady Pendragon*, *Aphrodite IX*, and *Tales of Honor*, as well as handling the company's business affairs.

RAHSAN EKEDAL
Rahsan Ekedal is an artist best known for his work on *Think Tank*, and the Harvey Award-nominated graphic novel *Echoes*. He has illustrated a variety of titles such as *Solomon Kane*, *Creepy Comics*, *The Cleaners*, and *Warhammer*, and worked with many publishers including Top Cow, Dark Horse, DC/Vertigo, and Boom! Studios. He was born in California and educated at the School of the Arts High School and the Academy of Art University, both in San Francisco. Rahsan currently lives in Berlin, Germany, with his wife, Shannon, and their big black cat, Flash.

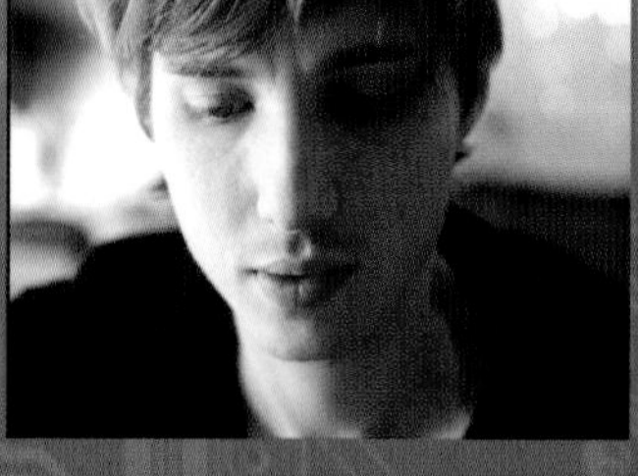

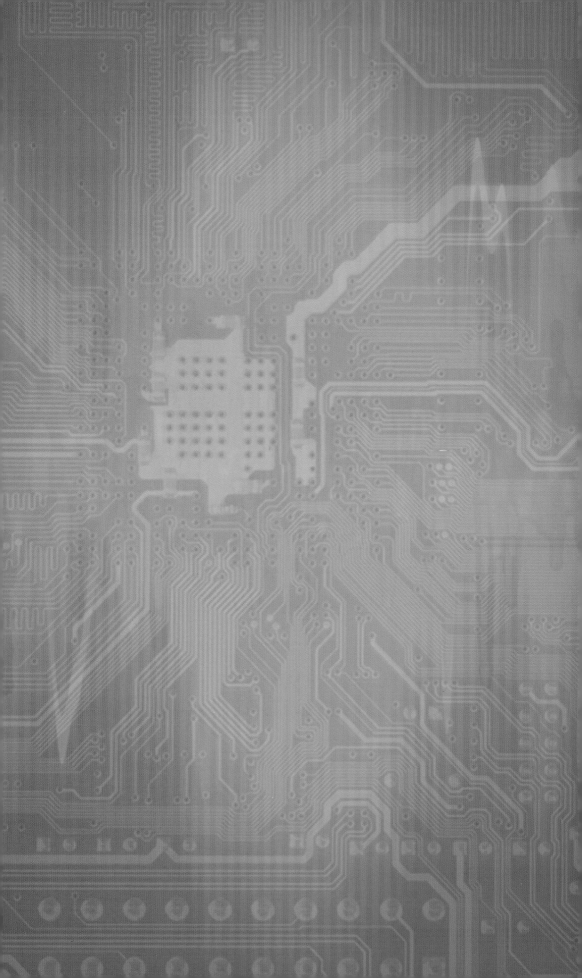

THINK TANK ANIMAL

2017

THE PRICE OF THIS VIGILANTE JUSTICE WILL BE PAID IN BLOOD.

MATT HAWKINS • BRYAN HILL • ATILIO ROJO

EDEN'S FALL™

AUGUST 2016

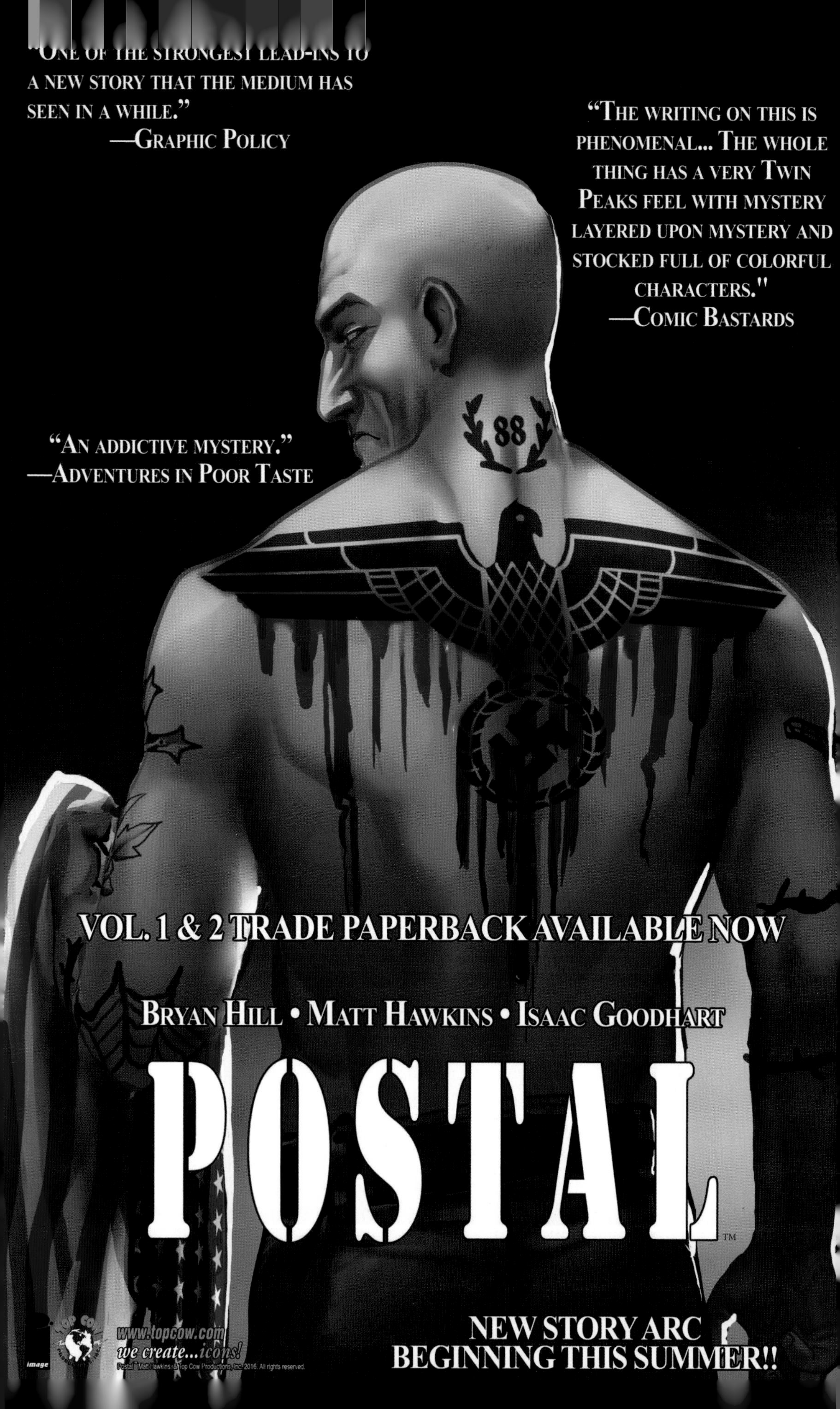

"ONE OF THE STRONGEST LEAD-INS TO A NEW STORY THAT THE MEDIUM HAS SEEN IN A WHILE."
—GRAPHIC POLICY
"THE WRITING ON THIS IS PHENOMENAL... THE WHOLE THING HAS A VERY TWIN PEAKS FEEL WITH MYSTERY LAYERED UPON MYSTERY AND STOCKED FULL OF COLORFUL CHARACTERS."
—COMIC BASTARDS
88
"AN ADDICTIVE MYSTERY."
—ADVENTURES IN POOR TASTE
VOL. 1 & 2 TRADE PAPERBACK AVAILABLE NOW
BRYAN HILL • MATT HAWKINS • ISAAC GOODHART
POSTAL™
NEW STORY ARC BEGINNING THIS SUMMER!!
www.topcow.com
we create...icons!
Postal™ Matt Hawkins & Top Cow Productions, Inc. 2016. All rights reserved.

The Top Cow essentials checklist:

IXth Generation, Volume 1
(ISBN: 978-1-63215-323-4)

Aphrodite IX: Complete Series
(ISBN: 978-1-63215-368-5)

Artifacts Origins: First Born
(ISBN: 978-1-60706-506-7)

Broken Trinity, Volume 1
(ISBN: 978-1-60706-051-2)

Cyber Force: Rebirth, Volume 1
(ISBN: 978-1-60706-671-2)

The Darkness: Accursed, Volume 1
(ISBN: 978-1-58240-958-0)

The Darkness: Rebirth, Volume 1
(ISBN: 978-1-60706-585-2)

Death Vigil, Volume 1
(ISBN: 978-1-63215-278-7)

Impaler, Volume 1
(ISBN: 978-1-58240-757-9)

Postal, Volume 1
(ISBN: 978-1-63215-342-5)

Rising Stars Compendium
(ISBN: 978-1-63215-246-6)

Sunstone, Volume 1
(ISBN: 978-1-63215-212-1)

Symmetry, Volume 1
(ISBN: 978-1-63215-699-0)

The Tithe, Volume 1
(ISBN: 978-1-63215-324-1)

Think Tank, Volume 1
(ISBN: 978-1-60706-660-6)

Wanted
(ISBN: 978-1-58240-497-4)

Wildfire, Volume 1
(ISBN: 978-1-63215-024-0)

Witchblade: Redemption, Volume 1
(ISBN: 978-1-60706-193-9)

Witchblade: Rebirth, Volume 1
(ISBN: 978-1-60706-532-6)

Witchblade: Borne Again, Volume 1
(ISBN: 978-1-63215-025-7)

For more ISBN and ordering information on our latest collections go to:

www.topcow.com

Ask your retailer about our catalogue of collected editions, digests, and hard covers or check the listings at:

Barnes and Noble, Amazon.com,
and other fine retailers.

To find your nearest comic shop go to:

www.comicshoplocator.com

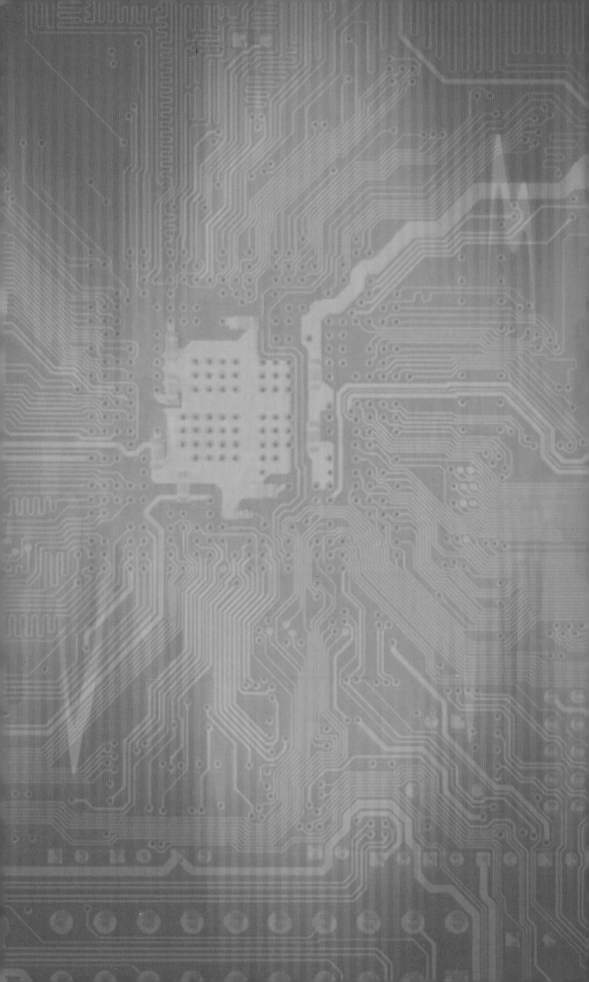